VINCENT CRONIN was born at Ampleforth and Harvard. He England and joined the Rifle he took a degree in Greats at Oxford. He has spent, at various times, five years in France, and has written three highly-praised biographies of French monarchs: *Louis XIV*, *Napoleon* and *Louis and Antoinette*. Many of his books have been translated into French, and a previous work, *The Florentine Renaissance*, was described by *The Times Educational Supplement* as 'probably the best book that has ever been written on the Renaissance'.

Vincent Cronin has won both the Richard Hillary Award and the Heinemann Award for Literature, and is on the Council of the Royal Society of Literature. He lives in London, is married, and has two sons and three daughters.

THE COMPANION GUIDES

LONDON *David Piper*
'It has strong claims to be among the best guide-books
ever written.'   *Sunday Telegraph*

ROME *Georgina Masson*
'The best guide to Rome published for many a long year.'
                        Elizabeth Nicholas, Sunday Times

THE SOUTH OF FRANCE *Archibald Lyall*
'He will fire one with curiosity until only a journey can
relieve it.'   *Cyril Connolly, Sunday Times*

VENICE *Hugh Honour*
'The best guide-book I have ever encountered.'
                        Angus Wilson, Observer

FLORENCE *Eve Borsook*
'A richly composed civic portrait . . . discriminating
guide.'   *New Statesman*

THE WEST HIGHLANDS OF SCOTLAND *W. H. Murray*
'The best thing of its kind.'   *Glasgow Herald*

THE COMPANION GUIDE TO

PARIS

■

VINCENT CRONIN

FONTANA · COLLINS

First published by Wm. Collins 1963
Second Edition 1968
Third Revised Edition 1973
Reprinted 1973
This edition first issued in Fontana books 1975

© Vincent Cronin, 1963, 1968, 1973

Made and printed in Great Britain by
William Collins Sons & Co. Ltd, Glasgow

FOR CHANTAL

Contents

❦

Illustrations

❦

Introduction

THIS book aims to help the visitor to begin to know and enjoy Paris. It is divided into eighteen chapters, each (save the fourth) corresponding to half a day's sightseeing. At the beginning of each chapter is a sketch map with a suggested route, not too long to be followed on foot. Each route begins and ends near a Métro station or bus stop.

The walks can be made in any order; most people will doubtless want to choose from them according to their mood, convenience and tastes. Others will prefer to make their own way through the city; by consulting the index they will be able to obtain information about the chief places of interest as they happen to arrive at them.

For those who wish to follow the walks in the order in which they stand, the plan of the book is as follows. Chapter 1 is an introductory walk designed for the day of arrival, while Chapter 4 makes suggestions for seeing Paris by night. All other chapters are grouped in pairs, each pair making a whole day's sightseeing. Thus Chapter 2 is a morning walk, and Chapter 3, an afternoon walk, begins close to where Chapter 2 leaves off; Chapter 5 is a morning walk, and Chapter 6, the walk for the same afternoon, begins close to where Chapter 5 ends. Thereafter throughout the book odd-numbered chapters are—ideally—morning walks, and even-numbered chapters afternoon walks. One of the reasons for this distinction is that a number of places of interest—for example, the Archives— are closed during the morning.

While on the subject of closing, it is important to remember that while many Paris museums are open on Sundays, virtually all are closed on Tuesdays.

The routes, the places visited, the works of art have been carefully chosen, but, it cannot be overemphasised, are only *recommended*: a framework from which it is hoped each person will wander at will. Moreover, value-judgements have been written down in the hope of stimulating, not of converting.

From London you can travel to Paris by boat and train on four different routes, the fastest service being the Golden Arrow on the Dover-Calais route, leaving from Victoria and arriving nine hours later at the Gare du Nord.

If you go by air, B.E.A. run hourly services from Heathrow to Orly, where a bus takes you through southern Paris to Les Invalides air terminal. This is very central on the Left Bank of the Seine, and has an Information office open weekdays from 9 a.m. to midnight, which will make immediate reservations of hotel rooms anywhere in the city by telex. There are also direct B.E.A. flights to Orly from Birmingham, Manchester and Glasgow.

At the time of writing there are two much less expensive services from London involving short flights. Skyways operate a service on which you can travel by coach from Victoria Coach Station to Ashford Airport, fly to Beauvais, and thence take a coach to the Place de la République Coach Station, in eastern Paris. The return fare is approximately half the Heathrow-Orly return fare. The other inexpensive service is the Silver Arrow: train from Victoria to Gatwick; plane to the Channel beach resort of Le Touquet, where a train is waiting to take you to the Gare du Nord. The whole journey takes four hours.

Before choosing a hotel, you will want to decide on a district. For someone intending to get to know Paris, there are roughly four: the Opéra-Grands Boulevards-Madeleine, bustling, noisy, international but conveniently central; the streets in and off the Champs Elysées, less noisy but more expensive; the quiet, fashionable, residential 16th arrondissement; and the Left Bank, informal and inexpensive.

A word first about luxury hotels. The Ritz, 15 Place Vendôme, enjoys the most beautiful site and, to use a favourite Parisian Anglicism, the highest *standing*. The Crillon is one of Gabriel's eighteenth-century palaces on the Place de la Concorde, originally designed for ambassadors and distinguished foreigners, now a favourite with Americans because near their embassy. Of the other luxury hotels the most Parisian and least flashy are the Lancaster, 7 Rue de Berri, and the George V, 31 Avenue George V, both close to the Champs Elysées.

In less luxurious categories here are some suggestions. In the Opéra-Madeleine district four-star hotels include the Westminster, 13 Rue de la Paix, and Louvois, 1 Rue Lulli;

three-star hotels the Saint Pétersbourg, 33 Rue Caumartin, and Arcade, 7 Rue de l'Arcade.[1]

In the Champs Elysées district four-star hotels include the Claridge, 74 Avenue des Champs Elysées and the recently-built Queen Elizabeth, 41 Avenue Pierre 1er de Serbie; three-star hotels the Elysées Palace, 12 Rue de Marignan, and Résidence Saint Philippe, 123 Rue du Faubourg St Honoré.

In the 16th arrondissement are the four-star La Pérouse, 40 Rue La Pérouse, and the three-star Régina de Passy, 6 Rue de la Tour.

One of the best hotels on the Left Bank is the Relais Bisson, 37 Quai des Grands Augustins, overlooking the Seine and close to Notre Dame. The delightful Rue Jacob has a number of moderately priced hotels, notably, at No. 44, Hôtel d'Angleterre (without restaurant). Another very pleasant, though slightly self-conscious, old hotel is the Saint Simon, 14 Rue Saint Simon (with restaurant). Finally, an inexpensive hotel in Paris's own 'house-boat': the Saint Louis, 75 Rue St Louis en l'Île.[2]

Most of these hotels offer a *prix à forfait*, covering the cost of room, Continental breakfast, service charges and taxes.

One other task remains before leaving. If you wish to attend a session of the National Assembly, you should write for a ticket three weeks beforehand to MM. les Questeurs de l'Assemblée Nationale, Palais Bourbon, Paris VII.

Once in Paris, how to get about? For the complete stranger the Métro is recommended because, thanks to crystal-clear maps, it is virtually impossible to lose one's way. The Métro also has these advantages: since Paris stands on limestone, it is built very shallow, hence few stairs; no part of Paris is more than half a mile from a station; and many of the stations are strikingly good examples of modern design. In the Louvre station, for example, works from the Museum are on display in showcases.

There are fourteen lines, each with two names after its two terminal stations. For example, line number 1, which traverses Paris close to the Seine is known as Pont de Neuilly if you are travelling west, Vincennes if you are travelling east. If you want to get from the Louvre to the Invalides, you take the Pont de Neuilly line as far as the Concorde, then change to

[1] Paris hotels are officially graded according to comfort and price: Luxury, four star, three star, two star and one star.
[2] A list of 100 conveniently-sited hotels will be found on pp. 232.

the Balard line, taking the passage marked *Correspondance*.

The fare is the same whatever the distance travelled, but a higher rate is charged for first class. You save money by buying a book of tickets (ten tickets each valid for one journey). Tickets are shown at the entrance-barrier, not given up at the exit.

Now, buses. The bus system is too complicated to be shown in a small plan, but a map of routes can be had at news-stands. Bus stops are marked by black and yellow signs, giving the number of the route, the direction and the main stops. The fare varies according to the number of stages travelled. Tickets may be bought on the bus, or at Métro stations, where you can also buy carnets of tickets valid for both bus and Métro travel. You give up the number of tickets appropriate to the number of fare stages in your journey.

Here are two useful bus routes: No. 21 (north-south and south-north), from Gare St Lazare, past the Opéra, down Avenue de l'Opéra, along Rue de Rivoli, past the Louvre, across the Île de la Cité, past the Luxembourg, and so south to Porte de Gentilly; No. 73 (east-west and west-east) passes the Hôtel de Ville, Rue de Rivoli, Champs Elysées, Place de l'Étoile, Avenue de la Grande Armée, to Pont de Neuilly.

By showing their passport, foreign visitors may obtain a reduced-price ticket entitling them to unlimited travel by bus or Métro (first class) for seven consecutive days. This can be had at the R.A.T.P. office in Place de la Madeleine (on the flower market side). It may also be obtained in Britain, from French Railways, 179 Piccadilly, London, W1V 0BA.

Taxis are plentiful except during the rush-hour and there are taxi-ranks at many key points of the city. After 11 p.m. the tariff rises by about 60%. Do not be surprised to find yourself being driven by a woman; as long ago as the Belle Époque some of the horse-drawn fiacres were driven by women. The usual tip is 12 to 15%.

Driving your own or a rented car in Paris is not the most peaceful of occupations, as traffic is either congested or moves very fast. If you are slow to start when the lights change to green, the driver behind may well give you an impatient nudge with his bumper. Parking is a problem and unless you are staying beyond the Étoile, where there is space to leave a car in the streets, taking your own car is not recommended. The whole of inner Paris on the Right Bank, and the Latin Quarter on the Left Bank are now a Blue Zone, which means that parking is limited to one hour, or one hour and a half. Obtain a cardboard dial or *disque* from a tobacconist, indicate on it the time you park, and the time you will collect your car, and display it at your windscreen.

Two things to be bought on arrival are a street-plan of Paris, and *Une Semaine de Paris*, which tells you what's on in Paris generally during the current week: at the theatre, with a short description of each play, at the cinema, and at the special exhibition halls, such as the Grand Palais. The second half of this magazine is devoted to night clubs, with flashy advertisements for them which give a misleading picture of Paris as a whole, and to restaurants. Restaurants which advertise here are, with a few exceptions, to be avoided. The excellent Paris restaurants do not need to advertise.

A last word in a different key. To enjoy Paris, there is one thing you should bring with you: plenty of imagination. It is not a literal or factual city. It cannot be adequately photographed. It cannot be reduced to statistics or even to words of unambiguous meaning. Nor approached tensely, as a chore to be done. The appropriate mood, it seems to me, is gaiety, fantasy and open-mindedness to values that are not ours and to a rich past that informs every aspect of the present.

CHAPTER ONE

Smart Paris

❦

*Place de la Concorde – the Obelisk – Place Vendôme – Boule-
vard de la Madeleine – the Madeleine – Rue du Faubourg St
Honoré – Palais de l'Elysée – Avenue Matignon – Rond Point
des Champs Elysées*

PARIS is a compact city, however vast and confusing it may
appear to those who arrive for the first time. This compactness adds to the pleasure of Paris, just as unity of place adds
to the effectiveness of a play. Because much is concentrated in
little, we are continually aware of being in Paris, and nowhere
else; and we are soon able to memorise a good many streets,
like the lines of a short poem.

Soon after arriving I like to go to the **Place de la Concorde**
and stand by the fountain nearest the river, or, if the traffic
makes it difficult to cross, at the edge of the Tuileries Gardens,
facing the river. Here much of Paris is clearly visible;
here it is possible to get one's bearings, visualise the city plan,
see where one's hotel lies in relation to the landmarks and
anticipate some of the pleasures to come.

Immediately to the left are the trees of the Tuileries
Gardens: hidden beyond those trees, a mile and a half away, is
an island, the Île de la Cité, where Paris began. That was the
centre of Paris during the Roman and medieval periods, and
on the island stands Notre Dame.

Turning clockwise, we notice a line of grey houses and
apartments on the far bank of the river. These belong to the
Faubourg St Germain, fashionable residential district of the
eighteenth and nineteenth centuries. To-day, the 'noble
Faubourg' has some claim to be called Official Paris, for many
of its houses have been turned into Ministries or Embassies,
while the building with a classical façade directly across the
Seine is the Palais Bourbon, seat of the Assemblée Nationale.

Beyond, slightly to the right, is the gilded dome of the
Invalides, under which lies Napoleon. Nearby, though out of
sight, is the École Militaire: so this district can be labelled

Military Paris. Farther west, if the day is clear, we shall glimpse the Eiffel Tower, most conspicuous of a group of buildings for long associated with Exhibition Paris.

Now for the Right Bank. The chestnut trees extending along the river border the Cours la Reine, which was laid out in 1616, the first avenue in Paris designed not for traffic but purely for pleasure-driving in that new invention, the sprung carriage. The next avenue, the Champs Elysées, is also a street for promenades: heralded by Coustou's champing horses and culminating in the Arc de Triomphe, monument to France's imperial ambitions.

Directly behind the obelisk stand two eighteenth-century mansions framing the church of the Madeleine. The Madeleine quarter is fashionable and expensive: Smart Paris, if you like. Beyond, on a clear day, a cloud-like building seems to hover in the haze. That is the basilica of Sacré Coeur, standing over a mile north of the Madeleine in the hill-top village called Montmartre—for half a century, until the nineteen-twenties, centre of Artistic Paris.

Finally, looking down the centre alley of the Tuileries, we shall be able to see in the distance part of the Louvre: Royal Paris from the middle of the sixteenth century until Louis XIV moved his court to Versailles.

Each of these Parises we shall explore in due course, as well as a number of others. For the moment let us look at the Place de la Concorde itself. It may well be called the centre of modern Paris, for here, on the very spot where we are standing, the guillotine cut off Louis XVI's head and, two years later, Robespierre's. Blood had wiped out blood, the terror ended and in the following year, 1795, Frenchmen could proclaim that they were united in concord.

Place Louis XV, Place de la Révolution, Place de la Concorde—the three names the square has borne proclaim its unique place in history. The square is unique also in appearance. First, the impression of space—can this really be the centre of a city of three million inhabitants? And the way space is organised into long, majestic vistas: the way buildings, statues and trees have been manipulated to make a complex work of art. These elaborate groupings, with perspectives like those in stage scenery, are a feature of the city and I think partly induce that heightened awareness felt by many visitors. The nineteenth-century group of statuary by which we stand contains a number of male and female figures, naiads and such-like, the whole representing **Marine Navigation.** Paris has many such statues to abstract concepts: for instance, the eight female figures on pavilions surrounding the square—the provincial cities of France. Elsewhere in Paris are statues to Prudence, Law, Eloquence, Admiration, Inspiration, Medieval Art, Cantata, Consular Jurisdiction, Family Joy and more than a hundred other abstractions. These statues have their amusing side but it is worth remembering that to the Parisian they cause no amusement nor are they in the least a mark of affectation. It is natural for the Parisian to make and admire such statues, for the tendency to personification is inherent in the French language. Marine Navigation is feminine —a woman, like the Seine itself. Nothing in the French language is neuter, and nothing in Paris is quite inanimate. Even its streets and squares usually bear the names of persons.

On the other side of the platform Marine Navigation has a twin in **Inland Navigation:** the names are different but to me at least the fountains have always appeared identical. Between the two fountains, on the spot where Louis XV's statue once stood, rises the **Obelisk.** A monolith of pink syenite dating from the thirteenth century B.C. it is the oldest monument in Paris. Its hieroglyphic ducks, owls and locusts glorify Rameses II, 'master of the earth, terrible golden falcon.' The obelisk was a gift from Mehmet Ali, viceroy of Egypt—a nineteenth-century Colonel Nasser with a weakness for giving away obelisks. Paris was first to erect hers, in 1836; London followed in 1878, New York in 1880.

Louis Philippe erected the obelisk on this key spot because an obelisk was considered a non-political monument, something quite neutral. But is it as neutral as all that? The inscription on the east face describes it as a monument to France's recent glory on the Nile—Napoleon's campaign, which freed Egypt from the Mamelukes. In 1836 Paris, starved by Louis Philippe of pomp and ceremony, was harking back to the glories of Napoleon. But the association with Napoleon is closer still. The young conqueror of Egypt had seen obelisks on campaign (though not this particular one, which stood far south, in Luxor); stirred and interested, he ordered reports. Rome, he knew, had her obelisks: Augustus had set up one in the Circus Maximus. Love of things Eastern and his ever-present urge to emulate Rome here coincided and Napoleon decreed that Paris too should have her

obelisk; he even chose its site, on the Left Bank beside the
Seine. Napoleon's obelisk was never built; it was left to
Louis Philippe to realise the Emperor's dream and in his
down-to-earth practical way explain in a series of carvings
exactly how the obelisk was lowered, transported and re-
erected. Napoleon would never have added those explanatory
carvings. The inscription on the west face records that the
engineer who erected it was a certain Monsieur Lebas and that
he did so 'to the applause of an immense crowd'.

Strong though the echoes of Napoleon may be, I always
think of the obelisk in quite another context. Its original use
was astronomical—to measure the shadow of the sun—and it
came to serve as a royal monument only because the Pharaohs
were associated with the Sun God. What the obelisk pro-
claims is that a king is king by divine right, that he is associated with the sun, that the king, in fact, is *le roi soleil*. Did
Louis Philippe have this at the back of his mind? Did he
associate the obelisk with Louis XIV? Perhaps not. At any
rate, there it stands in the centre of the world's greatest and
handsomest square, an indirect reminder, for those who care
to see it as such, of Louis XIV, *le roi soleil*, France's ruler for
seventy-two years, who more than any other man set his
stamp on Paris, whose taste and planning are still the pattern
for Paris, two of whose works, the Champs Elysées and
Tuileries Gardens, are among the most beautiful things before
our eyes at the moment.

Let us walk now to Louis XIV's own square, the Place
Vendôme, round by the Madeleine to the Champs Elysées,
through the heart of what we have termed Smart Paris; in
doing so we shall be able to see some of the best shops and a
few important buildings.

We cross to the **Tuileries** between winged horses by Coysevox (**Fame** and **Mercury**, each carved entire, even Fame's
trumpet, from a single block of marble). Horses we shall find
a recurrent feature of Parisian art: these balance the **Marly
horses**, on the other side of the square, the work of Coysevox's
nephew, Guillaume Coustou. A path across the corner of the
Tuileries leads to a stairway between bronze animal groups.
The long street flanking the gardens is **Rue de Rivoli**; the street
leading off it, opposite the stairway, is **Rue de Castiglione**.
Both were built by Napoleon and their deep arcades have an
Italian flavour, appropriately enough since they were named
after his victories in Italy.

The shops of Rue de Castiglione are, as it were, an apéritif to this smart quarter. They are elegant but not nearly as elegant as those to come. For men, very narrow silk ties and hand-made shirts with odd, rounded collars; gold lighters, foulards printed with 1900 motor cars or aeroplanes of the twenties—the difference matters in Paris, where fashion extends even to the obsolete. The ladies' shops display lizardskin handbags of so fine a grain they look like petit-point and umbrellas with long, precious handles. '*Frivolités*' the provincial French call such unessentials—what a delightful word!—but a Parisienne, who considers these trappings very important, would never call them that.

A word about street numbering. Walking up Rue de Castiglione we notice that numbering begins at the bottom, odd numbers on the left, even numbers on the right. Throughout Paris houses are numbered according to the following logical system: in streets such as this, which run at right angles to the Seine, numbering begins nearest the river, while in streets parallel to the Seine the numbering, following the current, begins in the east. Odd numbers are always on the left, even numbers always on the right.

Rue de Castiglione leads into the Place Vendôme, an octagonal square surrounded by houses of uniform design. It was laid out as a setting for an equestrian statue of Louis XIV and remains the most perfect group of seventeenth-century architecture in Paris. Louis's sun emblem can be seen on several of the balconies, against the reticent façades. How well the stone has aged—dry tertiary limestone quarried on the Left Bank, grey in colour, softening to white in the sun. It has a tendency to be grim, and so requires much space around it and, above, a wide sky. It lends itself hardly at all to intricate carving but admirably to line. As in a grey flannel suit, cut is everything.

Against the grey stone lies the gilt or polished brass of the shop names. Such discretion! Yet shop is hardly the word for the establishments surrounding this square, almost every one with a famous name. Rouff, celebrated for embroidered table linen; Charvet, where Edward VII used to buy his foulards (but this information, needless to add, is not displayed); Chaumet, Mauboussin, Boucheron, jewellers whose names are so evocative that they display in their black velvet cases merely a scattering of choice diamonds. Within many of the courtyards, which can just be glimpsed from the square, are

offices of banks and stockbrokers, all adding to the impression
of unostentatious wealth; on the other side of the square at
No. 15 is the Ritz Hotel.

In the centre stands the **Vendôme column**, erected by
Napoleon to commemorate the campaigns of 1805–7, the
spiral of reliefs originally cast from captured Russian and
Austrian cannon. The column was so much damaged when
Courbet and other revolutionaries pulled it down in 1871 that
it is now covered by new bronze plaques moulded from the
originals. The statue at the top represents Napoleon as Caesar.
The column was built in frank imitation of Trajan's column in
Rome: an imperial monument to glorify the new Empire. The
thread of the campaigns is, to say the least, difficult to follow,
but the number of mountains crossed and bridges built is
remarkable and brings out an aspect of Napoleon's genius
sometimes forgotten: his skill as an engineer.

Out of the Place Vendôme, Rue de la Paix leads into **Rue des
Capucines**. In this street we are midway between the first and
second arrondissements: the left pavement, like the Place
Vendôme, lies in the first arrondissement; the right pavement
in the second. One way to learn the arrondissements is to
imagine Paris as a spirally coiled shell, its apex pointing to the
sky at the centre of the Île de la Cité. The arrondissements
would then follow the line of its shell, unfolding clockwise in
three rings. Thus the two most fashionable residential districts, VIII and XVI, are contiguous, lying west along the Seine
from the first arrondissement.

At **Boulevard de la Madeleine** we enter quite a different
Paris: pass from the seventeenth to the twentieth century.
Wider streets, lined with trees, bustling shops and traffic,
cinemas and neon signs, kiosks, brasseries and cafés. The
Grands Boulevards, laid out along the line of fourteenth-
century fortifications or 'bulwarks', marked the limits of Paris
until the time of Louis XIV. They extend in a semicircle as
far as the Place de la Bastille. They are still lively, but their
heyday was under the Second Empire, when dandies with
gold-knobbed canes used to quiz the pretty girls and the Jockey
Club stood where Rue Scribe joins Boulevard des Capucines.
Literary, artistic and political Paris have now moved elsewhere, and the Boulevards are chiefly a shopping centre: not
for the very rich but for ordinary well-to-do women. At the
end of Rue Scribe lies Boulevard Haussmann, with the two
best Paris department stores: Le Printemps and Galeries

Lafayette, while down the Boulevard de la Madeleine stands a close rival, Les Trois Quartiers.

The throng of shoppers and others in the Boulevards, cafés with every outside table taken, cars speeding from one traffic-jam to the next: these are signs that Paris is the most densely populated city in the world. This density is not, I think, something to be regretted, for it arises from the compactness of Paris and the limit on the height of buildings. The city, being built to human scale, does not crush the individual: he never feels here, as in some capitals, that he is merely a unit in a vast sprawling urban aggregate.

At the end of Boulevard de la Madeleine stands the building which gives the street its name: the church of Ste Marie Madeleine, called La Madeleine; this saint being treated with the same apt familiarity in France as in England (Magdalen, Oxford and Magdalene, Cambridge). The plans for a Roman-style temple date from 1764: even before the Revolution art had prophetically turned from frivolity to the republican virtues. Napoleon continued the building, intending it as a Temple of Glory to the Grande Armée; after his death it was restored to divine worship. From the outside it is a cold, tight, rather stiff building: twice removed from its original inspiration, the Periclean temple, and lacking both Greek proportions and a burning Greek sun. The exterior is seen at its best on a bright summer Tuesday or Friday, when a flower market is held in the Place. As for the interior, it is best visited on a Sunday, when a smart congregation attends High Mass; for the church can boast little of artistic value save the bronze doors, with fine bas-reliefs of the Ten Commandments. They are the work of Triqueti, known also for his mosaic-work in Windsor Chapel.

High Mass at the Madeleine differs from masses elsewhere as a première of *Phèdre* at the Comédie Française differs from an evening, say, at the Châtelet or Olympia. The congregation is immaculately turned out without the slightest suggestion of flashiness. Families come even from Passy: children dressed as children, not as miniature grown-ups, small sons well-scrubbed, wearing neatly pressed suits with short trousers, daughters in plain or severe colours, with simple round hat or beret and white socks. Excellent organ music, the white and gilt fluted columns, comfortable hassocks create an atmosphere of reasonable, cheerful devotion.

The officiating clergy are led to the altar by the *suisse*, or beadle, magnificent in black frock-coat, with red sash and red cuffs, his head crowned by a white-frilled tricorne. He swaggers up the steps, flourishing his staff of office in white-gloved hands, and thereafter treats clergy and laity alike as though he were an orchestra conductor in charge of the whole rite. Only slightly less magnificent are the lesser *suisses* who pass the collection plates, halting at every pew, thumping their staffs on the floor and announcing the good cause: for example, '*Pour les pauvres de la paroisse*'—not that there are many poor in the Madeleine parish.

Why are they called *suisses*? It seems that a long friendship between France and her neighbour culminated in the Peace of Fribourg, whereby François I was permitted to recruit up to 16,000 Swiss soldiers—an élite which bravely gave its blood on the battlefield and guarded the monarchy until the massacre of the Tuileries. Members of the Swiss Guard were employed to keep order in church and the name is still applied to the Frenchmen who perform this office.

After the *suisse* has with a final flourish led the clergy back to the sacristy, the organist strikes up a daring, difficult piece and the congregation files out—to the *pâtisseries* which lie so conveniently close. Pastries are bought for lunch and the children—provided they have been *sages*—are occasionally allowed to eat in the shop an éclair or *mille-feuille*.

From the steps of the Madeleine there is a fine view of the Place de la Concorde and the Palais Bourbon, known also as the **Assemblée Nationale.** The façade, a portico with twelve Corinthian columns, was added to the *back* of the original mansion, which had then been standing for the better part of a hundred years, simply to balance the façade of the Madeleine. What other city in the world would drastically alter a public building merely to bring it into harmony with a church standing half a mile off?

We take Rue Royale, a wide street of eighteenth-century houses and famous shops, and turn into **Rue du Faubourg St Honoré**, named after a former church to a sixth-century bishop of Amiens who—no one knows why—is patron of pastry-makers. This is a street of shops like no other in the world. Each window is a work of art where goods are arranged as carefully and imaginatively as in a painting or *collage*. One window may display exotic flowers composed of white ostrich plumes, another's flowers are dried ears and leaves of maize, yet another's simply twisted paper—and the result is not artificial flowers but a certain mood designed to set off the goods in the window. In this street window-dressing reaches the level of stage-production, and window-shopping becomes as exciting as a visit to a theatre or ballet.

I like coming here on the first day of a visit to Paris because the style of the window-arrangements, which changes as markedly as the length of skirts or the popularity of a novelist, will reveal at once the present mood of Paris. For Paris is as moody as a woman, and her moods the world names fashions. One season she has to wear green, has to dine at the Petit Bedon, has to summer on a Brittany beach: next season green and the Petit Bedon and the Brittany beach have gone the way of the New Look.

Most of the shops are on the north, sunny side of the street, but I usually begin at No. 5, Henry à la Pensée, partly for its irresistible name, then cross to No. 20, the antique shop founded by Yvonne de Bremond d'Ars. Her adventures as an antique-dealer are described in a number of charming books —some have been translated. The shop is stocked with delectable objects, but like most Paris antiques they are more expensive than English antiques in England. Farther along is Hermès, whose windows are perhaps the most famous in the world. Hermès specialises in leather goods, saddles and riding foulards: should you desperately need, shall we say, a pair of wild ass-skin gloves, this is the place to come. Hermès also makes one of the best French scents: *Calèche*.

Her luxury goods are unsurpassed, and that is as it should be, since Paris has been making them since the Middle Ages. French kings had far more money to spend than other European sovereigns; they could afford luxury themselves and expected luxury in their courtiers. The inventory of Madame de Pompadour's possessions—dresses, silver, furniture, china and so on—took two lawyers more than a year to compile. With the fall of the Bourbons came simplicity, then a marked decline in taste, but now Paris has found a new market—in the rich of the whole world. To-day her best customers may well be an oil sheikh or a Brazilian coffee-planter, but her standards are unlowered. The goods are not necessarily better made than those to be found in other capital cities—they are certainly more expensive—but they are worth the price because nothing is standardised, everything has an individual touch which makes it precious. They also have that intangible quality: chic. Chic being a matter of good taste, sense of line and genius for detail: perhaps a small gilt buckle on the back of a glove, or a heart-shaped lock on a jewel-case.

This most marvellous of streets also possesses two of the finest buildings in Paris, the first being the **British Embassy,** an early eighteenth-century house designed by Mazin and bought in 1814 by the Duke of Wellington from Napoleon's second sister, Pauline Bonaparte. During the day its gates are open, giving a view of the inner courtyard. The house stands well back from the street and looks on to gardens behind. This is the basic plan of most private houses in Paris: almost nothing of them can be seen from the street and the inquisitive traveller must somehow find his way into the courtyard.

At No. 76, on the first floor, is the **Galerie Charpentier,** one of the world's leading art galleries, famous for its sales and exhibitions, either on a given theme (Bread and Wine, 1954) or of a particular master (Douanier Rousseau, 1961). Here and in other galleries of this neighbourhood illustrated posters will be on display announcing an exhibition in this or that gallery: hereabouts it is likely to be of established painters such as Buffet or Bazaine, while the Left Bank galleries show unknown or lesser known artists at correspondingly lower prices. One way of sampling the current exhibitions (they are numerous, for in Paris studios 50,000 artists are busy painting, drawing and sculpturing) is to watch these posters for a painting which catches your interest and note the address of the gallery; another way is to buy the best of the literary-artistic weeklies, *Arts*, which lists many of the exhibitions, with photographs of typical canvases—rather blurred photographs but enough to give you an idea.[1]

Farther along, an increasing number of *agents* in navy-blue capes, white truncheons at their hips, and the presence of armed sentries with white belts and red cockades mark the entrance to the **Palais de l'Elysée**, official residence of the President of the Republic. The palace was designed in 1718 by Molet for the Comte d'Evreux, a colonel-general in the cavalry, as the military trophies carved on the entrance archway recall—a sumptuous palace to be built for a notoriously parsimonious man, and the explanation is this. Evreux had occasion to ask a favour of the Regent who, to correct the Count's avarice, announced that he would deliver his reply in person. Now Evreux, although he had married an heiress,

[1] For a list of recommended galleries, see p. 246.

lived in a very modest house. His pride being touched, he sold much of his land, raised 800,000 *livres* and built the Elysée. Three years later the Regent made him a gift of much of the present garden.

The house was later bought by Madame de Pompadour, who had it decorated by Boucher and Van Loo, and extended the garden in a semicircle, which even to-day protrudes into the Champs Elysées. For ten years, under the Pompadour, it rang with laughter and play; then it was bought by Beaujon the banker, an invalid suffering from the stone, confined to a wheelchair and a diet of boiled spinach. To ensure good medical treatment Beaujon arranged for his doctor to be paid a princely annual salary, to cease immediately in case of his patient's death! After the Revolution the house again reverted to frivolity, becoming a restaurant and night club. In 1805 Murat bought it and, when he was made King of Naples, gave it to his brother-in-law, Napoleon. Here in 1815 Napoleon signed his second abdication. Thereafter, until 1873, it served chiefly as a residence for royalty on state visits to Paris, including Queen Victoria, when she attended the Great Exhibition of 1855.

We now arrive at **Avenue Matignon**: fewer shops, more art galleries and—chief feature of this street and the Rond Point —leading couturiers, such as Jacques Heim, Jean Dessès and Carven. The father of all French couturiers, Worth, is at No. 120 Rue du Faubourg St Honoré, just after the turning down Avenue Matignon. Charles Frederick Worth, a Lincolnshire man, started as an apprentice of Swan and Edgar, London. In 1846, at the age of twenty-one, he emigrated to Paris and after a dozen years with a silk mercer founded his own fashion house. He was soon patronised by the Empress Eugénie, to whom henceforth he showed every novelty. His original shop in Rue de la Paix set the fashion for wealthy Paris and made Worth a fortune, part of which he spent on buying some of the columns of the demolished Tuileries to decorate his own sumptuous villa.

There is little to distinguish these fashion houses in Avenue Matignon from private houses, for the couturier looks on himself as an artist, and indeed he is. The collections of spring suits and summer dresses are presented in February, of autumn and winter clothes in July. Except during the months of January, February, July and August it is possible to attend a showing at any of the twenty-odd big couturiers, either

through one's hotel concierge or by telephoning directly.[1]
The showing begins about three or three-thirty. On arrival you
may be asked for your passport, to be sure that your occupation is not listed as dress-designer. With evening dresses as
with atomic submarines—spies are not welcome! Then you
are put under the care of a *vendeuse*—this is a mere convenience; there is no obligation to buy—who seats you in one of
the rooms and gives you a card with up to 200 models listed.
The number and name of each model is called out as the
mannequin passes through the room. After the showing,
which lasts over two hours, you can try on a model you have
liked. If the model suits you, the cost of having a new creation,
an 'original' exactly like the model, will be upwards of
2,000 francs. It will entail three or four fittings, during which
twenty different measurements are taken. It is slightly less
expensive to reserve one of the models worn by a mannequin,
and considerably cheaper to patronise the boutiques on the
ground floor of the fashion houses. Here a smaller range of
clothes is to be had, made with only one or two fittings, at a
third or half the price of an 'original'. Here too, at the end of
December and July, sales are held.

At the corner of Avenue Matignon and Avenue Gabriel is
the Elysées Matignon, a restaurant and club favoured by the
film world. Many of the film-company offices, with the big
motorcar showrooms, are situated in the next street, the
Champs Elysées.

The name Champs Elysées was applied at the end of the
seventeenth century to a piece of marshy ground outside the
city, through which André Le Nôtre extended the perspective
from the Tuileries with an avenue lined by a double row of
elms. This went no farther than the Rond Point, where we now
stand. It became a popular carriage-drive, was improved and
enlarged by Madame de Pompadour's brother, and under the
Second Empire became virtually a parade-ground of fashion,
with a continual procession of smart broughams and gigs.
Sexagenarians can remember when there was not a single shop
among the houses lining the Champs Elysées; now there is
not a single house among the shops, show-rooms, cafés and
cinemas. But it remains primarily what it always was: a place
of promenade. From it we can get a good view up to the Arc
de Triomphe and down to our starting-point, the obelisk.

So much by way of introduction to this part of Paris. From

[1] For a list of couturiers, see p. 246.

the Rond Point the indefatigable visitor may want to stroll to one of the cafés farther up the Champs Elysées or join the promenade. Perhaps, surfeited with shops and streets, he may want to return to his hotel. There is a Métro station at the Rond Point and several bus lines pass here.

By now we have seen a good many Parisians, most of them well-to-do, for the poorer people seldom come west of Boulevard de Sébastopol. Who are they? Well, the majority were born in the provinces: only forty-seven out of a hundred are likely to be natives of Paris. This underlines an important point: Paris is rooted in the provinces: indeed much of her strength lies in the tension between northern vigour and southern verve, logic and swagger, discipline and fantasy, sense of line and sense of colour.

One of the most obvious features of these Parisians we have seen in street, shop and café is their self-assurance. They look assured because the odds are that they feel secure. They were probably brought up in a united family (divorce is still rare in France) according to certain unchallenged traditions, against the background of conservatism and continuity so evident, say, in the buildings of Paris.

Another obvious feature is that the men are aware of the women, and the women are aware that the men are aware of them. There is flirtation in the air (not for nothing are the café chairs arranged two by two). The women are well groomed and elegantly dressed. Clothes are expensive and so nothing, not even a belt, is bought without careful consideration. Will it go with my grey suit? Will it match my new suède shoes? So everything is just right. But the Parisian woman is rarely narcissistic. She dresses to give pleasure and to make the men aware of her.

The sense of line so evident in Parisian dress we have noticed already in the Place de la Concorde and the Place Vendôme; the flair for setting off beauty we have seen in the shops of the Faubourg St Honoré. Parisians have made Paris, and Paris in turn moulds them: stimulating, demanding an adequate response. Hence the speed of Paris life: the speed of traffic, the speed at which things are said and understood, the delight in curt epigrams, quick sentences with tailor-made lines. But enough. All this and more will become apparent, I hope, as Paris gradually unfolds.

CHAPTER TWO

The Cité

❧

*Pont au Change – Tour de l'Horloge – Notre Dame – Flower
Market – Sainte Chapelle – Law Courts*

SINCE Paris began on the Cité, let the Cité be our starting-
point. As we cross the **Pont au Change** from the Place du
Châtelet, there is time to glance quickly at the history of Paris
before buildings take over the story. At the coming of Julius
Caesar, who first mentions Paris under the name of Lutetia,
the island of the Cité was a fortified village belonging to the
Parisii, a tribe of perhaps 30,000 peasants, producing oats,
wheat and barley. Well-sited though it was, the island fortress
fell to Caesar's legions and the Parisii were brought within the
bounds of the Empire. An arena for gladiatorial shows, baths
and bridges were built (one immediately upstream from the
Pont au Change, where the Pont Notre Dame now stands).
On the island a Roman governor imposed Roman laws and
moved his occupying troops along new straight stone roads.
Yet all around lay savagery: on winter nights wolves and boar
would issue from the thick surrounding forests to roam the
town.

In the middle of the third century[1] an Athenian named
Dionysius—St Denis—introduced Christianity to Paris. St
Denis was beheaded but the new faith flourished. As Roman
power declined, abbeys and monasteries on the Left Bank of
the Seine replaced the legions' barracks. Local pride reasserted
itself. In the fourth century a milestone and a synodal letter
refer to the town for the first time as Paris.

In the fifth century Franks from the Rhine captured Paris,
but the Parisians, now stalwart Christians, converted their
new masters, though at first to the Franks Christ was merely
a new and more powerful tribal god. The early Frankish
kings lived little in Paris—they wandered, transported by long

[1] The date is uncertain. Monsieur R. Héron de Villefosse, an expert
on the Cité, speaks of the end of the first century, which would allow one
to accept the legend that St Denis was converted in Athens by St Paul.

teams of oxen. The town continued to grow, not in one piece but in patches clustered around the monasteries.

Charlemagne's empire demanded a capital near the centre of power: Aix-la-Chapelle. Only under Charlemagne's successors, when the empire fell apart, did Paris assume the leadership. It happened like this. A Norman army of forty thousand—women as well as men—sailed up the Seine in seven hundred warships. The Parisians barred their way—to Paris and to all France. The crucial battle was fought on a small bridge on the other side of the island, where the Petit Pont now stands. Here in 886 a dozen Parisians fought off an attack by flaxen-haired Normans using flaming arrows and burning pitch. By repulsing the Norman invasion, Count Odo, commander of the island fortress, gained immense authority: his nephew Hugh Capet had only to defeat the discredited Carlovingians to become king. And now Paris, capital of the duchy of France, that is to say of Île de France—the countryside around Paris—was recognised also as capital of the new kingdom.

Under the Capetian dynasty Paris spread to the Right Bank and for two centuries increased in size and wealth. It was well placed in the centre of Northern France, the Seine made trading easy, durable building stone lay in extensive quarries on the Left Bank. The kings began to build, and although a thousand years had passed since the arrival of Caesar, the site and purpose of their buildings were dictated by what the Romans had done.

As we cross the Pont au Change, we see three pepper-pot towers. These are the first visible vestiges of the past on this side of the island. The towers were built by St Louis in the thirteenth century as part of the fortifications of his palace. The tower on the left is called **Tour de César**: for this was the site of the Roman governor's palace, and here a visiting Emperor would stay. The middle tower, the **Tour d'Argent**, served as the king's treasury. The right-hand tower is called **Tour de Bonbec**, Bonbec meaning someone who talks a lot, in allusion to the confessions exacted here from prisoners under torture.

The buildings between and behind the towers are modern but the towers bear witness to the continuity of ideas. Roman power had been based on law and justice; and the medieval kings who lived here were regarded above all as dispensers of justice, St Louis being the best loved of French kings precisely

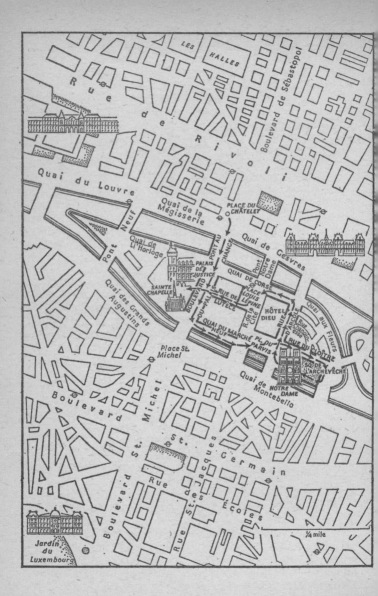

because of his proverbial justice. François I was the last king to reside in the island palace, but when the royal court crossed to the Right Bank, the courts of justice remained here. To-day, these buildings united by St Louis's towers are still the **Palais de Justice**, or Law Courts.

The square corner tower near the Pont au Change, called the **Tour de l'Horloge**, dates from the fourteenth century, its clock from the sixteenth, though the dial is a copy. It is the oldest public clock in the world, and the lower of its two Latin inscriptions alludes to the Law Courts: 'This clock which divides the day into twelve equal parts is a lesson that Justice must be protected and the law defended.'

Boulevard du Palais passes in front of the entrance to the Law Courts (to which we shall return later, when they open at noon) and ends in the Quai du Marché Neuf, which leads to the **Place du Parvis**. Here a bronze star marks the theoretical centre of Paris, from which are measured all road distances between the capital and other cities. *Parvis* is a corruption of *paradisus*, the earthly paradise, whence the cathedral, figure of the heavenly Jerusalem, can be seen in all its splendour.

Notre Dame it seems to me is the most original building in Paris, in the sense that it is the least derivative: this is the earliest Gothic cathedral, and the Gothic was conceived in Paris and the surrounding countryside. For a thousand years the rounded arch of Rome had been the basis of every important French building: like Roman law, it was unchallengeable. And suddenly, here in Paris, architects flung that heavy, rather earthy line into the air, hammered it out like a sword until it was long and fine. The body of the church, as though in response to St Bernard's ascetic sermons, became lean and airy and light. Paris has a northern climate, with few hot sunny days: for that reason also the Romanesque, squat and dark against the southern sun, had come to dissatisfy her. The Gothic is her quest for light.

The façade consists of three stories, the lower two tripartite. The first story comprises the portals, the gallery of twenty-eight Kings of Judah and a balustrade on which Mary, the new Eve, stands between Adam and Eve. The Kings are here because they were Mary's ancestors. But why such a prominent place to ancestors? The answer is that the thirteenth century believed nobility of birth to be intimately linked with nobility of soul. Mary's royal ancestors helped to confirm the idea of Mary's immaculate nature.

The second story comprises the rose-window flanked by double windows within arches, surmounted by a soaring, open arcade with slender columns. Above rise the towers, which look so complete although in fact they were intended to be crowned with spires. The spire, the flèche, the tapering pinnacle: these were the delight of the thirteenth and fourteenth centuries, as we can see in miniatures of Paris from that period.

Above the centre door, the **Porte du Jugement**, is carved the Second Coming. This was a traditional feature, for here on the west front it would catch the setting sun. On the left Abraham holds three of the elect in his bosom, while among the dead rising is a crusader in chain-mail, reminding us that the Crusades were largely a product of French chivalry, and that this doorway was built in the reign of St Louis, who led the seventh and eighth Crusades.

The sculptor gains his effect by contrasting calm and turbulence, first between the elect and damned, then, lower down, between the virtues and vices. The first medallion on the right is notable: a crusader personifies courage while, below, cowardice takes the form of a woman running away from a hare. These medallions figure here because they form the matter of man's last judgement.

The right doorway is the **Portal of St Anne**. The façade has already emphasised the historic aspect of Mary's role in the Redemption (Adam and Eve, the Kings of Judah): this portal is a continuation of the same line of thought. The closer to Mary, the closer to her fullness of grace, so that some theologians even asserted that Anne like her daughter was sinless. Scenes from the life of St Anne and the Virgin figure on the lintel. The kneeling figure on the right of the tympanum is Louis VII giving his charter to the new cathedral: it was during Louis VII's reign, in 1163, that the Pope laid the foundation-stone. The prelate on the right is Maurice de Sully, bishop of Paris, founder of the cathedral. The son of a poor woodcutter, his sermons show him to have been an energetic, direct and eminently sensible bishop, and history records that he was one of the staunchest defenders of Thomas à Becket in his struggle with Henry II. An earlier bishop of Paris, St Marcel, stands on the pier (the statue is a modern replacement): he tramples the river-dragon he killed after it had long ravaged Paris. All the west doors have beautiful hinges but the hinges on this door are the most intricate: legend has it that they were made not by men but by a horned she-devil of the name of Biscornette, to whom the smith had sold his soul.

The left-hand doorway, the **Portal of the Virgin,** has the best statues. On the central pier stands Mary herself, a grave, unsmiling, remote figure. On the lintel three prophets and three kings again emphasise that Mary was a woman foretold. The cupboard-shaped carving is the Ark of the Covenant, a favourite symbol of Mary's motherhood. Above are the Raising of Mary (the angels, out of respect, do not touch her body, but carry it in a cloth), the Assumption and Coronation. The devils squashed in the niches on either side of the door contrast tellingly with the calm saints standing above: the saint carrying his own head is Denis, first bishop of Paris. On the edge of the door are bas-reliefs showing the labours of the twelve months: the point being that work is good and a means to redemption. Similarly, the seven liberal arts used to be depicted on the central portal, but were removed in the eighteenth century.

The west front was built after the nave, so that to enter the cathedral is to go back a generation. The pillars are still heavy and short, while their capitals mostly lack the conventional foliage that marks thirteenth-century Gothic. Of the rose-windows, that in the north transept is composed of blues and reds which give an impression in some lights of mauve, in others of violet. The rose-window was a Gothic creation, its floral shape recalling Mary's title, 'Rose of Paradise.' The north rose is consecrated to the Old Testament, north being the region of cold and night. The Virgin is the centre of the rose, the petals being patriarchs, prophets and kings—a restatement in glass of the sculptors' theme. The west window is redder, the south (the region of light and therefore consecrated to the New Testament) much restored and lacking unity of colour.

Against the south-east pillar of the transept stands a fourteenth century statue of Notre Dame de Paris. Whereas the figure we have just seen on the left portal was straight, ageless, and emotionless, an aloof generic figure akin to the philosophers' universal, almost the idea of queenliness, here is a particular person, supple, turning tenderly to her child. Only a hundred years separate the two statues, but in that time St Francis of Assisi's teaching had turned the course of Christian art into more emotional channels.

Of the carved wooden **screen** which once surrounded the choir only two sections remain. That on the south shows appearances of Christ after His Resurrection (including the apocryphal appearance to St Peter), that on the north, the older, scenes from His early life. In the 'Flight into Egypt' two broken gilt figures on a pedestal are somewhat puzzling: they depict a then popular apocryphal tradition, that as the Holy Family passed on their journey, so pagan statues fell to the ground and were shattered.

Of later art in the cathedral the only remarkable works are the **stalls** (late seventeenth century) and the **Pietà** behind the High Altar, by Nicolas Coustou. Nicolas was elder brother of Guillaume, sculptor of the Marly Horses flanking the Champs Elysées. The tombs in the ambulatory are of little interest, for the place of burial of the French kings is Saint Denis, just as the place of coronation was Rheims.

Of the great ceremonies which took place in the Cathedral the first was the celebration of the first Mass at the High Altar by Heraclius of Jerusalem. Since the foundation-stone had been laid by the Bishop of Rome, the cathedral thus forcibly asserted the unity of Eastern and Western Christendom. The most spectacular ceremony was doubtless the crowning of Napoleon, David's painting of which hangs in the Louvre. But then Notre Dame was merely a décor. Personally, I like to imagine an earlier scene: a candle burning before the High Altar, not an ordinary candle but one five miles long, wound round a huge wooden bobbin. During the troubles of the Hundred Years War the Parisians vowed to offer annually to Notre Dame a candle as long as the circumference of the city. The custom was maintained for 250 years, until the size of the candle had really become unmanageable.

What the circumference of Paris was in the middle of the fourteenth century can be seen by climbing the 387 steps of the **North Tower** (*open* 10–4 *except Tuesday; entrance in Rue du Cloître Notre Dame*), and so gaining the most central, though not the most extensive, view of the city. The medieval walls extended in a circle from the Cour Carrée of the Louvre in the west, up and along the line of the Boulevards, then down across the Île St Louis, skirting the large expanse of green (the Luxembourg Gardens), then back to the Louvre. The tower also provides a close view of the grotesque gargoyles. These no longer carry rain-water clear of the walls, but presumably still exercise their other function of warding off from the precincts evil spirits.

Continuing along the north wall of the cathedral, we find the tympanum of the **North Porch** decorated with the miracle of St Theophilus, a story as familiar in the Middle Ages as the story of Bernadette of Lourdes to-day. Theophilus, it seems, was secular deputy of the Bishop of Adana, Turkey, in the sixth century: a man so pious that when the bishop died the people unanimously elected him successor. Such was his modesty, Theophilus declined the office and remained simple deputy to the new bishop. As such he appears in the top carving, seated on the right of his bishop.

The devil soon makes Theophilus long for the power he has declined. He consults a Jew skilled in black magic and agrees to damn his soul if Satan will give him worldly glory. The pact is drawn up on parchment, and Theophilus signs his name. The next carving shows Satan appearing at the magician's summons and carrying off the parchment. Thenceforth Theophilus enjoys worldly success. He soon supplants his bishop in popular favour; to him, as the next scene shows, come all the honours and gifts. But he begins to feel the pangs of remorse and one night after having prayed a long while before a statue of Mary, he goes to sleep in church. He dreams that Mary in radiant light appears to him, pardons his sin and gives him back the parchment which she has wrested from the devil. When he wakes, he discovers that his dream has really taken place, and that he is holding the parchment in his hand. So popular was this anticipation of the Faust legend that it again figures on bas-reliefs farther along this wall.

Beyond the North Portal is a little gem of carving, the **Porte Rouge**, with scenes from the life of St Marcel in the vaulting. This door was reserved for the canons, who lived in the narrow streets opposite. In one of the streets, Rue Chanoinesse, Abélard gave lessons to Héloïse in the house of her uncle, Fulbert, a canon of Notre Dame. Now the scarlet-clad canons walk there no more: instead black and white patrol cars file into this street twice a day, for here is the central police garage, conveniently near the Préfecture de Police in the Boulevard du Palais.

The garden behind the apse provides an excellent view of the flying buttresses—the bones of the building, as it were, thrust outside in the interests of light and space—and of the flèche—a restoration of Viollet le Duc—in the ball of which are relics of the True Cross and Crown of Thorns. The **South Porch** is decorated with scenes from the life of St Stephen, aptly so, for Notre Dame was built partly on the site of a fourth-century church of St Stephen, perhaps the mother-church of Paris.

To every medieval cathedral its school and hospital. Nothing remains of the school, which stood to the north, but the present Rue d'Arcole flanks the **Hôtel Dieu,** a nineteenth-century replacement. Originally, the bishop's own house was open to the needy, then a special building—Hôpital des Pauvres—was set aside, first mentioned in 829. In the fifteenth century its 303 beds could each receive two or three patients (not an unusual medieval practice: three in one bed was also a custom in inns). Treatment was free at the king's expense. The present building is dark and massive: the best one can say of it is that it does not clash with its Gothic neighbour.

From here it is a short walk to the Sainte Chapelle. The Quai de Corse and later Place Louis Lépine are likely to resemble a garden, with shrubs, cacti, flowers in pots, cut flowers and even fruit trees, roots swaddled in straw, branches neatly trained *en espalier* in the way French gardeners prefer. Even when the streets are deep in snow, here in the **flower market** you find the luxuriant colours of azaleas and mimosa, for Paris can draw directly on her Mediterranean coast. On Sundays the flower market becomes a bird market; and this too seems rather a Mediterranean importation. However gaily the linnets or canaries may chirp they surely cannot be happy and I like to recall that whenever a king made his first public entry into Paris, the bird sellers (gathered in those days on the Pont au Change) were paid to open their cages and release two thousand four hundred birds 'so that the air was darkened by the beating of their wings.'

Rue de Lutèce leads to the courtyard of the Palais de Justice, at the left of which is a vaulted passage to the **Sainte Chapelle.** (*Open daily except Tuesday*, 10–11.45; 1.30–5.30.) Because the Sainte Chapelle was a court oratory within the royal palace, lords and servants worshipped separately. The lower chapel, the roof of which is supported on forty single-shaft columns with fine carved bosses, is merely the squat muscular acrobat, on whose bent back is balanced, arms up-stretched, his soaring, radiant partner.

The approach to the upper chapel is by way of the left-hand spiral staircase, though originally, as we know from old engravings, there was a more imposing outer staircase. On the last step the stained glass appears, for which each person will want to choose his own superlatives. The sense of a single work of art, complete in itself and unified, stems perhaps from the fact that the chapel rose in a single élan, in thirty-three months (1245–8). It had to rise quickly, for the relics it was built to contain were already in Paris, waiting.

In 1238 the saintly Louis was shocked by news that the Crown of Thorns was a forfeited pledge at Venice for an unpaid loan advanced by Venetian merchants to the Emperor Baldwin of Constantinople. Louis paid the debt and secured the relic, to which a little later was added part of the True Cross. The last window on the right shows St Louis receiving the relics at Sens, helping to carry them barefoot, taking part at their exposition with his queen and his mother, receiving an embassy from the Emperor Baldwin, and carrying the Byzantine cross which holds part of the True Cross. We cannot see his features very clearly, but we know him to have been tall and spare, with fair hair and blue eyes and a winning smile. He had a liking for fine clothes, was a good horseman and generous to a fault. Generous—yes—this is a building where no cost has been spared.

The other windows (more than quarter of the glass is modern) depict the Mirror of Mankind and the Universe from the Creation to the Apocalypse in scenes meant to be read from left to right and from bottom to top. By the fourth window on the right is a small recess constructed by that cunning intriguer Louis XI so that he could hear Mass without being seen. The decorative motif on the stonework is the fleur-de-lis of St Louis and the Castilian tower, emblem of his Spanish mother, Blanche, whose strict principles laid the foundations of her son's sanctity.

The *tourelle* at the east end of the shrine still contains the actual wooden stair which St Louis climbed when he went to take from its tabernacle the relics which he alone was permitted to exhibit to the people below. And here is a clue to the building's chief function: it was built as a reliquary, and surely its architect, Pierre de Montereau, had other smaller reliquaries at the back of his mind when he designed this casket with its jewel-like windows. The true richness of the thirteenth-century glass is seen by contrast with the lemon-coloured rose-windows above the west porch, dating from the late fifteenth century. I sometimes wonder—there seems to be insufficient

evidence to form a conclusion—what motive determined the
choice of blue and red as the dominant colours of the early
glass. Was it simply that these were the easiest primary
colours to produce, or did the designers foresee how well this
bluish light would suit Gothic, or were the colours chosen,
like the gold of Byzantine mosaics, because they symbolised
heaven and the Holy Spirit?

As the Sainte Chapelle recalls St Louis the Crusader, so the
Palais de Justice (*the building is open daily except Sunday*, 10–
5) recalls Louis the peacemaker and legislator. Under an oak
tree he would administer justice to all-comers: so respected
were his decisions that even Henry III of England and his
barons submitted their dispute to Louis's judgement. 'If a
poor man quarrels with a rich one,' he says in his famous
testament, addressed to his son, 'support the poor man more
than the rich, until the truth is discovered.'

Steps in the Cour de Mai lead up to the **Salle des Pas Perdus**
(ominous name), formerly the great hall of the royal palace.
Here solicitors and barristers in black gowns with starched
white jabots—women among them—pace nervously up and
down with their clients, smoking a last anxious cigarette and
discussing final details or chances of victory before their case
is called. An atmosphere of tension and drama, yet all very
informal, and so too are the hearings, held from twelve to
four in small court-rooms off this big hall and other adjoining
corridors. The visitor is free to push through the leather-
padded swing doors, take a seat at the back of the court and
listen to as many cases as he will. It is one way of getting the
'feel' of Paris life and penetrating some of the faces glimpsed
in street and café and at the balcony of open windows.

No wigs, no coat of arms, none of the trappings of a
monarchy. The various parties are allowed to talk freely and
provocatively, on the principle that the truth is most likely to
emerge from an unguarded phrase. Witnesses are heard in a
chance sequence, not divided into friends and enemies.
Already, if the case is important, newspapers will have
heightened the emotional temperature by denouncing in
headlines a man not yet brought to trial as 'Monstrous
Satyr' or 'Bloodthirsty Bluebeard'. There is no such offence
as contempt of court in France.

To add to the drama the lawyer, when he addresses the
court, identifies himself with his client. 'On the morning of the
twenty-fourth of March,' he declaims indignantly, 'I visited

my farm, I examined the farmer's accounts and there discovered seventeen false entries.' And so on, cutting clean
through the tangle of assertions and counter-assertions. If
anyone wants to experience a strange combination of rigorous
logic and effusive show of feelings, let him visit the Paris law-
courts. And sitting there, at the back of the court, he may be
inclined to half-close his eyes and imagine on the tribune the
judge's forerunner, a Roman governor, two thousand years
before, giving rulings and judgement according to laws in
substance the same as those administered to-day.

CHAPTER THREE

Saint Germain des Prés

✤

Quai des Grands Augustins – Porte de Buci – Passage du Commerce – Cour de Rohan – Boulevard St Germain – Rue de Seine – Rue Visconti – St Germain des Prés – Place St Germain des Prés – Place Furstenberg

AFTER the Cité, the oldest part of Paris is that lying immediately to the south. It can be divided into an eastern half, along the Boulevard St Michel, centre of academic life, and a western half, around St Germain des Prés, centre of intellectual, artistic and literary movements. The western half is earlier in point of time and provides a good introduction to the eastern half, the Latin Quarter proper.

Pont St Michel leads to **Quai des Grands Augustins**, the first quay constructed in Paris, deriving its name from a thirteenth-century convent of Augustinians which stood at No. 55. The convent hall was one of the largest in the city, and Parlement sometimes met there. The only remains are a sundial on the fourth floor and, in the vestibule, a fine fourteenth-century tombstone.

Rue des Grands Augustins is also medieval. Nos. 5 and 7 are the **Hôtel d'Hercule**, named after the motif of its frescoes and tapestries. It belonged at one time to Louis XII, and here François I spent part of his youth: in the days when kings considered it no indignity to live in a narrow street. The two pretty courtyards are well worth a visit. Like much of old Paris, they are *classés*, that is, preserved and kept in repair by the State.

We come into **Rue St André des Arts** (the 'St' scratched out at the Revolution can still be seen). When Philippe Auguste sailed to join Richard the Lion-Hearted in the third Crusade, being a wary king he enclosed Paris in its first fortified wall. The wall cut off this district from its nearest church, St Germain des Prés, so a new church, St André des Arts, was built at the eastern end of this street, to which it gave its name. At No. 45, on the fourth floor, there lived during the Revolution Billaud-Varenne, known as the tiger with the yellow wig, largely responsible for the Terror and for Marie Antoinette's death. No. 52 is an eighteenth-century house with circular courtyard, wrought-iron banisters and balconies supported by rams' heads.

A few doors farther west we arrive at a locksmith's workshop and yard, A partly-ruined tower is hung with pieces of the locksmith's scrap metal. At first glance rather dull, but if we inspect the tower, we see that it is of medieval masonry. This was part of one of the twenty gates in Philippe Auguste's wall; it is strong and cunningly wrought, for Philippe Auguste was an engineer: he knew the power of siege engines, and even designed effective ones himself, as Saladin found to his cost.

This particular gate, the **Porte de Buci**, is famous in history because it was opened by a traitor to 800 Burgundians (the people's party), who thereby entered Paris and for three days and three nights massacred the Armagnacs (nobles and merchants) then in control of the city. Charles VII, a boy of fifteen, was hurried away and eighteen years were to elapse before he returned to rule over a reunited France.

The little **Rue Mazet** which runs off to the right was once the coach-terminus for traffic to the south-west, and No. 9 the famous Restaurant Magny, a favourite haunt of Flaubert, Sainte-Beuve and Turgeniev. We take the **Passage du Commerce**, opposite. All this district was inhabited during the Revolution by leading politicians, including Danton and Fabre d'Eglantine. No. 8 of the passage is a house of the second half of the eighteenth century, where Jean Paul Marat published his violent newspaper *L'Ami du Peuple*, in which he called for precisely 270,000 executions. Opposite, at No. 9, lived Dr Guillotin. The good doctor, a *député*, first attracted notice by his plans for making the meeting-hall of the States General more comfortable—rearranging the benches, installing stoves. In 1789 he submitted a philanthropic plan for replacing the many different modes of execution (gibbet, pyre, wheel, etc.) by a machine which would cut off the head, the prisoner feeling only 'a slight coolness about the neck.' The idea was shelved until 1792, when experiments were carried out on sheep in this courtyard. The guillotine was first used to execute a prisoner in Place de Grève, but spectators were disappointed at its speed and called for the restoration of the gibbet.

Off this passage is the **Cour de Rohan**, a garbling of Rouen,

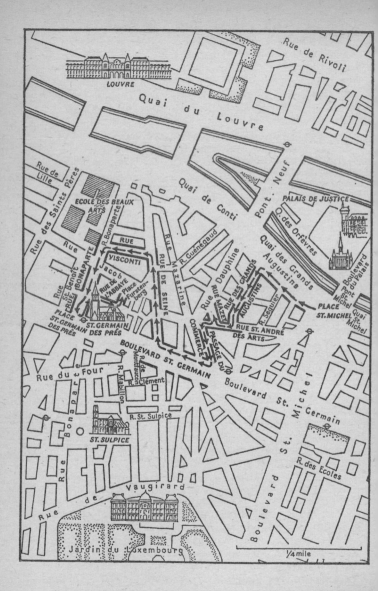

whose bishops had a town-house here. The second courtyard
is dominated by a sixteenth-century façade, with the bishops'
coat of arms visible under the base of one of the right-hand
ground-floor windows. Also noteworthy is the iron tripod
called *pas de mule*, from which many a portly bishop doubtless
struggled to mount his horse. The third courtyard has a pretty
old well and pulley.

The passage brings us down to **Boulevard St Germain**; at
what is now No. 85 Marat had his house and was assassinated.
When Haussmann built the boulevard less than a hundred
years ago he managed to retain a few historic buildings
(notably Nos. 153–175), but for me, at any rate, the interest
of this street lies in its bookshops. Paris counts upwards of
1,600 bookshops and a large proportion are in or just off the
Boulevard St Germain.

Browsing here has its own particular pleasures—the novels
grouped by publishing houses, each wearing the colours of its
'stable': red and white of Gallimard, Julliard's green and
white, Albin Michel's yellow and brown, grey and green of
Plon's *Feux Croisés*; the wide paper band boasting a literary
prize or claiming the author as '*plus beat que les beatniks*';
volumes of poetry published from a private house in Rennes,
say, or Toulouse. But there is one hazard: the uncut pages of
new books. It has been known for a poor student to carry and
use his own paper-knife actually in the shop, but this is not
recommended. If uncut pages thwart browsing in depth, they
add, I believe, to the pleasure of purchase: slitting them in-
creases one's sense of possession and of a work newly minted.

A papal bull of 1231 described Paris as 'the city of books'
and since the first was printed in 1470 a good many million
must have appeared, to be joined more recently by hundreds
of weeklies and monthlies expressive of every shade of political, literary and artistic opinion. Even the *charcuterie* shop is
not so colourful or abundant as the magazine racks in bookshop or newspaper kiosk; glance at the titles and you will
realise just how avidly the French read. The present vogue is
for history; three intelligent, well-illustrated reviews to
choose from, with sister publications devoted to music,
geography, science and religion. Literature alone counts three
weeklies and a score of monthlies, including *La Nouvelle
Revue Française*, once edited by Gide, Sartre's left-wing *Les
Temps Modernes, Esprit*, founded by Mounier, the inventor of
'personalism', and *Tel Quel*, so highbrow that half the articles

are written in a jargon invented in the current year and comprehensible only to initiates. Very striking is the number of magazines devoted to astrology, horoscopes and the irrational generally.

Again, there is a profusion of daily newspapers, of which the most consistently reliable is *Le Monde*. If these make for rather disappointing reading, the reason may be that French is not a racy, journalistic language. Indeed, more and more French newspapers try for vividness by using English and American words: sometimes in a way which amuses us but which doubtless would not amuse the Académie Française. A recent example: '*Les mémoires de Nixon seront* rewritées *par un journaliste américain.*'

Most of the luxury magazines, *L'Officiel*, *Vogue* and *L'Art et la Mode* are designed chiefly for women but perhaps the best of all, *Plaisir de France*, is of general interest. Here French civilisation (past, present and future) appraises herself critically in front of a looking-glass; colour photographs, for once, have the subdued look of reality and advertisers vie to employ leading artists. Text and illustration are perfectly harmonised, as in those limited *éditions de luxe* which are the glory of Paris publishing.

Indeed, letters and art are here not two things, but two aspects of a single whole. This becomes apparent as we turn off Boulevard St Germain down **Rue de Seine**, the young artists' street, with its print shops and shops selling specially illustrated editions—Racine's *Athalie* with drawings by Krol, Mallarmé's poems illustrated by Matisse, and dozens more. In this street also are to be found dealers in art and, above all, art galleries: Galerie Chardin at No. 36, Visconti at No. 35, Stiebel at No. 30 and Galerie Europe at No. 22. Nearby are a number of art schools.

Because of the immensely increased demand for painting and the fame of the school of Paris, the young Parisian artist of talent is no longer likely to be starving or pawning his last suit to buy paints. He is probably under contract to a dealer, who pays him a handsome annual fee in return for a stipulated number of canvases, which are then shown exclusively in that dealer's gallery. Much, then, depends on the taste of the 360-odd Parisian dealers. Those on the Right Bank tend to be conservative and affluent—the Galerie Maeght, for instance, which made a fortune through having the monopoly of **Georges Braque**—but hereabouts dealers risk their limited capital by backing original artists who may well fail to attract buyers.

Those who find no paintings to interest them in Rue de Seine may wish to explore galleries in the surrounding streets. Four of the best Parisian art-dealers are within easy walking distance: Paul Facchetti, 17 Rue de Lille; Karl Flinker, 34 Rue du Bac; Galerie J, 8 Rue de Montfaucon and Galerie St Placide, 41 Rue St Placide.

One could pass the whole afternoon browsing in Rue de Seine, but it is worth hurrying on, into **Rue Visconti**. The street was made godchild to Napoleon's architect only in 1864; its original name, Marais Saint Germain, can still be seen on No. 1. Quiet and secluded, the street was a favourite meeting-place of the Huguenots and used to be known as '*la petite Genève*'. At No. 17 Balzac, then aged twenty-eight, set up his printing and publishing business, living on the first floor above. He lost heavily with a de luxe edition of the classics, sold the press, and published the first novel to appear under his own name, *Le Dernier Chouan*. Balzaciana, such as the author's famous cane, its gold knob set with turquoises, are to be seen not here but out in Passy, in the Musée Balzac, 47 Rue Raynouard, where Balzac lived a dozen years later, still in debt (this time his pineapple plantations around Paris had failed) and disappearing at sight of a creditor either into an underground trapdoor or out through one of the house's two entrances. On the wall behind the Passy desk is a small frame enclosing a pathetic grey piece of cardboard inscribed 'Here a Rembrandt.' He surrounded himself with works of art 'to come'—when he would be rich. For Balzac, writing night after night on cups of coffee, the prize was nothing less than Paris—its glory, its money, its art, its pretty women.

The literary traditions of Rue Visconti go back even farther, for at No. 24 Racine passed the last seven years of his life. He had renounced the theatre—his plays were out of favour—and lived quietly with his pious wife, educating five daughters in the hope that they would become nuns.

We turn left into **Rue Bonaparte**, which has a number of old houses (especially Nos. 20–24) and is famous for its antique shops. In Rilke's words, 'if you glance inside, there the antique-dealers sit and read without a care (yet they are not rich); they take no thought for the morrow, do not worry about success, have a dog that sits contentedly before them, or a cat that makes the silence even greater by gliding along the rows of books as though she were wiping the names off the bindings.'[1]

Rue Bonaparte leads to the entrance of the **church of St Germain des Prés**. This was by far the highest, richest and largest building of the Dark Ages, not excepting the palace on the Île de la Cité. There grew up around it a whole suburb, fortified, living upon the wealth and dependent upon the protection of the Benedictine monks. It accepted the authority of no one but the Pope and owned all of what are now the 6th and 7th arrondissements.

When in 542 Childebert (son of Clovis) was besieging Saragossa in Spain, he was astonished to see that the inhabitants used no arms for their defence, but were satisfied with walking round the walls chanting and carrying the tunic of St Vincent. Childebert raised the siege on condition that he was given the tunic. Then, to house it, he built this church, which was consecrated as the Basilica of St Vincent and Ste Croix by St Germain, bishop of Paris, who was buried within its walls in 576. Thereafter it was called 'St Germain et St Vincent', and known from its splendour as 'the golden basilica'. This was pillaged and burned by the Normans. In the eleventh century a new church was built, much of which remains: the tower as far as the arches, the nave, the transept and finally the bases of two other towers, less high, which stood at the angles of the choir and transept—hence the popular name of 'the church with three bell-towers'—and pulled down in 1822 to avoid the expenses of repair.

So the church we see to-day is Romanesque, with a Gothic choir. The triforium of the choir was built with shafts from Childebert's original sixth-century church. The dimensions may appear surprisingly small until one remembers that this was only the abbey church, and the parish was served by St Sulpice.

For a millennium St Germain des Prés was a stronghold of learning. Erudite ecclesiastics were rare in the eighteenth century, but this abbey provided at least three of them— Mabillon, Clément and Montfaucon—whose names are commemorated in nearby streets. Under the Revolution and in the nineteenth century, as we have seen, the quarter was still a favourite with political thinkers and writers; while to-day the intellectual pursuits of cloister and scriptorium are

[1] *Selected Letters of Rainer Maria Rilke*, translated by R. F. C. Hull (Macmillan 1947).

continued from new presuppositions in the cafés of **Place St Germain des Prés**.

The move here began in 1940, when, during the blackout, intellectuals found it inconvenient to trek as far as Montparnasse, their rendezvous between the wars. For some fifteen years afterwards St Germain des Prés was the headquarters of French existentialism. Sartre and Simone de Beauvoir held court at one of the café tables, while the smoky cellars nearby were crowded with students in long loose sweaters wearily listening to *le iazz hot*. To-day, with the decline of existentialism, St Germain des Prés has become 'respectable', and one will probably look in vain for gamin-like girls wearing narrow black trousers and long, uncombed hair, frowning at the spring sunshine and trying hard to prevent cheerfulness from breaking in.

A gaudy new drug store and three cafés dominate the square: **Lipp,** frequented by lawyers and politicians; **Flore,** a favourite with philosophers and those who prefer their thought abstract; and **Deux Magots** (*Magot* meaning a grotesque Oriental figure), the rendezvous of writers (usually those aged over thirty-five) and of artists. The leading lights at the *Deux Magots* are the painter Tony Gonet and the sculptor Iquity, a strikingly good-looking young man with *rouflaquettes*, wearing a velvet jacket. Here and there mannequins sit to be seen and have themselves called on the telephone. The young men in perfectly-fitting suits who can afford to drink whisky are probably over from the 16th to make or meet intellectual friends.

Imaginative artists and their critics have come to these cafés not to stand each other drinks but to talk and exchange ideas. This they do with the utmost seriousness. New advances are planned on diverse fronts: *musique concrète*, glass architecture, sculpture in plastic and aluminium. The latest books and plays are evaluated by men who have weighed and reweighed every word. Anyone listening for half an hour will be struck by the recurrence of three terms of high praise—*fin, net* and *pur*—which are worth considering because they throw light on the values of intellectual Parisians.

Fin means sensitive and subtle, cut fine (as in the culinary phrase *fines herbes*), a combination of delicacy and sharpness. It describes the French ideal of sensibility and sense, with sensibility predominant (the one unpardonable sin in Paris is heartlessness). The use of a single word where we should use

two derives from an even more fundamental French characteristic: the refusal to draw a sharp line between matter and
form, as Anglo-Saxon peoples do. For the intelligent Frenchman a fact is inseparable from the way it is presented, and particularly from the pleasure its presentation happens to achieve.
Hence to be alive is thereby to be involved in the art of living.
Conversely, these people at the café tables are anything but
aesthetes or ivory-tower theoreticians: they take it as axio-
matic that life imitates art, and that they are fashioning a way
of life for the next generation. No wonder they look serious.

Net means clear and unconfused, reminding us that one of
the tags dearest to Frenchmen is: '*Ce que l'on conçoit bien
s'énonce clairement.*' This is certainly true as regards expression of shades of feeling and states of mind, to which the
French language is perfectly adapted. Ambiguity in these
spheres can be and usually is avoided, though it must be
admitted that French philosophical and political concepts are
often very confused. On the other hand, since the essence of
poetry is the ambiguity we call metaphor, French is an extremely difficult language for a poet, as opposed to a versifier,
to manipulate. Since Prévert's best verses, a generation ago,
Paris has sadly had to admit that she lacks a local poet, one
haunted by the lines and light of Paris.

Pur indicates that the style of a work of art is condensed, in
keeping with its subject matter and undiluted by extraneous
elements. The Frenchman who eats his green beans as a
separate course after his braised veal finds it difficult to admire
the fool in *King Lear*.

Given these values, which are seldom if ever questioned, the
talk is remarkable for its intellectual honesty and daring.
Daring is surely the adjective to describe the paintings of
Nicolas de Staël, Beckett's *Godot* or the group of Parisian
writers (Claude Mauriac, Robbe-Grillet, Butor, Sarraute),
who have evolved the anti-novel, for by agreeing to describe
their characters behaviouristically and to prohibit description
of feelings or states of mind, they have cut themselves off
from the whole tradition of French literature. *Alittérature*
this, and the only answer to *alittérature*, quip the assistant
producers and starlets who crowd the cabarets of the adjoining Rue St Benoît, is *alecture*!

At first, it must be admitted, the charm and brilliance of
this square may be difficult to discover. The witty talk, like the
men and women of talent, will probably be hidden behind a

dense undergrowth of stubbly beards, queer-smelling smoke
from pipes like small saxophones, leather jackets with padded
shoulders, nails varnished with white or perhaps mauve
lacquer, and a screen of pompous verbosity—all this belonging to the *poseurs* and hangers-on. St Germain des Prés
probably has more *poseurs* per café table than any other comparable area in the world. And some of the nonsense talked!
Parisian art criticism can rival German metaphysico-
nonsense as the world's most nonsensical gibberish—huge
tissues of abstract words which seem to balloon away, carrying their proponents in little swaying gondolas bencath.

But *poseurs* have always been part of the Paris scene, and
where there are originators, one will usually also find mimics.
They add colour and amusement without obstructing the main
action. For me, at any rate, this square is more interesting and
more exciting than the latest laboratory or the launching pads
of Cape Kennedy. The round café tables are the drawing-
board of future Western civilisation, where equivalents are
being found for new moods and new states of mind: the
images which are going to haunt our imagination, the categories in which we are going to think. Here it is always the
eighth day of creation. For many people all over the world
Paris stands for resistance to what is dull, flat, factitious,
banal and mediocre, and the centre of that resistance is the
Place St Germain des Prés. Perhaps that is why in the *Deux
Magots* even a glass of *bière blonde* can take on the qualities
of champagne.

As evening falls, it is pleasant to wander in the little side
streets off Boulevard St Germain. I am thinking particularly
of a little square behind the church of St Germain des Prés,
approached along Rue de l'Abbaye (at Nos. 3–5 stood the
sixteenth-century abbot's palace, in brick and stone). It is
called **Place Furstenberg**, after a cardinal-abbot of St Germain des Prés, and replaced the courtyard of the palace,
which formerly extended here. At the corner of Rue Jacob
and Rue Furstenberg a stone pillar can still be seen which was
part of the entrance archway to the courtyard. At No. 6, Delacroix spent the last six years of his life (he had lived earlier in
Balzac's house, Rue Visconti) and his studio is still preserved
as a museum. More likely than not you will have the square
to yourself. Parisians seldom come here: it is neither *net* nor
clair, and the meandering lines of the 1890 lamp-posts are
perhaps less than rigorously *pures*! But the little square has a

charm all its own: it is pleasant to rub one's hand along the pillar of the abbatial archway and bridge fourteen centuries of intellectual inquiry; pleasant to look at the wax-like flowers of the four magnolias; pleasant, by the warm glow of gas-light, to unwrap a newly-bought book and with as much excitement as though it were a telegram cut the opening page.

CHAPTER FOUR

Paris by Night

❧

The Seine and its Bridges – Restaurants – the Opéra – Concerts – Theatres – Music-halls – Chansonniers – Night clubs – Les Halles

AN easy way to get to know the Seine is to take a *Bateau Mouche* (named after their original owner, Monsieur Mouche) shortly before dusk. You will then have an opportunity of seeing the sun set behind the bridges, shadows deepen along the quays and, on the return journey, floodlights resurrect the main Paris monuments. *Bateaux Mouches* leave from the Pont de l'Alma on a one-and-a-half-hour journey, during which you can sip a cool drink or dine from one of several excellent menus. Another shorter service is run by the smaller Tour Eiffel *vedettes*, which leave from the Pont d'Iéna.

Avenue de la Seine—so one might call it, for the river is little wider than one of the great Parisian streets and, as Napoleon said, it is the main road between Paris, Rouen and Le Havre, a hundred miles away. The Seine of Paris is an inland river—no gulls or tang of salt, rather shallow and slow-flowing, for here it is only about a hundred feet above sea-level. It rises in Burgundy and with only two tributaries from the north, the Marne and Oise, has to drain the vast low-lying plain of northern France.

Not surprisingly, the river is often in flood. On the very bridge which marks our starting-point is carved the figure of a zouave, which Parisians watch anxiously when the river rises. During the famous 1910 flood, water reached its highest recorded point—the zouave's beard. According to geologists, once upon a time the river was in continual flood, was in fact a lagoon. In the lagoon flourished a small water creature, the nummulite, with a shell. Over millions of years myriads of shells formed a deposit, which became in time a dry limestone known as *calcaire grossier*. The lagoon drained to the ocean, the stone remained, was quarried and became houses, churches, and bridges. Like Venus, Paris was born from a sea-shell.

I like to recall this as the boat slips under some of the thirty-odd bridges of gleaming grey-white stone, each by its name or style evocative of its epoch, yet all blending well with their present surroundings. Their age can be reckoned roughly by the number of arches: the Pont Neuf, with twelve arches, being the oldest. The bridges are continually crossed and re-crossed by Parisians at work and play, so that the glint of light on water is one of their familiar sights, softening and refreshing. The Seine and the horse-chestnut trees—these seem the feminine side of Paris, as opposed to the bustling streets and offices.

The Seine gains much from the handsome stone quays, sometimes lined with trees, along both banks. As early as 1416 a decree recalls an age-old custom whereby these paths must be at least twenty-four feet wide, for the passage of horses towing barges. Now by night they are a favourite haunt of young couples, and by day of fishermen. Anyone can fish in the Seine for the price of a licence; but your true Parisian comes to meditate rather than to land a few small perch. Once the fishing was more jealously guarded. In the fourteenth century the king contested the exclusive rights of the monks of St Germain des Prés to fish from the Petit Pont as far west as Sèvres: an important issue when the Seine was well-stocked and Benedictines ate meat only four times a year.

As the boat heads up-river the first landmark is the **dome of the Invalides** on the south bank, which recalls Napoleon's love of the Seine. This love dates perhaps from his arrival, a military cadet of fifteen, who stepped ashore from the *coche d'eau* after its fifty-hour journey from Burgundy. For Napoleon, always probing to essentials, the important thing about Paris was the Seine. He built four of the bridges we shall pass under, improved the quays and lived in a riverside suite of the Tuileries. Finally, in his will he directed that his body should lie, not merely in Paris, but '*sur les bords de la Seine*.'

The *Bateau Mouche* passes under the elaborately ornate **Pont Alexandre III**, opened in 1900 in the heyday of Franco-Russian friendship. Facing upstream are the arms of Paris, facing downstream those of St Petersburg. The bronze decorations include a particularly life-like crab, which looks as though a sharp wrench would pull it away from its setting.

Thousands of Parisians crossing the bridge have wrenched; the crab is worn but still tenaciously holds.

The next bridge is the **Pont de la Concorde**, built from stones of the Bastille; after that the three-arched **Solférino**, with names of French victories in a forgotten Austrian war of 1859 inscribed on the cornice; then the slightly severe, clean-cut **Pont Royal**, paid for by Louis XIV. The Louvre is linked to the Left Bank by the **Pont du Carrousel**, erected in 1939, and the **Pont des Arts**, an iron footbridge built by Napoleon (he wanted only granite, iron and marble used in his monuments, so that they would last 'thousands of years').

The bridge decorated with masks is the **Pont Neuf**, the first to be built quite uncluttered by houses. As soon as the piles had been sunk and joined with loose planks, Henri IV decided to cross on a tour of inspection. When it was pointed out that several people had already tried this, fallen and been drowned, Henri replied, 'Yes, but they weren't kings!' And off he went to cross.

From the **Pont d'Arcole** to the **Pont d'Austerlitz** extends the commercial **port of Paris**. Here barges can be seen unloading building stone, timber from the Vosges, coal and steel from Flanders and Artois; indeed, goods from all France. For a network of canals and rivers connects Paris by water even with the Mediterranean. Paris is the third biggest commercial port in France, so the medieval arms of the city, a freighted ship on a sea argent, are still appropriate. The motto underneath the arms—'Fluctuat nec Mergitur'—can apply to a number of different things; perhaps originally it meant no more than that ships seldom sink on inland waterways.

After passing the oblique Pont de Sully we arrive at the **Halle aux Vins**, on the Left Bank. Here wines are unloaded and stored in vast warehouses connected by streets named after wine-growing districts: Touraine, Languedoc, Bordeaux, Champagne, Graves and so on.

Near the Pont d'Austerlitz the boat turns back. She has sailed roughly two miles without passing under a railway bridge or beside factories, gas-works or power-stations, though there are plenty of these in the suburbs.

As the boat heads downstream, the lavender and pewter tints disappear and floodlighting begins to set off the great buildings and focal points: Notre Dame, the Hôtel de Ville, the Louvre and thirty-one other sights. Floodlighting, it seems to me, is the twentieth-century's peculiar contribution to

Paris, giving the city a dramatic quality by night it has long
had by day, at least since the time of John Evelyn, who wrote:
'Whole streets . . . so incomparably fair and uniform, that you
would imagine yourself rather in some Italian opera, where
the diversity of scenes surprise the beholder, than believe
yourself to be in a real city.'

Son et Lumière has shown how effectively the artificial
moonlight of floodlamps can evoke the past. It takes place
most summer evenings in the courtyard of the Invalides,
while every Friday in the Louvre a room of sculpture is
illuminated. Here extraordinary results are obtained, so that
it can be said of any statue that it contains as many different
works of art as there are ways of lighting it.

The *Bateau Mouche* returns to its landing-stage near the
Pont de l'Alma and we find ourselves in streets lit by rather
soft and subdued lighting, not an attempt to turn night into
day, but suggestive of nocturnal pleasures. First of these in
point of time is dinner. Paris has some six thousand restaurants, very, very few of which serve meals that are less than
satisfying. Everyone has his own explanation of this consistently high standard. Three reasons occur to me: France
generally and Paris in particular recognise pleasure as a good,
so that your chef feels he is doing a commendable job by producing a culinary work of art which will please his customer.
Then again, the food itself is good—for the same reason as
French wine: both come from rich and varied soil, lovingly
cultivated to yield its special excellence. Finally, the food is
fresh: crisp, firm and full of flavour.

Which restaurants to choose?[1] That depends on one's
pocket-book. Personally, I try to choose a crowded restaurant,
and so follow the Parisians' flair for good cooking. Even in a
crowded restaurant service is quick. And in my experience you
get best value in the Latin Quarter restaurants: students living
on an allowance cannot afford to overspend.

Small bistros and smart restaurants rise and fall, but certain
gastronomic temples are part of the history of Paris. They are
as famous to epicures as the Cluny and Jeu de Paume to art-
lovers; and each has its specialities: a Parisian will speak of
the *soufflé au cointreau* at Lasserre's in the same tone as an art
connoisseur discussing the Prado Rubenses. I must admit
here and now that I write about matters culinary as a layman,
not as a fine-palated gastronome. But sometimes décor,

[1] For some restaurants near the Pont de l'Alma, see p. 236.

service, good food and imaginative cooking fuse to produce an experience not easily forgotten even by the layman. This is usually sure to happen in every one of the following restaurants.

Where else but in Paris would a king raise a restaurateur to the nobility simply because he enjoyed his heron-pies? This was the good fortune of a certain Monsieur Rourteau in the reign of Henri IV. Rourteau founded the **Tour d'Argent** at 15 Quai de la Tournelle, overlooking Notre Dame, in the days when forks were a novel importation from Italy, and a dinner might well include larks' tongues and roast swan. The well-known speciality here is *le canard pressé* (also known as *le canard au sang*), invented by the great chef Frédéric Delair, a former owner, in 1890. Half-wild ducks from the Vendée are smothered at the age of six weeks, roasted twenty minutes in a hot oven and brought out underdone. The duck is then carved and its carcass put through a silver press, the juice being caught in a dish. To the juice are added the mashed liver of a raw duck, a glass of port, a little Madeira, champagne, a few drops of lemon juice, salt, pepper and spices. The slices of duck are cooked in this for twenty-five minutes and served very hot from the silver plate.

Unusual gifts of invention and patience seem required in order to devise, over a period of years, from all the possible ways of cooking duck, one at first sight so unsavoury yet in fact so succulent. If the word artist has any meaning surely it must apply to the creative chef. Having seen and tasted *le canard pressé* I no longer smile, as I once smiled, when Parisians reverently evoke past meals and chefs whose every pinch of salt was a joy to the palate. This classic dish has been cooked in the Tour d'Argent some two hundred thousand times, and a register contains the names of those to whom it has been served, including Queen Elizabeth II and the Duke of Edinburgh.

Another restaurant proud of its famous clientele is **Le Grand Véfour**, 17 Rue de Beaujolais, behind the Palais Royal gardens. In the days of the Directory this was the Café de Chartres, and an engraved copper plate on the red benches marks the favourite place of each great habitué of the past— Joséphine and Bonaparte, Victor Hugo and Mademoiselle Mars. Now the owner-chef, Raymond Oliver, specialises in dishes from his native Gironde: ortolans, lampreys and Bordelaise mushrooms.

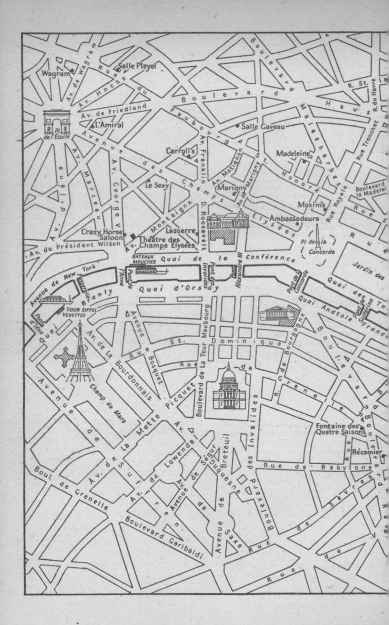

Lapérouse, 51 Quai des Grands Augustins, was once the town house of the Comtes de Brouillevert and has kept its present appearance since the eighteenth century: wrought-iron balcony railings, winding stairways, a homely smell of dust in the passages leading to intimate low-ceilinged private dining-rooms for two or four people, decorated with old wallpapers, faded tapestries, red carpets, plush curtains and mirrors. Lapérouse specialises in genuine French food rather than cosmopolitan delicacies; its particular boasts are *Gratin de Langoustines Georgette*, *Poulet Docteur*, *Canard Colette* and *Crêpes Mona*.

Maxim's, 3 Rue Royale, takes one back to the 1890's and the strains of *The Merry Widow*, in which Franz Lehar lyricised the most famous restaurant of his day. Stylised flowers and absinthe-coloured vegetation cluster round mirrors, dim, it seems, with memories of so many famous guests, while at the serving trolleys a final touch is added to such specialities as *Filets de Sole Albert*, *Tarte Tatin* and *Crêpes Veuve Joyeuse*. At night a gypsy orchestra plays and on Fridays, when evening dress is obligatory, Maxim's is one of the world's most opulent public places.

Lasserre, 17 Avenue Franklin D. Roosevelt, is no less smart, but in a more fantastic way. Downstairs, Louis XV *commodes* have been converted into cages for white doves, emblem of the Casserole Club, which meets here monthly to dine by candlelight. On the first floor the painted ceilings by Touchagues can be rolled back on summer evenings for starlight dancing.

Drouant, 18 Rue Gaillon, is famous not only for its cuisine but for its literary associations. Here at the turn of the century the original members of the Académie Goncourt met for dinner at a cost of twenty francs a head, as stipulated by their founders, the Goncourt Brothers. And here, one afternoon every December, the ten Academicians still meet and, suitably fortified with food and drink, announce the *prix Goncourt*. The monetary prize is tiny but the sales of his novel usually bring the winner a small fortune. At about the same time the Femina and Renaudot juries make similar choices, so that every year at least three novels of literary merit are assured of popular success.

There then are six great Parisian restaurants, which have handed on traditions from father to son or owner to owner. They are what the French would call classics. Hidden away are the débutants, the chefs whose art is known only to a few, the *patrons* who from a smile or a phrase can create a memorable, highly individual atmosphere. But here the traveller must turn explorer, picking up clues, from, say, the leisure page of one of the financial newspapers or even from an overheard conversation until he discovers for himself the restaurant which combines his favourite dishes with his favourite décor.

After dinner, presumably an opera, concert or theatre. Ideally, Garnier's **opera house** should be visited on a gala night. Then cockaded guards with drawn swords line the onyx balustrade of the grand staircase leading to the multi-coloured marble foyer, where crystal chandeliers and glass doors set off the ladies' evening dresses and jewels: jewels on a scale to be seen nowhere else in the world. The music may well be by Bizet or Gounod, Massenet or Chabrier: *Son et Lumière* on a sumptuous scale taking us back to the Second Empire: wealth from railways or mines, heavy meals served from mahogany sideboards, and pleasure-seeking behind official prudery so stiff it dared to demand the removal of Carpeaux's lovely group, 'The Dance', from the Opéra façade. Those who like Marc Chagall will be interested to see his much-discussed new ceiling in the opera house.

If the gala is a ballet, so much the better, for French ballet dancers are more pleasing than French singers, though both fall well short of excellence by international standards. And again I find it difficult to watch the ballerinas without being reminded of the Second Empire, though this time in a more agreeable form: Degas, sketching the little *rats* backstage, fighting his temperamental melancholy, confessing wistfully in his old age: 'My heart is sewn up in a ballerina's slipper.'

Asked in what style his opera house was designed, Garnier replied: 'In the style of Napoleon III.' It was too florid to last.

The **Comédie Française**, founded by Louis XIV, is the most important of the five Paris theatres subsidised by the State. The actual theatre, which stands near the junction of Rue Saint Honoré and Rue de Rivoli, is an eighteenth-century building with a nineteenth-century façade. Here, at prices about half those of unsubsidised theatres, you can see the classics of French drama: primarily Corneille, Molière and Racine, but also Marivaux and moderns such as Jean Giraudoux and Paul Claudel.

The Comédie Française has played and still plays an important part in French civilisation. Its purpose is to preserve certain attitudes, such as patriotism, esteem for chivalry, courage, glory and courtesy, and a certain kind of language, that evolved in the Grand Siècle, which the French esteem as much as we esteem that of the Authorised Version. Just as the French State each year sends to the Villa Medici in Rome the most promising young painters and sculptors in order that they may imbibe the classical aesthetic ideal at one of its sources, so the people of Paris are encouraged by low prices to come to the Comédie Française to imbibe similar classical traditions. Paradoxically, I think a visitor is close to the heart of Paris when he attends a performance at the Comédie Française of Corneille's *Cinna*: a play about Augustus Caesar, set in Rome, and the diction of which is very close to Latin. Parisians down the centuries have sought to continue and perfect the kind of life-style first evolved in Rome. *Cinna* was Napoleon's favourite play, he was fond of quoting from it, and once remarked that if Corneille had been still alive he would have made him a Prince of the French Empire.

Readers of de Gaulle's speeches and *Memoirs* will have noticed how much his language resembles that of Louis XIV. This is not direct borrowing so much as a tradition transmitted through the classical plays which have been performed since Louis XIV's time by the Comédie Française.

Modern playwrights consider it as much of an honour to have a play included in the repertoire of the Comédie Française as they do to be elected to the Académie. But the only plays likely to qualify are those with a recognisable affinity to those of the Great Three: Corneille, Molière and Racine. Quite a few of them, like Claudel's *Le Soulier de Satin* and Montherlant's *Le Maître de Santiago* are set in the age of chivalry, and thus immediately link up with the standards to be preserved. Henri de Montherlant is particularly esteemed by the Comédie Française: he modelled his life—and death— on the Roman Stoics, his thinking is lucid and logical, his language firm and melodious. He had the unusual distinction of seeing his *Reine Morte* receive its first performance, in 1942, at the Comédie Française, while in 1957 gramophone records of his *Port Royal*, a play about the Jansenist nuns' resistance to royal authority, were enshrined for posterity under a paving stone in the peristyle of the theatre.

The French like to see themselves supreme in the theatre, as in all the arts, and here the stumbling-block is William Shakespeare. Voltaire decried Shakespeare as a savage with sparks of genius, and it is remarkable how many modern playwrights try to poke fun at the great Shakespearean scenes: Sartre (following Dumas) in *Kean* and Anouilh in *Ne Réveillez pas Madame*. Shakespeare is seldom given a chance in Paris theatres: actors tend to play him over-heroically, as though all the characters had the same Greek nose, and with too much stylised posturing. The most successful French productions are of plays with a strong element of fantasy: *A Midsummer Night's Dream* and *The Tempest*.

The other State-subsidised theatres are: the T.N.P. at the Palais de Chaillot, Place du Trocadéro, the Théâtre National de l'Odéon, Place de l'Odéon, and the Théâtre de la Ville, 2 Place du Châtelet. The State-subsidised Théâtre de l'Est shows sometimes films, sometimes plays.

The anti-classical trend in the modern French theatre is represented by Ionesco and Beckett. Both were born and educated abroad: Ionesco in Rumania, Beckett in Ireland; so they escaped indoctrination by the Comédie Française. In Ionesco's most famous play, *Le Rhinocéros*, the characters one by one turn into rhinoceroses, while in Beckett's *Waiting for Godot* two tramps wait about for a third person, who never appears and may not even exist. This kind of play, sometimes known as the drama of the absurd, is a first cousin of the anti-novel, as practised by Robbe-Grillet, Sarrault and Claude Simon, in that the feelings, thoughts and moral development of the main characters—the very stuff of classical theatre and the classical novel—are no longer of importance. Instead, the author concentrates on things and their appearance, on the sound and the nonsense of words. It is too early to say whether this movement will prove fruitful or whether like Dadaism and Surrealism in the twenties it will turn out to be just a fad.

Theatres which usually stage plays worth seeing are the Antoine, the Atelier, the Comédie des Champs Elysées, where many of Anouilh's plays had their première, the Hébertot, where Montherlant's *Le Maître de Santiago* ran for 800 performances, La Huchette, associated with the plays of Ionesco, the Mathurins, and the Théâtre Rive Gauche. Jean Anouilh, whom I find the most attractive of living French playwrights, is typical in many ways of the city. The central dilemma of his best plays, such as the early *Eurydice*, is the conflict between the idealism of the young and the cynicism of the established and the ageing. This is in a sense one of the perennial conflicts of Paris: between the Left and Right Banks, the original artist and the academies, the poet and the man whose heart is unattainable behind a bulging pocket-book.

The music halls offer a varied programme of entertainment: singers, show girls, sometimes conjurors and acrobats. Most famous of the musical halls is the Olympia, 28 Boulevard des Capucines, associated in many people's memories with the greatest Parisian singer of the century, Edith Piaf, whose rich, racy voice is still often heard on gramophone records; others providing consistently good shows are the Casino de Paris, 16 Rue de Clichy, and the Folies Bergère, 32 Rue Richer.

Finally, there are the Chansonniers, formerly numerous, now down to three in number, which offer revues: here you will see clever impersonations, especially of political figures, and hear topical jokes which demand knowledge of the current French scene.

Of the Paris night clubs the best known are those featuring pretty dancing girls in various stages of undress. The beginnings go back to the eighteenth century. From 1200 to around 1715 Frenchmen had—at least in theory—set women on a pedestal, according to certain rules elaborated in the courts of Provence; at the beginning of the eighteenth century they 'discovered' sensual women. Philippe d'Orléans, nephew of Louis XIV and Regent for the boy Louis XV, gave dinner parties in the Palais Royal at which silver dishes were carried in to table and uncovered to reveal nude girls. Louis XV took the gaiety a stage further in his notorious deer-park. Under the Revolution and two Empires the pretty girls retreated, to re-emerge in the gay 'nineties dancing the can-can, notably at the Moulin Rouge, where Toulouse Lautrec drew some of them for posters.

The heyday of Paris strip-tease was the 1930s and 1950s. English, American and Latin American visitors enjoyed watching pretty girls undress tastefully and sometimes even artistically with a freedom forbidden in their own countries. The stories they brought home started the myth of 'naughty Paris'. I say 'myth' because Parisians have never sought to be naughty in the sense of challengingly indecent.

To-day the picture has changed. England and to some extent America have carried nudity to an extreme which is considered by Frenchmen tasteless, while France of the Fifth Republic has tightened up its moral code. Soho now has more nude

shows than Pigalle, and *Hair* had to be toned down for production in Paris. To-day Paris still has a variety of cabarets
featuring dancing girls but they are notable rather for pleasing
décor, costume and imaginative production than for outré
behaviour or deliberate attempts to shock.

There are three main categories of night club featuring girls:
large lavish locations such as the Lido, 78 Champs Elysées,
where the show is expensively mounted with one eye on
foreign visitors, and the flavour less French than international; the cabarets where Parisians themselves go—
Crazy Horse Saloon, 12 Avenue George V, has long been a
favourite; and the less expensive, more earthy entertainments
to be found chiefly in Pigalle and Montparnasse. These
mushroom up and disappear from year to year; any list would
be out of date before it was completed; but newly opened
establishments are usually the best.

At most of these night clubs you have the choice of sitting
down to dinner or supper, with champagne obligatory, or of
standing at the bar and watching the show from a distance.
Between shows there is dancing to an orchestra.

Paris offers another type of night club, where wit, not female beauty, is the bait. Most of them are on the Left Bank,
and performers will sometimes be students at the Sorbonne
or of the École des Beaux Arts. Their life-span is not much
longer than the butterfly's, they cannot afford to advertise
widely, but any hotel concierge worth his or her salt will be
able to indicate *une boîte où il y a des jeunes talents et de
l'esprit*. Some of these places serve dinner, some provide only
drinks in an informal atmosphere. The show will consist of
witty sketches and songs, sometimes by singers who in a
couple of years will be household names. At the old Fontaine
des Quatre Saisons I remember 19-year-old Nicole Louvier
singing her first songs to the guitar and the best puppet show I
have ever seen, the characters made solely from stylised, cut-
out newspapers. A small budget means that imagination and
originality replace the lavish visual effects which predominate
on the Right Bank.

The traditional way of rounding off a night out in Paris was
to sip onion soup (*gratinée*) at dawn in a restaurant beside the
Halles, the city's food market, bounded on the north by Rue
Rambuteau, and on the south by Rue Berger. Now the Halles
have disappeared. The markets have trifurcated and moved to
near Orly, Le Bourget and La Villette, and the site is at the

time of writing being redeveloped. Some of the old restaurants remain, such as **Au pied de cochon**, 6 Rue Coquillière, serving rich customers onion soup and pig's trotters as a kind of earthy contrast to the light quiche de saumon and soufflé au cointreau on which they may well have dined some hours earlier.

The Halles were so much part of Paris night life and figure so often in the memoirs of Parisians that they deserve a few words. They were begun in 1183 by Philippe Auguste, the king who paved and walled Paris and accompanied Richard the Lion-Hearted on crusade. Napoleon III built ten pavilions in the then fashionable wrought iron, roofed with glass, to cover the market stalls. There porters and the formidable *dames des Halles* used to handle the best food from all over France amid a constant banter of sometimes witty slang.

The merit of the Halles was that fresh country food came every morning but Sunday into the very centre of Paris, and so found its way into shops and restaurants. Under the new dispensation shopkeepers have to make the journey to the outlying markets and back at an early hour; formerly they could come to the Halles on foot, now they need a van. All but the very keenest restaurant proprietors are going to settle for food that is less fresh than it used to be in the days of the Halles. Yet the move out could not be avoided: traffic congestion in this part of Paris had become intolerable.

The Avenue d'Iéna and Arc de Triomphe, seen from the top of the Eiffel Tower

top A parade of the Garde Républicaine down the Champs Elysées
bottom The Place de la Concorde

Notre Dame . the Portal of the Virgin

top Notre Dame from the left bank
right A lamp on the Pont Alexandre III

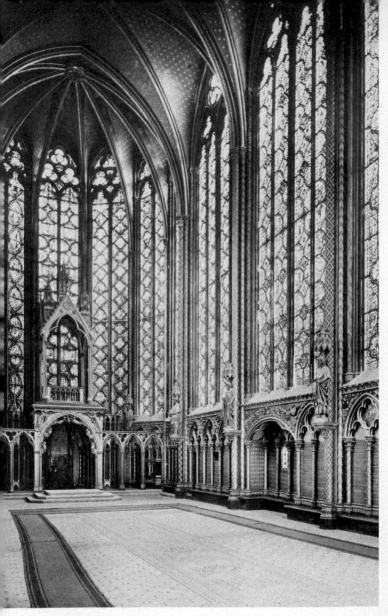

top The Sainte Chapelle
right 'La Danse', by Carpeaux, on the façade of the Opéra

top Arc du Carrousel
bottom left Arc de Triomphe
bottom right Porte St Denis

CHAPTER FIVE

The Latin Quarter

❧

St Julien le Pauvre – Square Viviani – St Séverin – Musée de Cluny – the Sorbonne – Church of the Sorbonne – Collège de France

FROM the modern Place St Michel let us follow Rue de la Huchette (Elliot Paul's 'Narrow Street'), pausing on the way to look along the picturesque Rue Zacharie and Rue de Chat qui Pêche, which owes its name to an old shop-sign. Rue de la Bûcherie leads into Rue St Julien le Pauvre, which brings us to the church of the same name. These narrow streets are among the oldest in Paris. As early as the sixth century Gregory of Tours says that when he came to Paris he stayed at the hospice for pilgrims at St Julien le Pauvre. Who was this St Julien? We can find the answer by walking a short way down Rue Galande to No. 42, where a thirteenth-century bas-relief shows a man and his wife rowing a traveller across a river. The figure on the left is our saint: in expiation of an unwitting crime he became a ferryman and offered his services free to the poor. The traveller is Christ disguised as a leper.

In the parvis in front of the church can be seen two large paving-stones. These formed part of the most important of the Roman roads, the Via Superior, now Rue St Jacques, which led south to Orléans. Although it was nine yards wide, the Via Superior became so crowded that another had to be laid parallel to it, slightly to the west. This second road, the Via Inferior, later garbled into Rue d'Enfer, is now Boulevard St Michel, which leads south from our starting-point, the Place St Michel. Two dead straight Roman roads leading out of the Cité, to which they were linked by wooden bridge or ferry. These roads were the busiest in Paris, because they led to Rome, and Paris first extended to the Left Bank, not the Right, because that was the side nearest Rome. Ever since, Paris has had a spiritual list towards the southern capital.

The church of St Julien le Pauvre was begun in 1170 and completed in 1240. The north apse was purposely built shorter

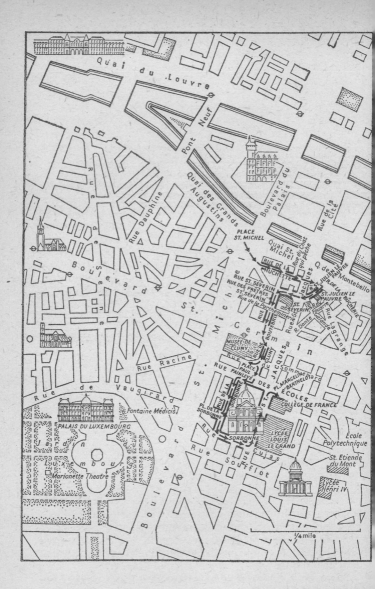

than the south, in order to preserve a miraculous well, now covered over by a cast-iron slab. The façade dates from 1651, when the church was reduced in size to save expense.

The interior is very curious: a formidable screen cuts off the nave from the choir, and this screen is hung with icons. For the church belongs to the Melchites, Greek Catholics subject to the Pope, using a liturgy in Greek and Arabic, baptising by total immersion and admitting to the priesthood married men. High Mass according to the Byzantine rite is sung here at eleven on Sundays and feast-days.

This Greek appearance, however, dates only from 1889. To trace the earlier history of St Julien, let us leave the icons and go into the little square north of the church: Square Viviani. That towering false acacia happens to be the oldest tree in Paris—brought back in 1601 from Guinea; however, it is not the tree we have come to look at, nor the quad, but the origins of the University.

From the square we get one of the best possible views of Notre Dame and at the same time see from the corner of our eye the little church of St Julien, in its present form roughly contemporary with the cathedral. We are still within the original twelfth-century walls of Paris. The question is, how did the centre of schooling, of intellectual Paris, shift from the Cité to the Left Bank, from the magnificent Notre Dame to the puny, self-effacing St Julien? The answer lies in the life of a single man, a highly typical Parisian, Peter Abélard.

Abélard was born in Brittany in 1079. As a young man he came to study in the school of Notre Dame (the Gothic cathedral had not yet been started). Here he came into conflict with the master on the question of universals. The master maintained the traditional view that general ideas, for example the idea of queenliness, exist and can be understood, even though we may never have met or heard about an actual queen. Abélard refused to accept this: he claimed that the idea of queenliness is merely something we deduce from actual knowledge of this or that queen. This was considered a dangerous attitude which detracted from objective truth and gave too much scope to human reason. To avoid disciplinary action, Abélard was obliged to flee to the abbey of Ste Geneviève, outside the city walls and free from the jurisdiction of the cathedral.

Here, on the highest point of the Left Bank, a little way south of St Julien, Abélard began to teach. He was a devout,

deeply religious man, but his religion was cold, subtle and
intellectual. Doubt was his starting-point, reason his guide to
certainty. His own reason, no one else's: hence his declaration
that educated men should be able to study Scripture for themselves with the help of the 'glosses' alone.

Abélard's reputation grew. Presently Fulbert, a canon of
Notre Dame, engaged him as tutor to his niece, Héloïse. It
was then that Abélard lived in Rue Chanoinesse, north of the
cathedral. Master and pupil soon fell in love with a passion
that has become legendary. Fulbert discovered the affair and
Héloïse was packed off to a convent where she gave birth to
Abélard's child. The strange, exalted nature of their love, the
sense of being at the very frontiers of knowledge and new
human experience is seen in the curious name Héloïse gave
her son: Astrolabe.

Abélard's punishment—emasculation—effectively put an
end to his hopes either of marrying Héloïse or of becoming a
priest. He continued teaching, going so far as to claim that we
believe an article of faith not because God has said it but
because we are convinced by reason that it is true. He came
into conflict with St Bernard and with the Pope—but he was
not a heretic, merely in advance of his age. In fact, the work
of his disciple, the famous *Sentences* of Peter Lombard,
became the accredited theological text-book in the Middle
Ages. He died in 1142, absolved and at peace.

Abélard set the pattern for subsequent philosophic speculation in Paris. He freed inquiry from the narrow island cloisters;
henceforth it led a roistering life on the Left Bank. Within a
generation of Abélard's death, in 1208, the University had
obtained its statutes, probably the first university in the
world (only Bologna disputes her title), and St Julien, because
it happened to stand so close, had become the University
church.

Here, in the tiny early-Gothic nave, the University first held
its sittings; twice a year the royal provost attended to swear to
preserve the privileges of the rector, master and scholars—
poor scholars from all over Europe. Behind St Julien is Rue
du Fouarre, which may owe its name to the straw on which
they sat at their outdoor lectures. Dante, who studied here,
refers to the street as '*vico degli strami*' (*Paradiso* x, 137); he
speaks of violent discussions in the street and adds that he
took comfort in going to St Julien to say his prayers.

St Julien's period of authority and respect lasted three

centuries. With the foundation of Renaissance colleges, the centre of University life moved steadily away, up the hill, and St Julien again became *le pauvre*. By 1650 St Julien had become merely the chapel of the Cité's Hôtel Dieu, itself in decline.

St Julien makes no artistic claims, but its neighbour, St Séverin, reached by a street of the same name, possesses a beautiful double ambulatory and the whole building is of interest as an illustration of the development of Gothic. The lower part of the west front (also the side door and porch below the tower) is early thirteenth-century; the upper stories flamboyant Gothic of the Renaissance. Inside, the first three bays of the nave and the triforium of the first four bays are thirteenth-century, while the outer aisles and apse are Renaissance. Renaissance too are the windows, one of which depicts the murder of Becket (who studied in Paris before Abélard was born). The seventeenth century, which disliked Gothic only a little less than did the eighteenth, coated the apse pillars with marble and gave the arches round heads. The side door on the south leads to a fifteenth-century charnel-house, in allusion to which an inscription on the façade of the church urges passers-by to pray for the dead. St Séverin, the students' parish church, has played a leading part in the recent liturgical revival. Dialogue Mass is said with the priest facing the people.

Rue des Prêtres St Séverin crosses Rue de la Parcheminerie, where medieval scholars bought their paper—a street worth more than a casual glance. Then Rue Boutebrie and Rue de Cluny bring us to **Place Paul Painlevé**; Painlevé, it appears, having been a mathematician famous enough in his day to be buried in the Panthéon. Here is a good place to look at the **Hôtel de Cluny**, the house of the abbots of Cluny. The position of the house was carefully chosen. It stands just off Rue St Jacques. This, as we have seen, was the main road south in Roman times and assumed its present name about 1230, because it was the road taken by travellers on the extremely popular pilgrimage to St James of Compostela.

The house was built in 1490. From the square we can see the crenellated walls, octagonal tower, openwork balcony, windows decorated as though with ruffs of carved stone. The carved shells are conspicuous (there are also shells in some of the mullioned windows): what the French still call *coquilles St Jacques*, because the shell was the pilgrim's emblem.

The impression of good taste, craftsmanship and lack of ostentation (Cluny was a synonym no longer for reform but for easy living) is confirmed by the interior (*open daily except Tuesday*, 10–12.45, 2–5). The rooms are small and well-proportioned, with oak-beam ceilings. They are arranged as a medieval museum, the chief glory of which is the tapestries. When Pol de Limbourg died (before 1434), the French miniature fell into decline, and only in the sixteenth century, under François I, did a new school of easel-painters arise. In between France did her best work with the needle.

Most of the tapestries have simple, straightforward subjects, but that in Room 2, showing a **Miracle of St Quentin**, requires some explanation. It is Gregory of Tours who tells how a thief was charged on the evidence of a priest and condemned to be hanged. Finding the punishment too severe, the priest now took the thief's part and asked the judges to mitigate their sentence. When they refused, he hurried to the sanctuary of St Quentin, a third-century Roman martyred for his faith in the town that bears his name, and begged the saint to intervene. And intervene he did, writes Gregory, for the hangman's chain broke before the wretch was dead; and the judges, seeing in this an act of God, pardoned the thief.

La Vie Seigneuriale, in Room 4, presents a vivid picture of daily life in the early sixteenth century on the banks of the Loire: reading, departure for the hunt, the walk, the bath. François I was on the throne and France was beginning to learn from Italy the joys of cultured living.

In the passage leading down to the Thermes are some miserere seats worth a moment's attention for that impish humour ever lurking below the surface of medieval art: two donkeys, one blowing the bellows, the other thumping the organ—close relatives of monkeys sporting in the margin of a *Book of Hours* and the gryphons high on Notre Dame.

The **Thermes** consists of the ruined baths of a Roman palace: apart from a rather decrepit amphitheatre the only important Roman remains in Paris. The Romans' insistence on hot baths is quite understandable, for the climate seems to have been colder then than it is to-day. Julian the Apostate, who was proclaimed Emperor perhaps in this very palace, speaks of blocks of ice 'like marble' hurtling down the Seine, of fig trees covered with straw to save them from the frost; of feeling too cold to work. Yet Julian was happy in Paris—a provincial town where the old virtues remained: he carried its memory with him to the east, where he died in battle: not an apostate, merely a gentle man, protesting in his way against the Christians' harsh persecution of pagans. Julian deserves to be remembered here, for he is the first of many foreigners to have loved Paris as a second home.

Two blocks from a Roman column stand in the Thermes, one set up between 14 and 37 A.D. by the watermen of Paris. The inscription runs: 'To Jupiter the great and the good, we, the Guild of Boatmen, founded this altar when Tiberius was Caesar.' Among the gods carved on the block are Keraunos, the horned god who protected cattle, and Esus, god of the Gaulish summer; he is reaping with a sickle in his hand—these are associated with two Roman gods, Jupiter and Vulcan: at this date the occupation was less than a century old and Roman culture had not yet totally imposed itself. The column, which stood at the eastern point of the Île de la Cité, shows the importance at that period of the water-traders.

On the site of the altar to Jupiter Notre Dame was built, and coming up from the Thermes into a large, well-lit room we find another reminder of the cathedral in the original statue of Adam from the west front. This rather narrow-shouldered man is no Greek athlete, but he is a credible figure, beautiful in his way, and surely discredits the myth that the thirteenth century was powerless to depict a nude body.

The next room is a treasury of images and paintings of the Middle Ages. Near the entrance stands a swooning Madonna from Spain, which by contrast shows up the admirable restraint of French art of the same period. Swooning Madonnas were happily never part of the mainstream of Christian art and were specifically forbidden at the Counter-Reformation. Among many fine pieces of sculpture a Jeanne de Laval and a St Barbara from Lower Normandy are of interest because of their contemporary head-dress. A saint in extravagant head-dress is rather unusual, particularly at this period. When Isabeau, black-eyed, fair-haired queen of France, introduced the hennin, a very tall conical head-dress with pendent muslin veil, a certain Friar Richard at the abbey of Ste Geneviève, just up the hill, preached against hennins for six hours on end and for nine days running, without, however, reducing their height!

Room 9 contains the best portrait of St Louis in existence: a statue from the Sainte Chapelle which gives an idea of that

charm which so impressed all who knew him. Then we take
stairs directly into the Rotonda, where the tapestries called La
Dame à la Licorne are displayed. If we are to understand their
meaning, we must look at them closely.

The first tapestry depicts 'The Sense of Sight'. On a blue-
green island a young woman is seated, holding an oval mirror
which reflects the head and neck of a unicorn. Opposite the
unicorn a lion supports a standard decorated with three
crescents. On the island are an oak tree and a holly bush;
these reappear in the other tapestries, which, perhaps because
they are higher, add two more trees: a pine and an orange.
Flowers and animals decorate the island and the red background. Part of the lady's hair is braided in front to form a
curious panache: this style has been found elsewhere only in
certain prints of Sibyls in a Florentine book published in
1470.

In the second tapestry, 'The Sense of Hearing', the unicorn
(less well depicted) becomes a standard-bearer. The central
position is now occupied by an organ, which the lady plays,
while her servant works the bellows. The organ is decorated
with a lion and a unicorn.

The third scene, 'The Sense of Smell', shows the lady making
a garland of carnations. She wears on her head a veil of pearls
and precious stones. Behind her, on a stool, a pet monkey is
smelling a rose, filched from her basket of flowers.

The fourth and perhaps most beautiful tapestry, 'The Sense
of Taste', shows the lady standing against a hedge of roses
between her animal standard-bearers. A parakeet is perched
on her left hand; with her right she takes a sweet from a gold
dish. On the train of her brocade dress sits a pet dog. Among
the background animals is a small unicorn, too young to have
grown a horn. A breeze flutters the lady's veil and the mantles
of lion and unicorn.

The fifth scene, 'The Sense of Touch', shows the lady holding her standard and the unicorn's horn. Her hair is worn long
under a crown. The unicorn's mane, in this tapestry alone, is
shown on the front of its neck.

The last scene is difficult to entitle. The lady stands in front
of a tent inscribed: 'A MON SEUL DESIR', the flaps of which
are held apart by the lion and unicorn. Above the tent, as in
the preceding tapestry, a belled falcon hunts a heron. Her dog
sits beside the lady on a cushioned stool. From a jewel-case

presented by her maid she is taking a necklace with great care, not handling it but lifting it in a piece of linen.

What does the series of tapestries mean? No one knows for certain. The most favoured interpretation is that they were offered as a gift by a young man to his fiancée (the inscription 'A mon seul Désir' was often used in the Middle Ages to accompany a gift to a loved one), perhaps by Jean de Chabannes when he married, about 1513, Claude Le Viste. The arms with three crescents are certainly the Le Viste arms. The lion would then represent the fiancé (whose arms featured a lion) and the unicorn his bride. One difficulty arises here. Claude Le Viste was a widow, while the unicorn, as is well known, was a medieval symbol of chastity; according to legend, it could be captured only by a virgin. However, the unicorn was also famous for its speed, its *visté*, to use the old French word, so it could well stand as a speaking symbol of the bride's name.

Others believe the tapestry depicts the Virgin Mary in obscure allegoric terms; the crescent was one of her symbols and in the last scene the jewelled necklace could represent the body of the dead Christ, the linen cloth his shroud.

Whatever the true interpretation, and whatever its origin (Bruges has been suggested), the tapestry is a masterpiece of its kind. The red background, very rare though not unique, adds greatly to its beauty, and it possesses a unity deriving partly from the composition, in each scene triangular, the lady's head at the apex. But it is above all in the details, the well-observed gestures, the life-like animals and flowers, that the work excels.

Finally, in case we were inclined to doubt whether a unicorn ever existed, at the far end of the room is displayed something very much like a real unicorn's horn. It is in fact a narwhal's horn, from the treasure of Saint Denis.

Room 12 is devoted to Limoges enamels, Room 13 to jewels. Among the Trésor Gaulois de la Grange Neuve, in Case 1 are some of the earliest Gallic coins, copies of staters of Philip of Macedon, then an international currency. The free, fanciful rendering of horses has been used as an argument by fanatical Gallicans to prove that Gaul's indigenous culture was superior to the Roman. Personally, I discount the argument, while yielding to none in my admiration of these pre-Roman horses, earliest variations on a theme we shall find many times in Paris.

In a neighbouring case three seventh-century Visigothic crowns, decorated with sapphires and other precious stones, provide a glimpse of craftsmanship during the Dark Ages. Room 18 gathers a number of combs, mirrors, table services, toys and such-like, to illustrate life in the Middle Ages, while Room 19 resumes the theme of metal-work in the Dark Ages with a magnificent eleventh-century golden reredos from Basle Cathedral. This room also contains notable Byzantine ivories and bindings.

The next room is the chapel, a little masterpiece of flamboyant Gothic, with a central pillar branching out into numerous ribs. Here begins the tapestry of **The Legend of St Stephen**, a series which is continued in Rooms 18 and 19. We have already noted the popularity of Stephen in France, notably the fact that the mother-church of Paris was probably built in his honour. As the tapestry shows, in the fifth century, as the result of a dream, his body was found and his bones carried to various countries, including France.

The garden provides another good view of the house. If we bear in mind that the early colleges probably looked much like this, we shall be better able to understand the growth of the University, as we cross to the other side of Place Painlevé and, at 7 Rue des Écoles, enter the Sorbonne (*open daily except on public holidays, 9–4, or 5 in summer*). The Grand Staircase brings us, on the first floor, to a group of murals. On the left is Abélard teaching; then St Louis presenting the charter of the original small theological college founded in 1253 by his chaplain Robert de Sorbon. Several such endowments were made in the reign of St Louis (one, the College of Constantinople, again recalls this king's connection with the East), but all were dominated by the Sorbonne, which came to be synonymous with the faculty of theology.

To win the coveted degree of '*docteur en Sorbonne*' a candidate had to defend his thesis against twenty professors, succeeding one another at half-hour intervals, from six in the morning until early evening, without being allowed food or drink. Since the professors included such geniuses as Duns Scotus, St Bonaventure and St Thomas Aquinas, it is a wonder that anyone received his doctorate.

As for the scholars, they were strictly disciplined. They had to attend matins (3 a.m. in summer, 4 a.m. in winter), Mass, vespers and compline, and retire to their dormitories when the curfew sounded from Notre Dame. They had to converse and write in Latin. They were allowed to play *jeu de longue paume*, but not cards and dice. They were fed chiefly on beans and birched often. Then, as now, they were poor, often woefully poor, so that they had to beg their meals.

Other foundations were made during the fourteenth and fifteenth centuries, not all of them religious. For instance, Philip the Tall's wife (she who spent orgiastic nights in a tower beside the Seine, into which she is said to have thrown her lovers) founded the Collège de Bourgogne (now the École de Médecine) for poor students, only natural sciences to be taught and metaphysics specifically excluded. The Renaissance brought the faculty of letters to the fore: one of the murals we are looking at shows the establishment of the first printing-press in the cellars of the Sorbonne. The first book printed there was, significantly enough, not a bible or religious work but a collection of letters (in Latin) by Gasparino Barzizza of Bergamo, then much admired for his style.

The Sorbonne was an unchallenged tribunal on points of dogma: it even forced Pope John XXII to retract his theory of the beatific vision. The Pope, it appears, held that the souls of the blessed do not see God until after the Last Judgement; the Sorbonne maintained the more orthodox view that they see God immediately after death.

By the sixteenth century the Sorbonne had hardened into religious bigotry, and it actually approved the Massacre of Protestants on St Bartholomew's Night. More amusingly, it declared quinquina '*l'écorce scélérate*' and had Parliament forbid its use as a medicine. Now, of course, quinquina, in St Raphael and other apéritifs, is one of the most popular French drinks.

The visitor may wander at will through the vestibules and galleries of the Sorbonne, nodding on the way to Homer and Archimedes, Chemistry and Archaeology (a high yield of statuary per acre in these nineteenth-century buildings) and even, if he wishes, attend one of the lectures, but to see Puvis de Chavannes's mural painting 'The Sacred Grove' in the Grand Amphithéâtre, or great lecture-hall, permission must be obtained from the office of the Académie de Paris, in the same building.

To reach the **church of the Sorbonne** (*open daily except Sunday and holidays*) it is necessary to retrace our steps to the street and turn left into Rue de la Sorbonne. The entrance is in

Place de la Sorbonne. This, the college chapel, was designed by Lemercier for Cardinal de Richelieu, who rebuilt the Sorbonne in 1629. Lemercier was, with François Mansart and Louis Le Vau, one of the three creators of French classical architecture. This church is an important example of his work, boasting as it does the first true dome in Paris, and two façades: one towards the street, and another on the north towards the college courtyard.

Richelieu's tomb, designed by Lebrun and sculptured by Girardon, shows the cardinal supported by Religion and Science. This late seventeenth-century group came within an ace of being destroyed in 1793: Alexander Lenoir, an art-lover, managed to save it by covering it with his body, but he sustained a wound from the bayonet of one of his fellow-revolutionaries. Lenoir (whose portrait by David hangs on the second floor of the Louvre) saved innumerable other works of art from the mob, who wanted to melt down what was bronze and break the rest.

Coming out into Place de la Sorbonne, if we walk anti-clockwise round the Sorbonne we shall arrive at Place Marcelin Berthelot. Here stands the Collège de France, founded by François I in 1530. The building dates from the seventeenth and eighteenth centuries—appropriately enough, for it was during this period, while the Sorbonne was sunk in torpid bigotry, that the Collège de France kept investigation and research alive. It is independent of the University and the lectures given by its fifty professors are open to all free of charge. A chair here is probably the ambition of every scholar in France. Renan and Michelet, Claude Bernard and Marcelin Berthelot, the chemist, have all taught at the Collège, and most of to-day's leading French scientists, such as Perrin, the atomic physicist, and Lévi-Strauss, the social anthropologist, are members.

The gateway of the Cour d'Honneur is inscribed 'Docet Omnia', though the original foundation taught only Latin, Greek and Hebrew: in fact, it was known then as Collège des Trois Langues. A statue of Guillaume Budé, the humanist who persuaded François I to found the college, can be seen in the courtyard, together with the names of all its professors, past and present. In the garden are more statues, notably one to Dante.

All the while we have been passing students, some of the sixty thousand now in Paris. We shall speak of them later.

Many lodge in the Cité Universitaire, on the southern outskirts, others in rooms nearby. Their material comforts would
astonish those medieval students who, like Dante, studied in
the shadow of St Julien. On the other hand, their studies are
proportionately more difficult: instead of the *trivium* and
quadrivium, electronics, heart and brain surgery, the theory of
nuclear fission. Like Abélard and Héloïse, men and women
study together, and their role in the city has changed little
since the University was founded. They still act as a ferment,
keeping Paris young, progressive and romantic. Indeed, the
history of Paris could be called a dialectic between the Latin
Quarter and the Right Bank, between the pen and the sword,
the young, poor and rebellious storming the preserves of the
rich and those who have arrived. If anyone doubts whether
this still holds good, let him listen to conversation at the café
tables near the Collège de France.

CHAPTER SIX

The Luxembourg and Panthéon

❧

*Palais du Luxembourg – Statues in the Luxembourg Gardens –
Fontaine Médicis – Boulevard St Michel – Lycée Louis le
Grand – St Étienne du Mont – Panthéon*

The Luxembourg is a palace with secrets. The coat of arms
above the main entrance is that of Marie de Médicis; it was
Marie de Médicis who ordered the palace built in 1612, she
who lived here six years, yet Parisians refused to call it by any
name but that of the former owner of the land. Then again,
building was begun at a time when the Tuileries was still half-
finished; the logical course would surely have been for Marie
de Médicis to complete the palace planned by her namesake
Catherine. Furthermore, the queen ordered a replica of the
Pitti Palace, where she had been born and grown up. An
architect was sent to study the Pitti and bring back plans. The
Luxembourg was built—and turned out to be just about as
different from the Pitti as was possible at that epoch—the
only similarity is that both palaces are fairly heavily rusticated.

The explanation lies in the character of Marie de Médicis.
Her childhood was bitterly unhappy. Two months after her
mother's death her father, Grand Duke of Tuscany, married
a slut and had nothing further to do with his children. Marie
grew into a beautiful though rather heavy young woman,
stupid and nervous, hiding her insecurity behind an excessive
stubbornness. At twenty-seven she was virtually sold to Henri
IV, her dowry being 600,000 *écus* and the promise of further
credit from the Médicis bank.

The amiable Henri loved her—he once said that were she
not his wife he would have given all his possessions to make
her his mistress—but his virile, gay, highly intelligent and fun-
loving nature demanded other women too. Scene after scene
embittered Marie de Médicis, who turned in on a small circle
of Italians, notably Leonora Galigai, a childhood friend
married to an intriguing politician, Concini.

In 1610 Henri IV was assassinated, and Marie de Médicis

found herself regent for the eldest of her five children, ten-year-old Louis XIII. She cared little for them: she was not a loving woman. Instead, her energy was now directed to political power. Too stupid to achieve it herself, she was drawn even more closely to the clever intriguers, Concini and Galigai. Since they lived on the Left Bank, she would live on the Left Bank too.

She planned a showy, magnificent palace and, feeling herself more than ever an exile, ordered a replica of the Pitti. Its rounded windows, flat roof and rather heavy, fortress-like appearance were antipathetic to French taste; the architect, Salomon de Brosse, begged for a free hand. Finally the queen consented: she was a weak woman.

Where was the money to be found? Already her extravagance—especially a passion for diamonds—was plunging her into debt annually to the tune of one million *livres*. Political opponents she was too weak to curb had to be bought off. Galigai helped by selling offices but, nailed to her bed by hysteria, Galigai was kept alive only by greed, and most of the bribes she took were salted away abroad. One source of money remained. Henri IV, with Sully's economies, had amassed a fortune in gold to pay for a projected war. This fortune, several millions in bullion, lay in the Bastille. For long the queen coveted it. Then one evening, 15th July, 1615, she took a step for which the thrifty French never forgave her: accompanied by her son, princes of the blood, dukes and peers of the realm, ministers and guards, she drove to the Bastille. Two heavy doors guarded the treasure. The first was unlocked by the lieutenant of the Bastille. The second had three locks. The queen produced her key to one, then turned to M. Jeannin, *conseiller général des finances*, and M. Phélippeaux, *trésorier de l'Épargne*, and invited them to hand over the other two keys. They refused, protesting that the Exchequeur had forbidden the withdrawal of bullion except in case of war. Flustered, the queen declared that her word overruled any existing order and again invited them to hand over their keys. This time they had no other course but to do so. The triple lock was turned, the door swung open. Forty-one gold bars were withdrawn and 1,200 sacks each containing one thousand *livres*. A month later the queen again committed this cool form of bank robbery, her loot on the second occasion amounting to 1,300,000 *livres*. Not one gold coin remained in the Bastille. But the walls of the Luxembourg Palace began to rise.

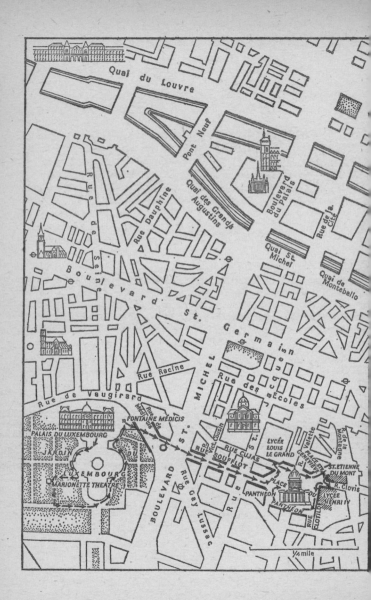

Meanwhile Louis XIII was growing up: silent, either very stupid or very cunning—no one understood him, least of all his mother. At the age of sixteen, two years after the plundering of the Bastille, he struck. Concini was murdered, Richelieu (the queen's new temporary ally) banished, to his bishopric, the queen exiled to Blois. Galigai was put on trial for sorcery. Believing herself possessed, she had been carried often to church screaming and kicking, in the hope that the Augustinians could exorcise what in fact was advanced hysteria. Exorcism failing, Jews had lately been summoned to recite cabbalistic verses. Hebrew books discovered in her apartment were enough to lose Galigai her head.

In 1625 Marie de Médicis came to live in the Luxembourg. She was reconciled with her son but had no real power. The Parisians hated her so much they would not call her palace 'Palais Médicis'. She intrigued against Richelieu, who had now become a rival, but without the guidance of her evil genius was on every hand outwitted. In 1631 Richelieu drove her from the Luxembourg, drove her from Paris, soon drove her from France.

Without loving art, she had ordered expensive, showy paintings for the Luxembourg. They are not there now. The series of twenty-one Rubenses has been transferred to the Louvre. There was never real power or beauty here, nor is there to-day. In rather dowdy surroundings the Senate meets and gravely passes ineffectual motions. The interior of the palace can be visited on written request (*open Sundays and holidays during sessions, daily during intervals between sessions*), chiefly for the sake of Delacroix murals in the library.

What matter more than the Luxembourg interior are the **Luxembourg gardens**, also designed by Brosse. They are the only Renaissance gardens in Paris: a cluster of distinct parts rather than a single whole like the Tuileries. As early as the reign of Louis XV the favourite topic of conversation here was literature. To-day students from the Sorbonne and Beaux-Arts can be heard discussing Sartre and Schoenberg in the shadow of monuments to Verlaine and Chopin.

The Luxembourg statues are worth more than a glance. Those on the terraces in front of the palace depict queens of France, including Marie de Médicis herself and François II's wife, Mary, Queen of Scots. As far as I know, Paris has only two statues of British women: this and the monument to Nurse Edith Cavell against the east end of the Jeu de Paume.

Of the French queens, Berthe was the mother of Charle-magne: known as *'au grand pied'* because she had one foot bigger than the other. Blanche de Castille and Anne of Austria were both pious Spaniards who gave their sons, St Louis and Louis XIV, an admirable education. Marguerite de Valois, Henri IV's first wife (*la reine Margot*), was beautiful, elegant, witty and a total libertine. Jeanne d'Albret was a strong-minded queen who, by instituting freedom of worship in her dominions, taught Henri IV the virtue of tolerance. With the exception of Anne of Brittany the French queens seem to have been better mothers than wives.

The children playing in the garden pay little attention to the stone queens, artists and authors. They have their own heroes in the nearby **marionette theatre**, chief of whom is a jovial, talkative, tipsy, quarrelsome hunchback given to beating his wife with a big stick. They call him Polichinelle, but we know him and his wife as Punch and Judy. The best time to watch the marionettes is Thursday afternoon, when there is no school and Mr Punch puts on a specially lively show. Children in Paris are lucky enough to have two other theatres: **Enfants Modèles**, 252 Rue du Faubourg St Honoré, and the Roland Pilain company at the **Gaîté Lyrique**, Rue Papin.

One of the pleasantest spots in the Luxembourg is the **Fontaine Médicis**, by Salomon de Brosse. It lies to the right of the palace façade, shaded by plane trees. The statuary shows the Cyclops about to crush Acis and Galatea with a rock. It is worth taking a close look at the Cyclops, for Rodin, who often passed the fountain in his youth, later produced a statue of the same subject, which contains echoes of Ottin's work.

If we continue walking, we shall come in to **Boulevard St Michel**, probably full of university students. Immediately after the war, when existentialism was the craze, girls went about with uncombed waist-length hair, wearing tight black trousers and a gloomy look. Then, during the depressing days when Bidault, Mendès-France and Pinay played political musical chairs, the students had a short spell of Americophilia. They drank milk with their meals, jived and jitterbugged, and went into rhapsodies over the Western film as an art form. Now that mood has been replaced by a new self-confidence. France has proved that she is still the world's leader in the arts, in design, in the art of living; she is prosperous, she hopes to become capital of a federated Europe. To-day's students tend to be-lieve that in a nuclear age, with war possibly an anachronism, heroism consists in fulfilling one's obligations as a person and as a citizen. Work and a sense of duty are the order of the day. Respectability is back with the virtues.

There is an extraordinary charm about this street. Most of the students are having their first taste of Paris, of freedom from a set time-table and of freedom to mix with girls of their own age. The enthusiasm and vivacity so generated, the sense of adventure and discovering life make the Boulevard St Michel a place to linger in.

This is the University, here at the café tables. Students are not obliged to attend lectures and prefer to buy stencilled verbatim reports in a bookshop. The only tutors they have are their own companions. Here, discussing, arguing, joking over cups of coffee, they exchange ideas among themselves and learn to be articulate. They receive State grants, insufficient however to keep them in a city as expensive as Paris. Even with cheap restaurants, reduced rail fares and theatre tickets, about half of the 60,000 students have to earn their living, for example as dish-washers, baby-sitters or by giving lessons. Some share single attic bedrooms with night-workers, sleeping in shifts.

Too many enrol and about thirty per cent are weeded out at the end of the first year. The remainder continue the three-year course for a *licence* or degree, culminating in a final examination—not a series of factual questions, but a dissertation, lasting four hours or more, on a single set subject, in which form counts almost as much as matter.

By their 'revolution' of May, 1968, students won the right to participate in University policy-making, but very few have the time and inclination to exercise it. The temper of most students is still strongly left-wing, and they hero-worship Marxists such as Sartre and Roland Barthes. Barthes is the current intellectual star, because it is he who has analysed various aspects of everyday living—sport, advertising, the theatre, the cinema, the reporting of social events—to show how the apparent surface message, whether expressed in language or in images, half-conceals a secondary message tending towards the confirmation of the political *status quo*.

The students tend to be more adult and self-reliant than Anglo-Saxon undergraduates: they have grown up more quickly. Indeed, the crucial intellectual hurdle occurs not at University but earlier, at seventeen or eighteen, when candidates sit for one of the *grandes écoles*, of which the most famous is the Polytechnique. A *polytechnicien* is to the ordinary University student what a racing Ferrari is to a Dauphine. He is pampered and carefully trained for the great competitive examinations which, more than the University degree, give entrance to key jobs. France still believes in an élite, but an élite open to all.

Qualifications for a teaching post in the Sorbonne are still the highest in the world. A minimum of ten years' personal research is demanded of any candidate seeking a permanent appointment. France is short of teachers and the Sorbonne has been asked to provide them. But naturally enough professors of this calibre refuse to multiply teachers at the cost of lowering standards. The result is that more and more students come up to the Sorbonne with insufficient grounding in the three Rs. Who cares? Have another drink.

Rue Soufflot leads east off the Boulevard. No. 14 was once a Dominican convent where St Albert the Great and St Thomas Aquinas taught. The building at the end of Rue Soufflot is the Panthéon, to which we shall come presently. Turning for a moment to the left into Rue Cujas we get a view of the Lycée Louis le Grand, called after the fourteenth Louis who gave his patronage to the Jesuit school housed here. Of the original buildings the façades looking on to the courtyard still remain. Molière, Voltaire and many of the Parisian nobility received their education here until the suppression of the Society in 1762.

At No. 2 Rue Cujas is the Collège Ste Barbe, founded in 1460 for Spanish scholars, and the oldest extant school in France, counting among its alumni St Ignatius de Loyola and St Francis Xavier.

Rue Cujas leads to Place Ste Geneviève and the church of St Etienne du Mont. On the way we pass the Panthéon, which stands on the site of the abbey church of Ste Geneviève. The fact is of some importance, for all the land hereabouts belonged to the powerful Genovefan abbots, who did their best to restrict the new church of St Etienne, rendered necessary by the growth of the University. Indeed, the church of St Etienne was allowed no entrance of its own, parishioners being obliged to enter through the church of Ste Geneviève, nor did it have the right to administer baptism.

The façade of the present church stands at an axis, cramped because the Genovefan abbots were niggardly about yielding land. The exterior is mainly Renaissance work, the first stone of the portal having been laid by Queen Margot in 1610. On the left of the doorway stands a statue of St Stephen, on the right one of Ste Geneviève. The interior is flamboyant Gothic, remarkable chiefly for its sixteenth-century rood-screen. Notre Dame and other Paris churches boasted similar screens, all but this one being removed in the eighteenth century. In the Lady Chapel are buried Pascal and Racine. Beside the sacristy two marble tablets tell the history of the abbey church of Ste Geneviève, which her younger and weaker sister has outlived. The Chapel of Ste Geneviève contains a modern shrine of the saint—during January, the month of her feast, brilliant with votive candles. The saint's bones, carried processionally round Paris on no less than 114 occasions of calamity, were burned during the Revolution. Finally, a series of twelve sixteenth-century painted windows in a gallery of the old charnel-house, attributed to Pinaigrier, should not be missed.

Rue Clovis is modern, but the bas-relief at No. 1, representing a lion on a blazon surrounded by thistles, recalls that this land once belonged to the Scots College, founded in the fourteenth century and transferred in 1662 to the nearby Rue Cardinal Lemoine.

The **Lycée Henri IV**, one of the most famous secondary schools in France, embodies much of the former abbey of Ste Geneviève, while the tower, called the Tour de Clovis, after the sixth-century king who founded the abbey, is all that remains of the Gothic abbey church.

That church, precisely because it was Gothic, displeased its eighteenth-century abbot and canons. So that when he was lying dangerously ill at Metz, Louis XV was persuaded to vow a new church if he recovered. That was the beginning of the **Panthéon** (*open daily except Tuesday*, 10–4, 5 *or* 6, *according to season*), the fortunes of which provide one of the most amusing see-saws in the history of Paris.

Louis XV's church of Ste Geneviève was completed only in 1790. The following year the church was turned into a Panthéon, where Mirabeau, who had just died, and other distinguished Frenchmen should be buried. The pediment bas-relief of Cross and angels was pulled down and replaced by France crowning Virtue, crushing Despotism, etc., etc. An inscription proclaimed: 'Aux grands hommes, la Patrie reconnaissante.'

Mirabeau was duly buried here, followed by Voltaire and

Rousseau. In 1794 documents came to light which suggested that Mirabeau had corresponded less than patriotically with the English. His body was ejected and replaced by that of Marat. Five months later Marat suffered a similar fate. La Patrie was evidently far from infallible in her judgement of the dead.

In 1806 Napoleon restored the building to its original use as a church, while retaining the vaults for the burial of great Frenchmen. But only in 1823 was the church inaugurated; a new pediment was installed, with Cross and angels.

In 1830 Louis Philippe changed the church back into a Panthéon. A fourth pediment—the present one, by David d'Angers—was put up: France distributes laurel-wreaths between Liberty and History. Wonder of wonders, Mirabeau has now been reinstated—he stands on the left, nearest but one to the figure of France. Close by, in a tall hat like that of Queen Nefertiti, stands Fénelon; farther along, seated and turning his head, Voltaire. On the right side of the pediment are soldiers led by Napoleon.

In 1851 the Panthéon was changed back into a church, this time a national basilica.

In 1885, for the funeral of Victor Hugo, the Third Republic again transformed the church into a Panthéon, and a Panthéon it has since remained. But this time the Cross on top of the cupola, regularly removed when the building was profaned, has been allowed to stand.

I remember, when I first entered the Panthéon, feeling suddenly cold and hollow. Nothing seemed to welcome me, and I felt an intruder. This must surely be the emptiest building in the world. As for the cold, it comes partly from the sparseness of windows (the original forty-two windows were walled up during the Revolution), partly from the lack of furnishings: no woodwork, no carpets, no hangings.

Next I wondered, what sort of building is this? What is it for? It is not a church; not primarily a mausoleum, for the tombs are hidden away in the crypt. Where the altar should be stands a group of statuary, dedicated to the Convention Nationale. In the left transept, murals of St Louis and St Jeanne d'Arc. But they are not performing holy deeds: they are saving or forwarding France.

In the right transept are murals depicting the battle of Tolbiac and the baptism of Clovis (it was then that Clotilda, wife of Clovis, had her vision of an angel bringing three lilies, one each for her, for Clovis and for St Rémy, and the device on the banner of France was changed from three toads to three lilies—the fleurs-de-lis). Opposite, Charlemagne is crowned Emperor by the Pope. A theme is being developed: not merely France, but the Holy Roman Empire, led by France.

And then, a very significant mural: the miracle of the *ardents*: when the French king healed his subjects with a more than human power. Yes, the point is becoming clear now: Imperial France is the new divinity; *La Patrie* eclipses the Christian God.

This impression is confirmed in the choir murals of Ste Geneviève by Puvis de Chavannes, exactly suited to the cold building. Pale greens, icy blues, greys and white: the scenes seem to have been painted under a wintry moon. But who was she, this girl who gave her name to the hill and first great abbey of Paris? She was probably of noble birth (the seventeenth century popularised the story that she was a shepherdess), for Germanus, Bishop of Auxerre, stayed with her family at Nanterre (now in the western suburbs) on his way to convert the Pelagian Bretons. She was then a little girl of seven, but her innocence and sweet character so impressed Germanus that there and then he consecrated her to God.

We next hear of Geneviève at the age of twenty-five, when Attila was riding westwards from Metz with half a million Huns. Geneviève had visions of the terrible horsemen, but prophesied that Paris would be spared. Later, in 480, when Paris was besieged by the Franks, Geneviève put herself at the head of eleven ships which passed through the enemy lines, sailed to Troyes and brought back corn for the starving Parisians. In short, like Jeanne d'Arc, Geneviève was a midwife of *La Patrie*.

In the apse, instead of the Christus Pantocrator demanded by tradition, we find a small mosaic, too small for the conch, but charged with significance: 'Christ shows the Angel of France the great destiny of the French People!'

A bare building, hardly a great work of art in the whole place, yet extraordinarily revealing of that cult of *La Patrie* which assumed quasi-religious proportions in 1794, flourished through much of the nineteenth century and was abased in 1870 at Sedan.

The entrance to the crypt is up near the apse. You cannot go down alone, but must buy a ticket and wait for one of the *agents* who, every half-hour or so, escorts a group. Voltaire and Rousseau are here, Hugo and Zola side by side, improbable bedfellows. Then Braille, benefactor of the blind, the latest to have his remains reinterred in the Panthéon.

In another wing of the crypt lie generals of the First Empire. So the *agent* says: but we cannot see the tombs for ourselves, cannot run our fingers over stone effigies. Decidedly something is missing in this cold aloof building. Could it be—the human touch: as opposed to the touch of humanity?

'I suppose de Gaulle will lie here one day?' I recall asking in 1960. The *agent* mused a moment. 'That depends on the National Assembly. The Assembly will decide.' As for the *agent's* own opinion, he believed de Gaulle would prefer the churchyard of Colombey-les-deux-Eglises. So cold, so impersonal the Panthéon!

CHAPTER SEVEN

The Louvre: Palace and Paintings

❧

*Cour Carrée – Cour du Carrousel – Salle des Sept Mètres –
Salon Carré – Grande Galerie – Salle des États – Petits
Cabinets – Galerie Médicis – Salle Daru – Salle Denon – Salle
Mollien*

THE visitor who enters the Louvre courtyard, the **Cour
Carrée,** from the Rue de Rivoli by the Pavillon Marengo, will
see the oldest part in the far right-hand corner. Here in 1204
Philippe Auguste built a small but strong fortress to protect
Paris on the west. Its name, **Louvre,** was derived probably
from Lupars, a wolf-hunters' rendezvous, or from Leovar, the
Saxon word for fortified camp. Under François I, Pierre
Lescot pulled down the keep and rebuilt the west and south
sides of the old fortress: and it is Lescot's work we are looking
at now. Lescot was an architect of genius, and it was his two
wings that set the pattern for the buildings of the Louvre until
their completion three centuries later, just as Goujon's carvings and ornaments, seen at their best on the west wing to the
left of the clock, set the pattern for decoration.

The Louvre is a dynastic work, part of whose growth can be
traced in the monograms of the kings who built it. High on
Lescot's south-west wing, finished under Henri II, we find an
H crowned, surmounting a cipher composed of an H and two
crescents. The cipher can be read either as two D's or two C's.
In this way Henri linked his name with his mistress, Diane de
Poitiers, without outraging convention, for the monogram
could equally well refer to his queen, Catherine de Médicis.

The north-west corner is signed with an interlaced L and A:
Louis XIII and Anne of Austria, for it was under Louis XIII
that Cardinal de Richelieu's architect Jacques Lemercier, in
order to quadruple the area of the original fortress, demolished
its two remaining sides, prolonged Lescot's wing to the north,
and began the north side of the present *cour*. The quadrangle
was completed, at Colbert's orders, during the minority of
Louis XIV, by Louis Le Vau.

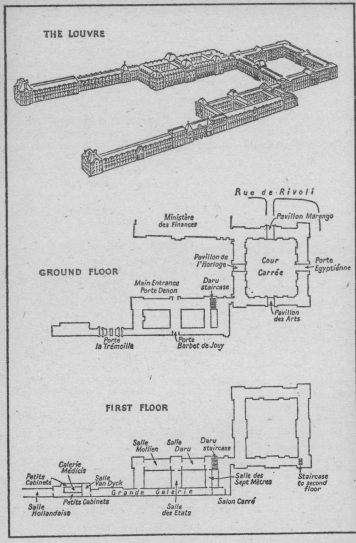

THE LOUVRE

GROUND FLOOR

Rue de Rivoli

Ministère des Finances

Pavillon Marengo

Pavillon de l'Horloge

Cour Carrée

Porte Egyptiénne

Main Entrance
Porte Denon

Daru staircase

Pavillon des Arts

Porte la Trémoille

Porte Barbet de Jouy

FIRST FLOOR

Salle Mollien

Salle Daru

Daru staircase

Staircase to second floor

Salle des Sept Mètres

Petits Cabinets

Galerie Médicis

Salle Van Dyck

Grande Galerie

Petits Cabinets

Salle des Etats

Salon Carré

Salle Hollandaise

Turning through the Pavillon de l'Horloge, we find that the later growth of the Louvre was governed by the desire to extend the palace, both to the north and south, until it joined the other royal palace of the Tuileries. The Tuileries, which no longer exists, stood at right angles to the Seine on the other side of the Arc du Carrousel. Catherine de Médicis began this grandiose design with the south gallery, continued and completed to the west by Henri IV. Where are Henri's monograms? Marie de Médicis carefully effaced them, but one, under the cornice, escaped her notice: an H and two G's: Henri and his mistress Gabrielle d'Estrées, whose portrait we shall discover later in the palace. Opposite, the wing on the far north side was built by Napoleon; the rest of the buildings were added by Visconti and Lefuel under Napoleon III.

Within a few years of the completion of the immense courtyard, a quarter of a mile long, the Communards burned down the Tuileries, leaving the Louvre open to the west. Strangely enough, there is no sense of anything lacking, and the north and south galleries scarcely seem too long for the immense vista towards which they direct the eye.

The Louvre collection (*open daily except Tuesday*, 10–5) is divided into six departments: (1) Greek and Roman Antiquities, (2) Egyptian Antiquities, (3) Oriental Antiquities, (4) Paintings and Drawings, (5) Medieval, Renaissance and Modern Sculpture, (6) Medieval, Renaissance and Modern *Objets d'Art*.

On this visit I recommend looking at some of the paintings, and on a second visit at some of the Greek and Roman antiquities, as well as at the medieval, Renaissance and modern sculpture and *objets d'art*. The Egyptian and Oriental rooms seem to me enclaves, like the Egyptian or Syrian Embassies no part of French soil, and therefore out of place in a book seeking the spirit of Paris. But for those who are interested, the masterpieces are said to be: among the Egyptian antiquities, the Mastaba, the stele of the Serpent King, the stele of Princess Nefertabiet, the statue called 'Crouching Scribe', a bas-relief of King Seti I and the Goddess Hathor—all on the ground floor; the dagger of Djebel el Arak and statues of Queen Karomana and the God Horus with falcon's head—on the first floor.

Among the Oriental antiquities (all on the ground floor): the vulture stele, the stele of King Naram Sin, ten statues of Gudea, a statue of Ebih-il, the code of Hammurabi, a colossal statue from the Palace of Artaxerxes, the frieze of the King of Persia's archers in glazed brick, and the sarcophagus of Eshmunazar.

The main entrance to the museum is by the Pavillon Denon; the paintings are reached by turning left and going up the Daru staircase. The palace became a museum in 1793, when the royal collections became the people's property. Indeed the whole notion of a museum, of beauty belonging to the State and set apart in uninhabited rooms stems from the Revolution.

François I was the first ardent royal collector. His taste for the Italian Renaissance painters and his collection of Leonardos and Raphaels have exercised an abiding influence on three centuries of French art. The main theme of the Louvre collection, as it is hung to-day, is the development of European art as a whole. I shall follow this theme here, focusing attention on French art and on important examples of other schools which have influenced French art, mentioning also certain well-known masterpieces and paintings which can be better appreciated with the help of explanatory remarks.

Very dramatically, the curator has arranged that a momentous step in the history of painting shall correspond to the visitor's entry into the Salle des Sept Mètres. Outside on the landing hangs **The Virgin with Angels**, by Cimabue, who flourished after 1272. The figures are elongated, hieratic, cold, aloof. Although by an artist of the Florentine school, this is an Eastern painting. The main figure is not radically different from Byzantine Madonnas in any one of the preceding nine centuries. And it was, of course, the artist's intention to repeat a familiar figure: first, because the more a painting seemed eternal, the more it partook of its subject's power, and secondly, because the traditional way to show the heavenly nature of heavenly beings was to depict them above and beyond human emotion.

Now, when we enter the Salle des Sept Mètres, the very first painting we come to, **The Carrying of the Cross**, by Simone Martini, of the generation after Cimabue, shows a radically different aim. Here Christ is depicted not as an impassive lord, but as a human being suffering human emotions.

This new emotionalism was noticeable in fourteenth-century sculpture at Notre Dame and I mentioned there one of its possible causes: the teaching of St Francis. Another painting in this room, Giotto's **St Francis Receiving the Stig-**

mata, makes the point dramatically. St Francis was privileged
to experience Christ's wounds in his own flesh; thereafter it
became extremely difficult if not impossible to depict God, or
His Mother and saints, as aloof and totally superhuman
beings. Emotion, of course, can be expressed in other ways
than by painting facial expression of joy or sorrow: in the
Coronation of the Virgin Fra Angelico achieves it through his
blues; Ghirlandaio, in his Old Man and his Grandson, by
means of symbols—the craggy rock and small trim trees re-
inforcing the notions of age and youth.

Antonello's Il Condottiere, the portrait of an unknown man
which owes its title to the fierce expression and aggressive jaw,
introduces a new element—oil paint—into the Italian mainstream. Henceforward most important paintings in the
Louvre will be in oils. A glance back at Fra Angelico's
'Coronation', painted in tempera, reveals the gain and loss.

In the next room, the Salon Carré, painters of the Académie
Royale first held an exhibition; hence the word 'salon', now
used of any group exhibition. Here hang a number of French
paintings in which we can trace Italian influence, such as the
Birth of St John the Baptist, with its Renaissance décor, a
product of the school of Fontainebleau formed by François I.
Caron's Sibyl of Tibur is a highly original painting in the
mannerist tradition. The Sibyl designates to the Emperor
Augustus the Virgin and Child seated on a crescent moon: an
allusion to pagan prophecies of the Messiah. The choice of
subject recalls the interest in astrology, horoscopes and magic
in the circle round Catherine de Médicis.

We now enter the Grande Galerie, begun by Catherine de
Médicis and completed by Henri IV, who was married in the
Louvre. In the Grande Galerie five times a year Henri and his
successors 'touched' for the King's Evil, scrofula, while a
chamberlain called out 'God will heal you, the King touches
you.' And it was Henri IV who began the association of the
Louvre with artists by setting aside a number of lodgings in
and off this very gallery for painters, sculptors and art
craftsmen.

In the first bays of this gallery hang two important Man-
tegnas. The Virgin of Victory commemorates a battle in
Charles VIII's Italian campaign—a crucial event in French
political and artistic history, for it revealed to France some
of the glories of the Italian Renaissance and awakened a
desire to annex part at least of Italy. The kneeling figure at

the left is Francis de Gonzaga, who actually lost the battle but saved face by building a church and having this picture painted in commemoration of what he chose to call his victory. As for the pendent piece of coral, that was a talisman believed to ward off evil spirits.

The well-known **St Sebastian** reveals Mantegna's interest in perspective, anatomy and architecture: in the background curious castles on tottering cliffs admirably enhance the sense of doom. Perspective, too, is Uccello's chief concern in the **Battle of San Romano**, a Florentine victory over the Siennese. This is one of three panels, the others being in the National Gallery, London and in the Uffizi.

We now arrive at the first of the Leonardos: the glory of the Grande Galerie. At the invitation of François I Leonardo spent the last few years of his life in France, where he died in 1519. One of the works which Leonardo brought with him was **The Virgin, Child and Saint Anne.** The traditional way of treating this subject—setting a small, puppet-like but adult Mary on Anne's lap—naturally did not satisfy Leonardo, but he seems to have had difficulty with the composition. In a cartoon for this painting (in the National Gallery) Mary is half-seated on her mother's right knee, and it is her sweetly-smiling face which dominates the picture. Here on the other hand Anne has again become the main figure, but Mary's position has meanwhile become unnatural. So unnatural in fact that Freud attempted to see in her drapery and foot the shape of an eagle. By bending one's head to the left it is indeed possible to detect the shape of an eagle, but whether, as Freud concludes, Leonardo was frightened by an eagle in infancy seems, at best, highly doubtful.

I think we learn more about Leonardo from **The Virgin of the Rocks.** We know that in the course of his geological studies Leonardo had become obsessed by cracked, split and eroded rocks which suggested that the earth, like man and plants and light itself, was in a state of universal flux. Neither mathematics nor any other science was capable of explaining this planetary disorder, which seems to have troubled Leonardo deeply. The rocks in this painting are more than mere rocks; they evoke the natural disasters which recur in Leonardo's *Notebooks*: earthquake and avalanche, volcano and waterspout. Their immense age sets off the youthful appearance of the human figures, while their unusual shape, combined with the eerie light and shade evokes a mood of mystery which is intensified by the crouching, sphinx-like position of the angel. A cosmic Madonna this seems to be, calming genius menaced by insanity.

To the right, in the Salle des États, hang a number of mainly Venetian canvases, including Titian's **Entombment**, once the property of Charles I, and **The Marriage at Cana**, by Veronese, Napoleonic loot. Many of the hundred and thirty figures, including the musicians, are said to be portraits of great men of the time. The grey-haired Titian, in red damask, plays the contra-bass; Tintoretto plays a violin, Jacopo Bassano the flute, while the figure playing the viola is Veronese himself. Critics who complain that the Gospel spirit is absent from this huge canvas forget that it was painted for a refectory. Moreover, at this period many artists, notably the elder Brueghel, were finding that a new pathos could be obtained by showing the Holy Family unrecognised and almost anonymous, just as they would have been in real life.

In the Tribune of the Grande Galerie are gathered six masterpieces from the collections of François I and Louis XIV.

The **Mona Lisa** is traditionally admitted to be the portrait of Monna Lisa Gherardini, wife of Francesco di Zanobi del Giocondo. Leonardo worked at the portrait, which is painted on an oak-panel, for at least four years and brought it with him to France. Much has been written about the mysterious expression of the 'Mona Lisa'—and mystery is a constant feature of Leonardo's work, whether it be the smile, expressing feelings or thoughts hidden from the spectator, or the pointing finger, indicating a power outside the spectator's field of vision—but less has been said about the other elements of the composition. The winding road and river, the craggy rocks, the unusually wrinkled sleeves and finely-pleated bodice, the veil so closely entwined with the hair it is difficult to tell where they merge—these details increase the sense of mystery. I believe, perhaps overfancifully, that even the parting in the centre of the hair is a deliberate act of non-committal, while the position of the hands suggests someone unforthcoming and self-sufficient.

The 'Mona Lisa' was stolen in 1911 by an Italian workman and recovered two years later in Florence. More recently a young man tried to destroy that baffling smile: he threw a stone which broke the glass and slightly tore the picture on one side. The 'Mona Lisa' is said to be one of the three most popular works of art in Paris, the others being the 'Venus de Milo' and Rousseau's 'Snake Charmer'. Each represents a woman and each, for different reasons, is slightly mysterious —but only slightly. (Surrealist works, being private and totally mysterious, are not popular.) The spectator is tantalised—he feels he can complete the character or story, solve the riddle; but in fact he seldom can. And so, provoked, he may end by throwing stones.

In Raphael's portrait of **Balthazar Castiglione** a gentle artist has painted a gentle subject. Castiglione, like Raphael, came from Urbino: he was Ambassador of the Duke of Urbino to the court of Louis XII, and author of *The Courtier*, a handbook of refined manners which includes the first—and still valid—definition of a gentleman.

On the opposite wall hangs a portrait of **Jeanne d'Aragon**, only the head of which is by Raphael; Correggio's **Mystic Marriage of St Catherine of Alexandria**, one of the paintings in Louis XIV's collection at Versailles, and Titian's **François I**. Titian never saw the king and as a character study this seems to me far inferior to Clouet's portrait, which we will come to later.

After a number of works of the Spanish school begins the first great period of French painting. The Roman baroque style epitomised by Caravaggio had at first been slavishly imitated by French painters, but in the first half of the seventeenth century, under royal patronage, they began to evolve a style more suited to national temperament: less theatrical, more sober and rational.

The great portraitist of this seventeenth-century group is Philippe de Champaigne, whose masterpiece, the **Ex-voto of 1662**, was painted at the age of sixty. It depicts the miraculous cure of his daughter, Sister Catherine de Ste Suzanne, a nun of Port Royal, in answer to the prayers of Mother Catherine Agnès Arnauld, the stern Jansenist reformer known as Mère Angélique. The pale faces, rough habits and absence of ornament admirably set off the light of faith in the nuns' eyes, while the crucifix without Christ suggests the severe, ascetic life of Port Royal, which exerted such an influence in Champaigne's day.

A similar rather severe devoutness is found on the other side of France, in Georges de la Tour of Lorraine. The Mary of La Tour's **Adoration of the Shepherds** wears a coarse dress like those of the Jansenist nuns, though its colour is here a smoky nocturnal red. Joseph's gesture of shielding the flickering candle-flame is a good symbol of his protective role towards the vulnerable sleeping infant. No other painter, I think, has made us so aware that the Nativity took place at midnight, or so well imparted the qualities of night: stillness and silence.

La Tour's reputation suffered a decline after his death so that almost nothing is known about his tastes or methods of work. But many of his figures have a density, almost a solidity which, with their stillness, makes us think of the sculptor rather than the painter. Now Lorraine is a region of wood-carving, and it may well be that La Tour took as his starting-point for this canvas the wooden figures of a village crib.

The marvellous Poussins and Claude Lorraines hang well together, for both men settled in Rome, though Poussin returned for a short while to decorate this very gallery. Some of the Poussins have darkened considerably because of his habit of underpainting in red. The most famous perhaps is his **Shepherds of Arcadia**, deciphering the inscription 'Et in Arcadia ego', which might well serve as Poussin's own epitaph. Poussin's method of painting not from life but from antique sculpture is admirably suited to scenes of classical mythology. We know that he grouped his figures in order to obtain harmony and greatest clarity of exposition: we are in the same generation as Corneille, with his rhyming hexameters, and Descartes, with his injunction to seek *l'idée claire*.

In Claude Lorraine atmosphere—the colour of light—becomes more important than figures. As Ruskin said, 'Claude set the sun in heaven and was, I suppose, the first who attempted anything like the realisation of actual sunshine in misty air.' Henceforth this is an important theme in the French tradition, to be taken up notably by Watteau and the Impressionists.

At the end of the gallery, lording it over what after all was his own palace, stands **Louis XIV**, painted at the age of sixty-two by Rigaud. *Le roi soleil* wears his coronation robes, while the sword at his side can still be seen in the Galerie d'Apollon. The stance and bearing reveal the stickler for etiquette, the plumpness reminds us that he was a voracious eater, in spite of stomach troubles which tormented him from early youth. The shapely legs are those of a horseman and dancer. Indeed there is something of the ballet dancer in the position of the feet, shod with rather high red heels, and the king did in fact take part in ballets, attired in mythological costumes, well into middle age.

In the next room hangs the most perfect of Van Dyck's portraits of **Charles I** of England, a painting which, curiously enough, slightly influenced French history. Manon Vaubernier, afterwards Comtesse du Barry, was discovered by one of the royal myrmidons, when she was a copyist in the Grande Galerie of the Louvre. After she had become his mistress, Louis XV bought this portrait for her boudoir in the belief that it was a family picture, since the page holding the horse was named Barry. Later it found its way to the apartments of Louis XVI, where the king had it daily before his eyes. The vacillation of Louis towards his advisers was much influenced by a fixed idea that Charles I lost his head for having made war upon his people, and James II lost his crown for having abandoned them.

The historical order is now interrupted by a series of Petits Cabinets, which begin on the left or southern side. The portrait of **Jean le Bon** is the earliest true portrait by a northern artist in the Louvre. Gérard d'Orléans probably painted it in England where the king was held prisoner for three years after Poitiers. The features are treated with an uncompromising realism which was to become a hallmark of French portraiture, while the rather sad expression recalls a disastrous reign, during which the currency was more than once devalued and Paris witnessed the first French revolution, that led by Etienne Marcel.

Jan van Eyck's **Virgin with Chancellor Rolin**, painted about 1436, is a key work in the development of Marian iconography. Just as the Middle Ages had brought knowledge, history and nature to praise the Mother of God, so now early Renaissance Flanders, with its new skill in manufacturing, praises her in terms of luxury goods—brocade and goldwork, stained glass and jewellery. A new equivalent of spiritual values has been found in the world of man-made objects. The painting is also remarkable for its portrait of Rolin, chancellor of Burgundy, a vigorous, shrewd, intelligent administrator in his sixties, who, as one might guess from his face, was something of a climber.

From about the same period dates the **Pietà** painted by an unknown artist for the charterhouse of Villeneuve lès Avignon, a rendering of the subject which precisely because of its restraint and simple, seemingly inevitable composition has

never been surpassed. The town in the background is probably Jerusalem, its crescent-topped minarets a reminder that
the Holy Places were still in infidel hands. In the same room
the **Pietà de St Germain des Prés** provides a glimpse of
fifteenth-century Paris, with the old Louvre and abbey of St
Germain des Prés.

The chief work in the Cabinet Fouquet is the portrait of a
man with a long red nose, looking sad, sick and sour. Can this
really be Charles VII, whom Joan of Arc fought to crown?
Why wasn't the artist arraigned for *lèse-majesté*? And then
we recall that this is the realistic fifteenth century, an age
which eschewed dreams, unless of the Danse Macabre.

Completing the tour of the Petits Cabinets we enter four
rooms of Dutch masters. In the fourth hangs Rembrandt's
Pilgrims of Emmaus, considered his greatest religious painting, remarkable for the expressions of the servant and the
pilgrim on the right: emotion caught at the crest of its wave.

In the Clouet room is the superb portrait of **François I**
aged about thirty. Physically, the king was tall, brave and
vigorous, with slanting eyes and a prominent nose. Clouet has
succeeded in showing his gay and open nature, while hinting
at his selfishness and basic ineffectiveness. Spoiled outrage-
ously by his mother and sister, he grew up with no moral
sense and even dared to ally himself with the Turk. But his
artistic sense was impeccable, and no king has been a more
generous patron to painters and architects, poets and savants.

The portrait of **Gabrielle d'Estrées and Her Sister** belongs
to the school of Fontainebleau. As we have seen in the Cluny,
this kind of bath scene figures already in an early sixteenth-
century tapestry. Henri IV's mistress holds a ring in her hand
—for the King had promised to make her his wife as soon as
his marriage to Marguerite de Valois was annulled—while her
sister's gesture is an allusion to the birth of César, Duc de
Vendôme, whose house would later give its name to the Place
Vendôme. This portrait was painted about 1594, five years
before Gabrielle's death at the age of twenty-six.

In the last Cabinet hang four portraits by Holbein, including one of **Erasmus**, where the line of the pointed nose is
continued into the pen, and so to the text, the first lines of
Erasmus's *Commentary on St Mark's Gospel*, admirably suggesting an acute and powerful intelligence. The portrait of
Anne of Cleves is of particular interest because it was this
painting which pleased Henry VIII and decided him to send

for her. When Henry met his fiancée's ship he was so much abashed at her appearance as to forget to present the gift he had brought for her. The next day he complained about her looks and said 'she was no better than a Flanders mare.' Indeed Anne had no looks and her only accomplishment was needlework. After her divorce she spent her life happily at Richmond and Bletchingley, where she is said to have worn a new dress every day.

Another engagement picture is Dürer's **Self-portrait** at the age of twenty-two. The flower he holds is what the Germans call 'conjugal fidelity', which makes it likely that the picture was painted after his engagement to Agnes Frey. The shape of the flower, the artist's tangled hair, his dress and tasselled cap: all combine to evoke Dürer's intense but haywire character.

After the small-scale perfection of the Cabinets, the **Galerie Médicis** comes as a rather too grandiose experiment in self-glorification. This series of twenty-one paintings illustrating her own life was commissioned for the Luxembourg Palace by Marie de Médicis, and painted from 1622 to 1625 by Rubens and his workshop. They are remarkable chiefly for their invention—Rubens has transformed a frankly banal and uneventful life into a series of dramatic, even heroic tableaux —and for their influence on subsequent French art. Among the noteworthy details are (in picture number ii) the coat of arms stamped with a red lily, this flower being the emblem of Florence, and (in number vii) the horn of abundance, which contains the queen's five future children. Number vi is generally considered the best: the Tritons and Naiads which will later influence Renoir have that marvellous flesh colouring which prompted Reynolds to say that Rubens's figures looked as though they fed on roses. Number x, 'The Coronation,' is worth bearing in mind, for it will invite comparison with David's 'Coronation of Napoleon'.

The Galerie Rembrandt contains an admirably crisp, clear portrait of **Descartes** by Franz Hals: almost in black and white, with hardly a trace of colour to excite emotion. It was painted towards the close of Descartes's long, self-imposed exile in Holland, shortly before Christina of Sweden's invitation summoned him to Stockholm—and philosophy lessons at five o'clock in the morning, 'when her Majesty's mind is freshest'.

Among the Rembrandts are a portrait of **Hendrickje**

Stoffels, the poor, loyal companion of the artist's last years, who also poses for **Bathsheba in the Bath**—a painting which excited such wrath that Hendrickje was summarily excluded from the local church. Marvellous paintings, but also inimitable, and that is perhaps why of all the masters in the Louvre Rembrandt has had fewest artistic descendants in France.

Rembrandt's **Venus and Cupid** provides a good transition to the next part of the gallery—eighteenth-century French art—for whereas Rembrandt failed in this subject, it became a stock-in-trade of the new generation of French painters. We seem to have entered an elegant, mannered, witty salon. The children, like François Drouais's **Comte de Nogent**, are likely to be dressed in rose satin, and the ladies, like Perronneau's **Madame de Sorquainville**, will have exceedingly witty eyes. Life will tend to be something of an evasion, as in Ollivier's **English Tea at the Prince of Conti's**: the scene is at the now demolished Temple, where Louis XVI and Marie Antoinette were later imprisoned, and the boy at the clavecin is Mozart. Finally the archetypal painting of the period, **Embarkation for the Isle of Cythera**, by the restless, consumptive Watteau. The title is that of a stage play, so that here we have a painting of the enactment of a myth. Reality is very far away, indeed the statue on the right seems to be hovering in space. The sun is setting; in a moment the figures like actors from a stage will have vanished, and when we take up French painting again on the eve of the Revolution, the scene will have shifted from Versailles to Rome.

To find the next group of French paintings it is necessary to retrace one's steps, which incidentally provides an opportunity of looking again at old favourites. Coming out of the Salle des Sept Mètres we turn into the Salle Daru and David's **Oath of the Horatii**. This shows the three Roman brothers who fought and triumphed over three brothers from Alba, thus giving Rome her early supremacy. In short, like another canvas in this room, **Leonidas at Thermopylae**, a hymn to patriotism. Exhibited in the Salon of 1785, it became the manifesto of the new antique, virtuous school which replaced the dalliance of Boucher and Fragonard with the austere virtues of Rome. Unlike Poussin's timeless classical figures, David's warriors seem to be alive now, models to be followed. The dramatic episode, the size of the canvas, the over-simplification—all show this to be committed art; the artist intends not so much to please as to influence his age.

The unfinished portrait of **Madame Récamier** at the age of twenty-three dates from after the Revolution, in which David had played a leading part, being at one time President of the Convention. Now the painter's ideals have been realised: Madame Récamier is even wearing an antique dress which owes much to David's own designs for a 'civic uniform' based on Etruscan, Greek and Roman clothes. Madame Récamier's Salon may have brought together writers as great as Chateaubriand and Benjamin Constant, but she herself though virtuous was an insipid woman. One misses the flashing wit of Madame de Sorquainville's eyes.

The Coronation of Napoleon depicts the Emperor, who has already firmly taken the crown from Pope Pius's hands and placed it on his own brows, about to crown Josephine. Gone now are Rubens's allegorical figures tossing gold coins: here the historical fact is so unique and important it contains its own sufficiency of drama.

To David also we owe perhaps the best portrait of **Napoleon** in existence. It was painted about 1797-8 after Napoleon's lightning successes in Italy. The original plan was to show Napoleon contemplating the Alps from the plain of Rivoli, while a groom led his horse to headquarters, designed to occupy the right corner of the canvas. But Napoleon would pose for only three hours: in that time David caught his likeness, but the painting was left unfinished. Finally, a **Self-portrait** painted by David at the age of forty-six, during his imprisonment after the death of Robespierre. Like Fragonard and Greuze, David occupied one of the twenty-six apartments in the Grande Galerie set apart for artists and their wives, but with the return of the Bourbons he had to flee France—he had voted for Louis XVI's death—and he died in exile in Brussels.

The last great painter to be represented in this part of the Louvre is Ingres. Like David, Poussin and so many of the French classicists, he studied in Rome, but that his classical style had already been formed is seen in his portrait of **Madame Rivière**, painted before he left France at the age of twenty-five. The portrait of **M. Bertin l'Aîné** is a later work, in which the painter has admirably caught the fiery, combative bourgeois journalist who preferred to be sent to prison rather than abandon his political opinions.

Five centuries of French painting, from Gérard d'Orléans to Ingres. Certain features seem constant: sobriety of composition, a preference for line over colour and chiaroscuro, a penetrating interest in character; certain features recur: an austere simplicity and a love of antique sculpture. Above all, French painting is very intelligent painting. The appeal is to the head, not to the heart. Romantics, such as Watteau and Delacroix, do occasionally appear but leave little mark. Leonardo's sense of mystery and Rembrandt's tragic vision are as inconceivable in Paris as El Greco's austere mysticism, the grotesqueness of Bosch or Grünewald's strident emphasis on pain. In fact the reason why there are so few Spanish and German paintings in the Louvre is that these do not appeal to French taste. French classicism is based on the golden mean. Time and again we see French painters toning down and bringing into balance their more extreme Italian models. It is, moreover, until 1860 very much an urban art: there are few signs of affection for fields, flowers, and trees which add much to the backgrounds of Venetian, English or German paintings.

The cream of the Impressionists we shall see later in the Jeu de Paume. Enthusiastic admirers of nineteenth-century French paintings may want to go to the gallery on the second floor, which contains Ingres's 'La Source' and various bathers and odalisques by the same painter, landscapes by Corot, tigers and seraglios of Delacroix, Whistler's 'Portrait of his Mother' and a few minor Impressionist works (Collection Antonin Personnaz). This gallery is reached by returning to our starting-point at the head of the Daru staircase, then walking east through the Egyptian rooms to a little staircase leading up from the easternmost Egyptian room. At the end of the gallery a staircase leads directly down to the Cour Carrée.

CHAPTER EIGHT

The Palais Royal to the Fontaine des Innocents

❧

Comédie Française – Palais Royal – Hôtel Drouot – Passage des Panoramas – Bourse – St Eustache – Bourse de Commerce – Fontaine des Innocents – Rue de la Ferronnerie

THE massive building with porticos in Rue St Honoré is the Théâtre Français, or **Comédie Française**. It was built by Philippe Egalité in 1786, four years after the Odéon, but neither of these is the oldest Paris theatre—that honour goes to Notre Dame, with its mysteries. When plays became not bawdier but more trivial they moved from the church to the church-square, then to tennis courts and sometimes to the Louvre or a private house.

We are coming to recognise that any great Parisian institution is more likely than not to have been founded by Louis XIV. The Comédie Française is no exception. In 1680 the king signed a decree amalgamating Molière's old company with the actors of the Hôtel de Bourgogne and gave the new company exclusive acting rights in Paris, '*pour leur donner moyen de se perfectionner de plus en plus.*' Curious, the idea that absence of competition would make for better art. After moving four times, the royal company eventually made its home in this theatre in 1799, opening with productions of *Le Cid* and *L'École des Maris*.

Molière had been dead seven years when the Comédie Française was started but it was his plays and high standards of acting which inspired the foundation. It says much for the king's character that he should have protected Molière. The court hated him for having made the marquis, not the lackey, the new buffoon. Even when Molière, in *L'Amphitryon*, satirised the king's right to take at will the wives of his subjects, Louis XIV himself ordered the play to be produced.

On 15th October, 1812, from Moscow in flames, Napoleon signed a decree whereby the company at this theatre, while remaining private, was to enjoy a handsome state subsidy. This

Moscow decree is still in force. Napoleon loved the theatre as well as actresses, particularly classical French tragedy. Something of an actor himself, he understood theatrical principles, once remarking to Talma: 'To turn tragedy into comedy you have only to sit down.'

To-day the Comédie Française has two theatres: this one, officially Salle Richelieu, but known to the public as Le Français, and the Salle Luxembourg, Place de l'Odéon, known since the Fifth Republic as Théâtre de France. Both are noted for impeccable, beautifully-dressed productions: the wardrobe of the Comédie Française is said to con ain no less than 15,000 costumes (some dating from Louis XVI) and 6,000 wigs.

In the foyer of the Salle Richelieu is Houdon's **statue of Voltaire**, who seems to be smiling at human folly. This is the Voltaire we know, the scathing wit and author of *Candide*, but Voltaire himself believed his true genius lay in tragedy. Both *Oedipe*, written at twenty-three, and *Agathocle*, written when he was over eighty, were well received, though even his best plays, such as *Alizire*, are now seldom staged. Two lesser statues, 'Tragedy' and 'Comedy', depict Rachel as Phèdre and Mademoiselle Mars as Célimène.

The eighteenth-century building in the Place du Palais Royal is now the seat of the Conseil d'Etat and cannot be visited. Adjoining the theatre is the **Palais Royal**. The original palace, at the end of the first courtyard Richelieu built for himself in 1629. The architect was Lemercier, whose work we have seen in the Cour Carrée and Sorbonne Church. After Richelieu's death Anne of Austria lived here and the suffix 'Royal' was added.

In 1781 Philippe Egalité, in the hope of raising money to satisfy his creditors, ordered the construction of the cafés, shops and apartments now surrounding the gardens, which caused Louis XVI to say to him, 'Now that you are setting up shop, Cousin, we shall see you only on Sundays, I suppose?'

Each Paris garden had its favourite topic of conversation. Here, in the long shadow of Richelieu, people talked about home politics. They sat in the cafés and discussed the latest extravagances of Queen Marie Antoinette, how she dared to dress up and play theatrical parts on the Trianon stage, how she gambled away the people's hard-earned taxes at faro. It was at one of these cafés, the Café Foy, that Camille Des-

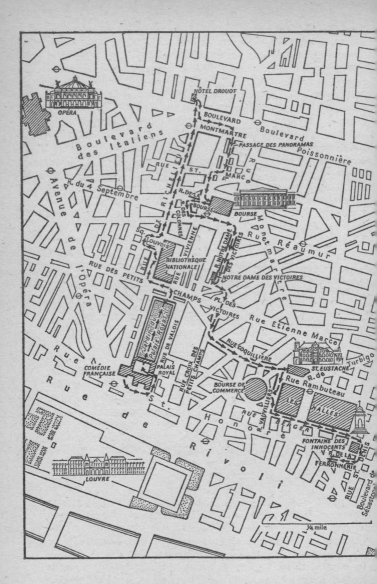

moulins snatched a leaf from a horse-chestnut tree and leaping on to his table flourished it to the crowd as a badge of revolt. That happened on July 12th, 1789.

Four years and two days later a young Norman girl came into the gardens at six in the morning to make a purchase at 177 Galerie de Valois. She was dressed in a brown dress and large black hat which set off her auburn hair and light blue eyes. She had to wander an hour in the gardens before the shutters were pulled down. Then she entered the shop and bought a heavy kitchen knife. Hiding it in the folds of her dress she took a cab to the Left Bank: to 20 Rue des Cordeliers. There lived Jean Paul Marat, a revolutionary turned arch-terrorist through bitterness at finding that he lacked powers of leadership over able men. The young Norman girl had read Marat's violent news-sheet, *L'Ami du Peuple*, and shuddered as he sent the moderate Girondins to the scaffold. This man was betraying the Revolution! And so she took out her kitchen knife and stabbed Jean Paul Marat to death as he sat correcting proofs in his sulphur bath. Three days later she was on her way to the guillotine, with a line by her ancestor Corneille ringing in her ears: 'It is crime which is shameful, not the scaffold.'

In the time of Philippe Egalité the gardens had had a bad name; after the Revolution they became more dissolute than ever. Here, under the arcades, the Merveilleuses paraded in transparent gauze tunics on the arms of their escorts—affected, lisping royalists in bottle-green suits whose stock phrase, '*C'est incroyable! ma parole d'honneur*,' earned them the name Incroyables. A hundred years ago the shops were a favourite haunt of the foreign visitor: now the place is deserted, a quiet, pleasant backwater in the centre of commercial Paris.

Steps at the north end of the gardens lead to Rue Vivienne. **Rue des Petits Champs**, which passes in front of Cardinal Mazarin's palace (now part of the Bibliothèque Nationale), used to be a famous centre of wig-makers. Binct, wig-maker to Louis XIV, lived here in 1692: he used to send round France to buy silvered blond hair (the best came from the north) which was then gathered and glued in the different shapes required for receptions, dinners and hunts. The wig was invented in Paris and the more one considers this fashion of wearing other men's hair the more extraordinary does it seem. Its point, I think, lay not so much in its artificiality as in its curls. No matter its shape, every wig had curls: blond ringlets that were airy, graceful and, above all, gay. The wearing of a wig was a promise to be witty and gay.

At No. 58 Rue de Richelieu is the entrance to the **Bibliothèque Nationale**, a mostly nineteenth-century building (*open to readers daily except Sunday and holidays*, 9–6). Its collection contains nearly every French work published since François I signed a decree compelling all publishers to send two copies of each book to the Bibliothèque Nationale. The exhibition rooms (*open daily except Sunday and holidays*, 10–4), containing some precious antique cameos, bindings and illuminated manuscripts, are likely to interest the antiquarian and bibliophile more than the ordinary visitor.

Rue de Richelieu passes the delightful small **Square Louvois**, with a fountain and statues of four French rivers. Farther up the street, at No. 75, is a carved coat of arms; No. 101 has a balcony decorated with masks and sculptured columns. On the other side of the Boulevard it becomes Rue Drouot, and here is the famous sale-room of the same name. Sad though it is to see the contents of private houses being scattered, the **Hôtel Drouot** is well worth a visit, especially in these days of inflation, when it has become something of an aesthete's gambling den. The lots—the best in French art, furniture and *objets d'art*—are on view the afternoon before the sale (sales are announced in *Le Figaro*) and when they come up for bidding may fetch five or ten times the price they made only a decade before. Buyers realise that probably never again will craftsmen spare the time and love which went into a Boulle Commode or a Louis XIV fauteuil upholstered in petit-point.

Thence along Boulevard Montmartre; the second turning on the right is **Passage des Panoramas**, so called because of the two circular buildings erected in 1799 by the American inventor, Robert Fulton. Here Fulton displayed cycloramas (eighteenth-century 'wide screen') of Rome, Naples, Florence and Jerusalem, using his takings to try to interest the Directory in a torpedo and a submarine which he called 'Nautilus'. France, while welcoming foreign philosophies and art, is more chauvinistic in the field of science—she is not supreme there—and the authorities turned a deaf ear to Fulton. However, a few years later with American backing Fulton successfully launched and sailed the first steamboat—on the Seine.

Rue St Marc and Rue Vivienne lead to **the Bourse**, begun nder Napoleon in imitation of a Roman temple. The **Bourse**

is open for business daily except Saturdays, Sundays and holidays from noon until three p.m. and during those hours visitors
are admitted to the public gallery. From there you look down
on an enormous round wrought-iron basket filled with sand.
This basket of sand is the centre of the room. Along the top of
the basket is a plush rail, like that on a prie-dieu. The basket
stands in the centre of a large, polished parquet floor, relatively bare of people. This floor is virtually surrounded in the
shape of a scroll by a continuous desk, capable of seating
fifty men with ease.

The parquet flooring is reserved for sixty-eight gentlemen in
dark suits. These are the *agents de change*, an élite of stockbrokers allowed to deal in certain shares known as *parquet*.
They alone are privileged to rest their arms on the plush rail
and to toss their cigarette butts into the sand—not a fetish but
a giant ashtray, refilled once a year with whitish sand from
Fontainebleau.

Outside the peripheral desk and at an angle to it is a raised
platform, where *coteurs* at incredible speed chalk up on black-
boards the changing prices of shares. Here and elsewhere on
the fringes of the building, known as the *coulisse*, the bulk of
stockbrokers, the *courtiers*, buy and sell. The distinction
between *parquet* and *coulisse* shares is purely conventional
and is shortly to be abolished.

Noise is a sure sign of the volume of business. Notebook in
hand, *courtiers* hurry in from the telephone, shouting and
gesticulating: finger pointed means sell, open hand means
buy. '*Johnny, je prends*'—someone is buying Johannesburg
diamond mines; '*Le bouc, j'ai*'—someone selling the Ramadier
loan of 1956. The language, the gestures, the magic words—
Rio Tinto, Royal, Mokta—may be known only to initiates,
but even a casual visitor is likely to be impressed by this
teeming mass of five thousand smartly-dressed, well-educated
brokers shouting as though at a boxing match, jostling,
elbowing, pulling as they struggle to make a fortune—not for
themselves but for the cool, financial wizards who sit at home
listening perhaps to Mozart. Business, as Dumas said, is other
people's money.

Women are not admitted to the Bourse. At the time when
John Law, the Scots banker, was blowing his 'Mississippi
Bubble', women mingled with the speculators on the pavement
of Rue Quincampoix, and their charms helped to make the
riches of Mississippi seem even more fabulous than rumour

reported. Then the bubble burst and in 1724 the Regent signed a decree forbidding women to take part directly in financial speculation. The gambling now has switched from pepper and spices to petrol, uranium and electronics, but the rule still holds.

Before a session the stockbrokers can be seen at cafés like Feydeau, the Vaudeville or Chez Galopin, noting a last-minute order, exchanging news from the teleprinter, and I, for one, find that these sharp-eyed, up-to-the-minute chain-smokers—twentieth-century magicians—have some of the glamour attaching to the huge sums of money in which they deal.

After the bustle of these cafés or the Bourse itself it is pleasant to make a short detour up Rue de la Bourse to glance along the pretty arcaded Rue des Colonnes, built on the eve of the Revolution.

There are two ways now of reaching the Halles district, one is by way of Rue Réaumur and Rue Montmartre, the favourite haunt of journalists (many newspapers are published near here); the second, by way of Rue Notre Dame des Victoires, leaves the commercial world to enter for a moment the seventeenth century. The church of Notre Dame des Victoires commemorates the capture of La Rochelle from the Huguenots in 1627 and is famous for having served as a stock exchange during the Revolution and for its large collection of votive offerings. The Place des Victoires commemorates the passage of the Rhine and other battles won by Louis XIV, whose equestrian statue stands in the centre.

Rue Croix des Petits Champs and Rue Coquillière lead to the church of St Eustache, which was begun in 1532 and took 132 years to complete. It is curious to think of Louis XIV's bewigged courtiers watching masons at work on Gothic flying buttresses. Paris-born Gothic lingered longer in Paris than anywhere else. The main west doorway is a classical addition dating from just before the Revolution. In the centre of the west gable is a small rose-window, surmounted by a stag's head with a crucifix between the horns—just such a stag as Eustace, a Roman general, saw one day while out hunting. The stag exhorted Eustace to amend his life: and amend it he did. The same meeting with a stag recurs in the legend of another popular French saint, Hubert, patron of hunting men.

The interior of St Eustache imitates the general plan of Notre Dame, even to the double side-aisles. But Parisians come here less for the architecture or even the apse windows (from cartoons by Philippe de Champaigne), than for the music. Liszt and Berlioz played on the organ, the best in Paris, and the singing, especially on Christmas Eve and St Cecilia's Day,[1] is justly famous. Those to whom French and Italian nineteenth-century church music is uncongenial may prefer to hear Gregorian in the Benedictine abbey, Rue de la Source, or chant *a capella* in the Russian Church, Rue Daru or in the Armenian Church, 15 Rue Jean Goujon.

In the north aisle stands Lebrun's tomb to the man who made possible so much of Louis XIV's Paris. It was Mazarin who brought Colbert, then a mere accountant, to the King's notice. 'Sire,' he said, 'I owe you everything, but I think I can pay my debt by giving you Colbert.' Colbert's subsidies encouraged mines, glassworks and factories for working wool and silk. He established state manufactures and monopolies which still exist (Gobelins tapestries, the striking of coins and medals, the royal printing houses and gunpowder) while the fact that we can buy postage-stamps to-day at a *tabac* is an indirect result of Colbert, who made tobacco a state monopoly. Coysevox's statue of 'Abundance' by his tomb is more than mere rhetoric. Yet Colbert was hated for his taxes—the taxes which we admire now in the Comédie Française or Place Vendôme—particularly by the farmers for forbidding the export of cereals; this may explain the hostility of the people of the Halles. He had to be buried by night, for fear the cortège be pelted with rotten eggs and tomatoes.

Across the way, Rue Oblin leads to the **Bourse de Commerce,** or Corn Exchange. This is an eighteenth-century building unusual for its circular shape. Behind rises a monumental column, all that remains of a house built by Catherine de Médicis. Some interlaced monograms, C and H, are still visible. The queen mother lived here for fourteen years and is said to have observed the signs of the zodiac from the top of the column.

Paris has long been drawn to magic practices—even to-day a surprising number of well-known Parisians consult faith-healers, healers by touch, astrologers and fakirs—and this dark, irrational side is particularly evident hereabouts. Rue Berger leads to the **Square des Innocents**. The name derives from a twelfth-century church dedicated to the Holy Innocents. Until the Revolution this was the most important

[1] 22nd November.

cemetery in Paris: those arches on the south side of Rue des Innocents are part of the vaults, and were once painted with the *Danse Macabre*. Here François Villon loved to wander in that fifteenth century which was so fascinated by death, and here, long before Sartre and Camus, he discovered the absurd, bequeathing his spectacles to blind paupers '*Pour mettre à part, aux Innocents, les gens de bien des deshonnestes.*' For all through Paris's history has run this strain of violence, bloodshed and preoccupation with tortures, executions, and death. It even lasted until the nineteenth century, when the marble slabs of the morgue drew crowds of ghoulish visitors.

Now the street is made pretty by a Renaissance **fountain**, moved here recently from a nearby street. It was designed by Lescot, with reliefs on three sides by Goujon, the fourth relief being eighteenth-century. But this is Villon's haunt, and at night it is his tormented spirit which walks here.

The next street south is **Rue de la Ferronnerie**, site of one of the tragedies of French history. In the year 1610 Henri IV was at the height of his powers: a sensible tolerant man of fifty-six with a zest for living, and adored by his subjects. The fourteenth of May, 1610 was a Friday. The Duc de Vendôme came to the Louvre to warn the king his father that an astrologer, La Brosse, had foretold that that day would prove fatal to him. 'La Brosse,' answered the king, 'is a cunning old knave who wants to get hold of your money, and you are a young fool to believe him. Our days are counted before God.' The king pretended to make light of the warning but he was so troubled he could not work. Already there had been seventeen attempts to take his life.

Restless and lonely, the king sent for his prime minister, but Sully replied that he was ill and confined to his bed. So Henri ordered his coach and drove out of the Louvre in the direction of the Arsenal, where Sully lived. Seven friends accompanied him. Because it was a fine day the leather hood of the coach was drawn back. When the coachman asked which route to follow, Henri replied, 'Go by the Croix du Trahoir'—a place of execution near the Halles. Not the shortest route, but Henri wanted to inspect preparations for a state welcome to the queen, due to take place that Sunday along Rue St Denis.

A sinister figure dogged the coach: a tall strapping fellow of thirty-two, with red hair and sunken, burning eyes. By profession a schoolmaster from Angoulême, he was also a madman and mystic. Under his green clothes his breast was covered with amulets. A vision had led him to Paris, a vision in which he had been warned that the king planned war on the Pope, and that he, Ravaillac, the chosen instrument of justice, must kill the king. Hidden in his green coat was a stolen double-bladed knife with a stag-horn handle.

Entering Rue de la Ferronnerie, the royal coach was pressed by two carts, one loaded with wine, the other with hay, and obliged to draw in against the shop at No. 11. Ravaillac sprang on to a stone post by the roadside and, stretching his arm over the coach wheel, landed two knife-thrusts. The second pierced the king's rib and severed an artery. He was hurried back to the Louvre, dying on arrival. That night Parisians wept as they had never wept since the death of St Louis.

A caster of horoscopes noted afterwards that Henri IV was born 14 centuries, 14 decades and 14 years after the Nativity, on the 14th December; he died on the 14th May, after living four times 14 years, 14 weeks and 14 days. Finally, his name, Henri de Bourbon, contained 14 letters. What is even more extraordinary is that the sign of the shop at No. 11 Rue de la Ferronnerie bore this name and device: '*Cœur couronné percé d'un flèche.*' No wonder Paris half-believes in magic.

CHAPTER NINE

The Marais

❧

Rue des Tournelles – Place des Vosges – Victor Hugo's House – Hôtel Carnavalet – Hôtel d'Hollande – Hôtel de Rohan – Cabinet des Singes

The Marais is a large triangle of land, its corners the Place de la République, the Hôtel de Ville and the Place de la Bastille. The name means 'marsh', for this is low-lying ground which often used to be flooded by the Seine. Alluvial deposits made it well suited to growing vegetables, its chief function until Henri IV drained the district and started building. The Marais remained fashionable until the middle of the eighteenth century, when society began to prefer the Faubourg St Germain. Now it is a working-class district; at the window of some princess's boudoir a cobbler will be hammering nails into a boot, a lorry will be backing into a ducal courtyard to load three tons of factory overalls, but these sights seem to enhance its historic associations. The gulf between past and present is more pronounced in the Marais than anywhere else in Paris: the old atmosphere, instead of being transmuted, has remained unchanged, side by side with the new. Here every turn in the street is likely to produce some contrast, touching, gay or absurd, between the vanished world of the Précieuses and the direct, business-like speech of a wholesaler in bedside lamps.

A good way to approach the Marais is to take the Métro to the station called Chemin Vert, then turn into Rue des Tournelles: No. 28 was built for himself by Jules Hardouin-Mansart (who designed the Place Vendôme) and No. 31 has a fine façade. Rue du Pas de la Mule leads into the Place des Vosges. As this is one of the pleasantest squares in Paris, I like to take a chair in the garden, for which, in a moment or two, an amiable woman with none of the trappings of authority will sell me a ticket.

If the day is sunny, mothers will be sitting under the trees, knitting as they talk (French women are seldom idle and these come from the working class), while their children—lively and tough—play in the sandy paths between the grass. Sooner or later, in my experience, one boy will start to dare another to walk along the top of the low railing, the boy will refuse or fail, a chase will ensue and finally a scuffle. Always there seems to be a scuffle in the garden or along the arcades where school-boys gang together on roller-skates. Perhaps it is wild fancy, but I sometimes wonder whether there isn't, about this square, the pull of history.

The very first important event here was a tournament in which Montgomery, captain in the Scottish guard, accidentally thrust his lance through Henri II's eye, a wound from which the king died twelve days later. In the next reign three of Henri III's *mignons*, or boy-friends, were here challenged by partisans of the Duc de Guise; on the day when his favourite Quélus died of wounds received in the contest, Henri III went to lay the foundation-stone of the Pont Neuf; his grief was such that the people said the bridge would be better called Pont des Pleurs. Later, on the very day when Richelieu declared duelling a capital offence, six noblemen fought a duel outside Richelieu's house (No. 21); one was killed, one wounded, two escaped to England, and the two ringleaders were caught and beheaded, in spite of appeals by the nobles to King and Cardinal. Place des Tournois or Place des Combats would better describe the square than its present name, given in 1799 in honour of the first *département* to pay its taxes.

For most of its history it has been Place Royale, in honour of Henri IV, who built the uniform square of rose-red brick houses faced with ivory stone. The king planned to live in the central house on the south side; his queen, Marie de Médicis, was to live on the opposite side of the square, for Henri IV had lately quarrelled with his fat banker's daughter. Gabrielle d'Estrées was no longer alive but there would have been no lack of feminine company in that southern pavilion: besides Gabrielle Henri IV is known to have had fifty-five other mistresses. His common sense and upright nature are evident in the square's tall, solidly-built houses: his romanticism in the choice of rose-red brick. Brick is an exceptional material in central Paris, seldom recurring until the 1930s, by which time it has become thin and orange-brown in colour. I think it is the shutters which give the square a slightly provincial air. Yet the design is strictly Parisian: four stories, steeply-

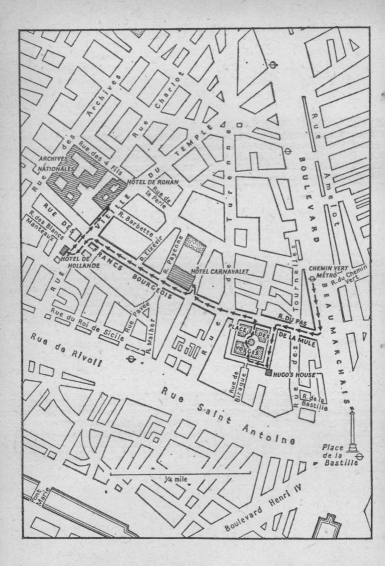

sloping roofs with dormer windows—these are the elements, a century later, of the Place Vendôme.

A portrait by Pourbus in the Louvre shows what Henri IV looked like. He was a chunky man with beard and long thin moustache: lively, quick, high-spirited and frank. He promised Frenchmen a chicken in the pot on Sunday and kept his promise; what is more important, by his own example of tolerance he ended forty years of religious war. His son, Louis XIII, continued to build, to pave the Paris streets in stone, but the people never forgave him for letting Richelieu rule. Louis XIII's statue stands in the centre of the square, erected by the Cardinal, whose inscription on the pedestal is more eloquent of his own virtues than of the king's. The Parisians later proposed to emend the inscription as follows: '*Il eut cent vertus de valet Et pas une vertu de maître,*' alluding to Louis XIII's habit of shaving himself, roasting his own meat and making jam; and to his stinginess and gossiping.

In the reign of Louis XIII Paris underwent a permanent change: the society woman was born. No. 20 provides a clue, for in this house lived Nicolas d'Angennes, Seigneur de Rambouillet. His son married a half-Italian girl, Catherine de Vivonne, who, as Marquise de Rambouillet, founded the Paris salon. The Marquise de Rambouillet changed the colour of drawing-rooms from blood-red to pale blue velvet, enriched with gold and silver; she brought together on an easy footing writers and nobles; she taught men to make their points not with swords and daggers but with witty epigrams. One of her intimate friends, Mademoiselle de Scudéry, the 'new Sappho', headed the group of ultra-polite literary women known as the Précieuses, who tried to refine the French language and pronunciation: certain words such as '*car*' being stigmatised as 'non-U'. Mademoiselle de Scudéry also devised the clever map of the Country of Tenderness wherein you might progress from the village of New Friendship either to Tenderness-on-Inclination, or to Tenderness-on-Respect, unless, missing your way, you fell into the Lake of Indifference or the Sea of Enmity.

The Place Royale was a centre of the Précieuses, so this square can be said to mark the change from the rough, masculine society of Henri IV to the witty society revolving around certain gifted or beautiful women which still prevails to-day, with the Duchesse de La Rochefoucauld uniting writers and influential Parisians on her famous Thursdays.

As women became more important socially, so the great courtesans flourished. Ninon de Lenclos lived here, so did Marion Delorme. Marion Delorme was well-born, beautiful, rich, extravagant—she changed her gloves every three hours —and a skilled player on a lute called the theorbo. She would not take money from her lovers, who included Cinq Mars, Richelieu and Louis XIII, only presents such as fine pieces of silver. In 1650 she was ordered to be arrested by Mazarin for her complicity in the Fronde disorders. She took a dose of antimony and, gravely ill, called the curé, who heard her confession. As soon as he had returned to the presbytery, the curé was summoned again, to hear a postscript or codicil to the confession. Once again he returned, once again he was recalled to hear a second postscript. And so on, ten times. When Mazarin's officers arrived, Marion Delorme appeared to be dead. She was only thirty-seven.

This 'death', however, is said by many to have been a ruse. A legend runs that Marion Delorme fled to Scotland, married an English lord, returned to France after the death of Mazarin, was held up by a bandit with whom she fell in love, and so on through numerous adventures until the age of well over a hundred. She was so much a part of Paris that Parisians refused to believe she had died.

Marion Delorme had lived at No. 6. When Hugo, drawn by its romantic associations, came to live in the Square in 1833 there were several reasons why he should choose house No. 6. He had written a play about Marion Delorme, and also he was peculiarly sensitive to atmosphere, 'auras' and the lingering-on of spirits: indeed, he believed in transmigration, and was convinced that he himself had once been Isaiah, Aeschylus and Juvenal. 'Do you know,' he exclaimed on a famous occasion, 'I've caught Juvenal using one of my lines. It's a perfect Latin translation of what I have written in French.' One sees the point of Cocteau's quip: 'Victor Hugo was a madman who believed himself to be Victor Hugo.'

Hugo lived on the second floor of No. 6 from the ages of thirty-one to forty-six. His house is well worth a visit (**Musée Victor Hugo**, *open daily except Tuesday and public holidays*, *10–12, 2–5, or 6 in summer*). In the entrance hall hangs his portrait in old age by Bonnat (it used to appear on the 5-franc bank-notes, known as '*misérables*'); beside the staircase hang drawings and caricatures relating to his literary and political activities. But the interest begins in Rooms I and II on the first floor, with Hugo's own drawings, gouaches and paintings. What a revelation! So dark and gloomy, black being almost the only paint in his palette; and the subjects! Tree-trunks, a dolmen, a giant mushroom, and castles, castles, castles—on land, in the sea, in the middle of Zurich Lake. Even Eddystone Lighthouse becomes a rickety castle tower. A ship caught on a huge breaking wave is entitled *Ma Destinée*.

I wonder whether we possess any other such startling record of a poet for short periods at the mercy of his subconscious. They do not illustrate his poems: far from it. They give an impression of dark, brooding power, morbid and without any affirmative note. They seem almost to be the compost from which the poetry flowered.

Room III contains illustrations to Hugo's books and plays, as well as designs for costumes. There is also a somewhat cruel drawing of Mademoiselle George, Napoleon's mistress, *en déshabillé galant*, a bust by Rodin and the beautiful hand-embroidered bottle-green uniform worn by Hugo when elected to the Académie at the early age of thirty-nine.

The second floor contains furniture arranged by Hugo from old panels, and the Chinese drawing-room from the Guernsey house where he lived in exile. Hugo did the Chinese carvings and decorations himself. I wonder whether this was one of his famous premonitions, for to-day Cao-Daism, the Universal Religion of Indo-China, honours Hugo as a saint and even believes that the master's sublimest works were written *after* his death. There is indeed an official edition of what is claimed to be Hugo's posthumous work, communicated by spiritualism. The claim seems scarcely upheld by two sample lines, concluding a séance:

> *Mais vous avez, Ho-Phap, une crampe à la main,*
> *Renvoyons notre causerie pour demain.*

Finally, the bedroom, upholstered in red damask, where Hugo died in Avenue d'Eylau. He was no longer the young idealist of Place des Vosges days: he had become pompous and inordinately vain. A story, apocryphal but still revealing, tells how a wag proffered the news that the municipal authorities were planning to change the name of the city from Paris to Hugo. The great man nodded gravely and said, 'Yes, it may well come to that.'

The actual change was slighter: Avenue d'Eylau became Avenue Victor Hugo. However, the poet-politician lay in state at the Arc de Triomphe, and 400,000 mourners accompanied his body to its grave in the Panthéon. He is still the most popular poet in France, as Henri IV is the most popular king. Both had a touch of coarseness, but both knew how to strike certain chords in the people's soul. Both loved Paris, and no one better than Hugo has made the city conscious of her own past. *Notre Dame de Paris* was an epoch-making book; without the popular interest it aroused Viollet le Duc would never have been allowed the funds to restore French Gothic.

The north-west corner of the square adjoins Rue de Turenne: Nos. 23 and 41 have seventeenth-century fountains. Rue des Francs-Bourgeois meets Rue de Sévigné, and the entrance to the **Hôtel Carnavalet**. (*Open daily except Tuesday*, 10–12, 2–6.)

On the gateway keystone is a winged figure of Abundance standing on a glove which was later carved into a carnival mask, in punning allusion to Carnavalet, a Parisian garbling of the Breton name of one of the first owners: Kernevenoy. The courtyard of the original house is seen on entering: it was built in 1546 by Lescot and Goujon, whose work we have already noticed at the Louvre. Only sixty years after Cluny— but what changes! The inner courtyard is now more important than the exterior; windows have been stripped of their lace-like ruffs; and the vertical line is provided by tall bas-reliefs instead of by a tower.

In the centre of the courtyard stands a bronze statue of Louis XIV by Coysevox, the only royal statue to escape the Revolution, because it had been commissioned and paid for by the municipality. The remaining three courtyards are modern, with some antique importations, notably the façade of the Drapers Company on the west side of the garden.

The house has been laid out as a museum of the history of Paris. There is a wealth of shop-signs, models of buildings, costumes, souvenirs of actors and actresses, and relics of the Revolution, as well as a number of good portraits, including 'Two Magistrates' by Largillière and 'Maréchal de Saxe' by La Tour. The Museum has many distinguished devotees and I know that I am in a minority in saying that there seem to me rather too many paintings recording forgotten state drives, and that it is more amusing to discover the history of Paris, directly if at random, in her own streets, houses and monuments.

Personally, then, I hurry to the first floor, where in the corner room Madame de Sévigné had her drawing-room, and where her portrait by Robert Nanteuil still hangs. She was born at 1 bis Place des Vosges in 1626; her father was killed in a duel and so was her husband, after seven years of marriage. She rented this house in 1677 and lived here nineteen years, though she made frequent journeys to her country house in Brittany, and to Provence. She had lively blue eyes, a mass of golden hair and a gift for conversation; according to Mademoiselle de Scudéry, there was no more faithful or more generous friend, and Saint Simon says: 'By her easy wit, natural grace and pleasant disposition, she seemed to impart the same qualities to anyone she conversed with, even when Nature had denied them.' She loved the Carnavalet, its garden, the good air—as she loved most things in life, savouring the everyday trifles and writing about them to her rather hard-hearted daughter, Madame de Grignan, whose portrait hangs opposite. In one of the autographs on display she is making her daughter a present of a diamond: so affectionate is the style that she seems to have inherited the totally selfless yet warm nature of her grandmother, Ste Jeanne de Chantal. Her letters have outlived the more pompous works of her friends the Précieuses because of their sincerity, eye for detail and zest for life. 'We cannot have too many things to love, real or imaginary, it doesn't matter which.'

Madame de Sévigné entered fully into the life of the time and it is in her letters that we find some of the most vivid and accurate reports of the age. For instance, the royal performance of Racine's *Esther* in 1689, when Louis XIV deigned to speak to her, and Madame de Maintenon gave her a smile; or the execution of Madame de Brinvilliers the poisoner; or how chocolate has superseded coffee in popular favour: 'Madame de Coetlogon took so much coffee that her little baby was black as an imp, and it died.' Madame de Sévigné's rheumatism gets worse, and she goes to try the waters at Bourbon; this displeases her daughter, who has urged Vichy instead; the impossible daughter is shocked that her mother reads romances, is barely polite to her mother's friends, failing, for instance, to thank La Rochefoucauld for a gift of sugar-plums.

Madame de Sévigné suffers in silence and replies with another tender, amusing letter. So that you feel that this house, which she loved, must have been a gay and happy place, arranged with taste and ringing with the conversation of loyal friends. Of all the old houses in Paris the Carnavalet is the one into which I should most like to have been born.

The small room adjoining Madame de Sévigné's drawing-room is a fine example of *chinoiserie*, but belongs to the eighteenth century: it is worth fixing in one's memory, for in a moment we shall find another comparable example in the Hôtel de Rohan. We see now the sort of effect Hugo was aiming at but could not achieve: the titanic hand perforce lacking in delicacy.

We continue along Rue des Francs-Bourgeois—No. 31, the Hôtel d'Albret, has a fine eighteenth-century façade—and turn left down Rue Vieille du Temple. At No. 47 is the seventeenth-century Hôtel d'Hollande, formerly the house of the Dutch ambassador, with a fine bas-relief of Romulus and Remus in the courtyard. Turning up the street, we come at No. 87 to the **Hôtel de Rohan**, completed by Delamair in 1713 for Armand de Rohan. (*Daily visits by groups. Apply to M. le Directeur Général des Archives de France, 60 Rue des Francs-Bourgeois. Tel.* TUR 94–90.) The name over the doorway, Hôtel de Strasbourg, recalls that he and his three successors of the same family were all Cardinals of Strasbourg.

Before entering the house, by turning right into a courtyard, formerly the stables, we can see a bas-relief by Robert Le Lorrain, a pupil of Girardon and perhaps even greater than his master, depicting the **Horses of Apollo**. The horses, which are being watered, only partly emerge from the stone, but so living is the line of their neck and heads, they seem to be straining and snorting for release.

On the first floor of the Hôtel de Rohan is the **Cabinet des Singes**, decorated by Christophe Huet, one of the prettiest rooms in Paris, and also one of the most revealing and important. No one was assassinated here, no one married, no intrigues plotted: and yet it tells as much of the mentality which led up to the French Revolution as any book by Rousseau or Voltaire.

The room, painted in 1745, is pure rococo. Now rococo was the age of fêtes, firework displays, opera, fancy-dress balls, light comedies, pastoral poetry: the age of the wig, its curls suggestive of gaiety, fantasy and airy movement; above all, the age of the mask. 'Nothing,' the rococo declares, 'must seem

to be what it really is.' Just as ebony furniture is inlaid with
brass and tortoiseshell until its ebony qualities disappear, so
masked dancers lose themselves in their masquerade. No one
has a 'real' face, only a succession of ball-masks.

The masks vary. Marie Antoinette plays at being a dairy-
maid; her court at being shepherd and tripping shepherdess;
some wear English clothes and at five o'clock take tea *à
l'anglaise*; others favour Turkish modes. But the favourite
fantasy-land of all is China. Garden-grottoes, hump-backed
bridges, fans, pagodas, silk hangings: yes, from these can be
woven dreams.

Now the most striking thing about the figures in the
Cabinet des Singes is that the little boys, their top-knots, their
clothes, their games are not Chinese at all. How could they be,
for no one in Paris society had ever been to China. They are
French versions of what the Chinese ought to be like.
Chinoiserie, in fact. The figures are all young and they are all
happy. For over a hundred years missionaries, many of them
French, had been sending back glowing reports of China. The
Chinese were virtuous, they had evolved a stable system of
government, they waged no aggressive wars—and yet they had
little or no organised religion.

This news had a profound effect in Europe. Here were men
and women *naturally good*. The Chinese had invented gunpowder, yet originally used it only for fireworks. Advance-
ment in Chinese society was not by bribery and corruption
but by an orderly system of written examinations. Now it is
this natural goodness which the artist shows in the Cabinet
des Singes. The Chinese boys are all *at play*—but playing
kindly, smiling. The inclusion of monkeys is very significant.
Nature is good: men and women, left to their natural in-
stincts, do not hurt each other or misbehave: they sport, free
from care, just as monkeys sport in the branches of the
jungle. Like animals, they do not need to toil: China was
believed to be a country of leisure.

Now if the Chinese are naturally good, how can Europeans
achieve the same happiness? They must live 'according to
Nature', interpreted as meaning, first and foremost, that
which corresponds to the assumption of uniformity. 'The
purpose of Nature,' wrote Spinoza, 'is to make men uniform,
as children of a common mother.' The consequences of this
belief were important. In religion as in aesthetics the only
acceptable principles, to quote Thomas Warton, were those

by no peculiar taste confined,
Whose universal pattern strikes the mind.

Gothic was condemned; likewise all revealed religion. 'The
worship God wants is that of the heart; when this is sincere, it
is something common to all mankind.' When the Church tried
to point out the folly of such an ethic, her objection could be
ruled out of court by pointing to the Chinese boys playing so
happily, so peacefully together without any knowledge of
Scripture. The ideal became standardisation, a lowest common
denominator, ideals and virtues so vague as to be mere mish-
mash. The way was paved for the death of God and the death
of the King.

The Cabinet des Singes was commissioned for a Cardinal's
house. Stranger still, this was not just a bedroom or salon, it
was the oratory. The cardinals prayed with their eyes fixed on
the little Chinese boys playing blind man's buff. No wonder
they came to believe that life itself was a masquerade, that
their own cardinal's robes were part of a masquerade, that
their robes could be laid aside and they too, like the Chinese
boys, could indulge in pastime. It was the last cardinal of the
four, Louis de Rohan, who succumbed finally to the tempta-
tions of this dream world.

Louis de Rohan was set on becoming a new Richelieu, but
for all his wealth, good looks and high birth he could not win
the good graces of Marie Antoinette. In 1784 Louis de Rohan
was fifty and as far from realising his ambition as ever, for the
queen disliked his intemperance and gross luxury, disliked
him so much that it was enough for her to see his handwriting upon a note to make her burn the thing unread. Now
among the Cardinal's friends was the self-styled Comtesse de
La Motte, a pretty intriguer heavily in debt. She called herself
the last of the Valois and claimed to be received at court. She
promised to put in a good word for the Cardinal with 'her
friend the Queen.' Jeanne de La Motte, with the help of her
lover, an ex-gendarme, then devised a trick. In the garden of
the Palais Royal they found a streetwalker who looked a little
like Marie Antoinette. After dressing her up and rehearsing
her, Jeanne took the girl to Versailles, staying at an inn
called by a curious coincidence *Belle Image*. From there on
the evening of 24th July, 1784, the intriguers hurried the girl to
the *bosquet de Vénus*, in the park of Versailles.

Within the grove, wearing a broad soft hat and a dark-blue

cloak over his lace-frilled purple, paced the Cardinal. He was in a daze of pleasant excitement, for he had been told by Jeanne that he would see the Queen. Presently Jeanne joined him and led him along a path to a hedge. Here, in the darkness, they were met by a woman in white. Rohan knelt before her. The woman whispered, 'You know what this means,' and let a rose fall at his feet. The Cardinal seized the hem of the white dress and kissed it passionately. But now a man—another of the intriguers—rushed up and warned the figure in white that d'Artois—Louis XVI's youngest brother—was near. Jeanne said, 'Quick! quick! . . .' The figure in white slipped back into the shadows, and Rohan was hurried away.

The fatuous cardinal was in a rapture of joy. The Queen had not spoken to him for eight years—and now this! When the Comtesse, who had brought his dream true, asked for money —and again more money, he showered it on her with grateful words.

Now at that time two Parisian jewellers had a valuable necklace on their hands. Louis XV had ordered it for Madame du Barry but died before buying it. The jewellers had tried to sell it to Marie Antoinette, for she had a passion for faro and gems, but the price was so high she declared the money would be better spent on a new warship.

Six months after the meeting in the *bosquet de Vénus*, the Comtesse told the Cardinal that the Queen wanted him to obtain the necklace for her, unknown to the King. The Cardinal fixed a price of one million six hundred thousand *livres*, the first instalment to be paid the following August. He wrote down the terms in a letter to the Queen which the Comtesse took away and later returned, signed: 'Approved; Marie Antoinette de France.' This had been clumsily forged by Jeanne's lover, for the Queen never added 'de France' to her name. The Cardinal did not spot the slip, nor did the jewellers, who handed over the necklace to the Cardinal; Jeanne's lover then called for it dressed in the livery of a palace footman. The La Mottes then broke up the necklace and sold the stones separately.

In August the jewellers demanded their money, the whole story came out and the Cardinal was imprisoned in the Bastille: likewise the Comtesse, who accused Cagliostro of being implicated (in fact Cagliostro had expressly warned the Cardinal to beware of Jeanne).

The case was heard before Parlement in the great hall of the

Palais de Justice. The Comtesse was sentenced to be branded with a V (*voleuse*) and imprisoned for life in the Salpêtrière (she later escaped, only to die of a fall). Cagliostro was acquitted and so was the Cardinal, who promised to indemnify the jewellers. He returned for one brief night to this house; perhaps he gave thanks in the Cabinet des Singes; then the next day the King ordered him to leave Paris for the country. He never returned. At the Revolution his house was turned into a powder store-room; its interior spoiled, all but the room of *chinoiserie*, the mischief-making innocents, the naturally good Chinese, still playing, still enjoying life, with no one to disturb them, no one to wreck their dream.

CHAPTER TEN

The Archives to Porte Saint Denis

❧

Hôtel de Soubise – Archives – Quartier du Temple – Rue Quincampoix – St Nicolas des Champs Conservatoire des Arts et Métiers – Rue Volta – Porte St Martin – Porte St Denis

THE **Hôtel de Soubise**—its entrance is at 60 Rue des Francs-Bourgeois—commemorates the love of an ageing king for a young redheaded beauty: to be precise, of Louis XIV for Princess Anne Chabot de Rohan, wife of François de Soubise. The Sun King, a generous lover, showered presents and money on his favourite, who in 1700 was wealthy enough to exchange her own house (now 13 Place des Vosges) for that of the Guises and transform it into a palace worthy of the Rohan family. The architect chosen was Pierre Alexis Delamair, who later designed the Hôtel de Rohan. Delamair built the new façade on the back of the old Hôtel de Guise, and the horse-shoe-shaped *cour d'honneur*, surrounded by a Corinthian colonnade. It is one of the most perfect ensembles in Paris but precisely because of its originality the Princess found fault with it.

The lavish interior (*open daily except Tuesday*, 2–5) dates from the next reign, when another young Princess, Marie Sophie de Courcillon, married a Rohan and came to live here. Boffrand was entrusted with the decoration and hung Delamair's sober walls with sculpture, panels and stucco, creating curves where he could, as in the oval salon on the ground floor. Next to this salon is the Prince's bedroom: though he was well over sixty, the panels make allusions to his strength (Hercules), authority and power (Neptune), courage (Mars), and skill at hunting (Cephalus).

The Hôtel de Soubise now houses the **National Archives** (*open daily except Tuesday*, 2–5); some of the most interesting documents and objects being displayed on the first floor. They are set out chronologically, the medieval exhibits in the **Great Antechamber**, which retains only one or two traces of its

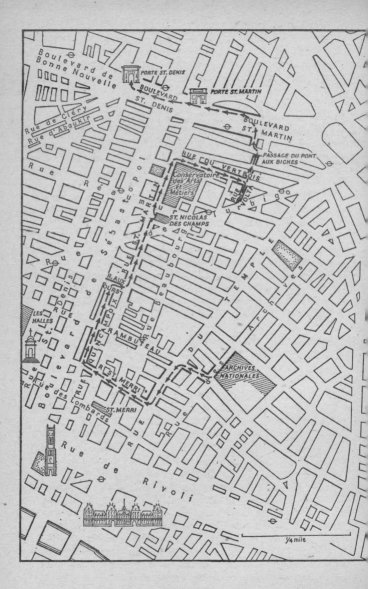

original decoration. Some may find these dull and pass at once to more dramatic rooms illustrating the Revolution and First Empire, but I for one enjoy the wrinkled parchments written in a language no longer Latin yet not French, the water-concession made to the convent of Célèstins, the heavy seal dangling from a charter like a medal on a faded ribbon. Here, then, are some of the notable exhibits.

Case 2 (to light the cases, it is sometimes necessary to press a button at one side) recalls an epoch when the western half of France belonged to England: a letter of Richard the Lion-Hearted concerning a peace-treaty recently signed with Philippe Auguste is dated 1196, three years before Richard was killed by an arrow at Châlus; also Philippe Auguste's will, written in his own hand, bequeathing the crown jewels to the abbey of St Denis.

Case 3 contains St Louis's list of alms to be distributed during Lent: 2,119 *livres*, 63 measures of corn and—Lenten fare indeed—68,000 herrings. Here too is Henry III of England's request that St Louis should act as peacemaker between him and his barons. Finally, the rub of sanctity: thirty-eight years after his death and soon after his canonisation the King's body is distributed in the form of relics: the Sainte Chapelle receives his head, Notre Dame a rib, and so on down the scale.

Case 4 contains an act of Philippe le Bel, dated May 1295, introducing the first of those devaluations of currency which have plagued France up to the present day.

Case 6 contains the papal bull (1219) authorising the Dominicans to celebrate their offices at Paris in the church recently given them by the University. This church was the former hostel of pilgrims bound for St James of Compostela (at the corner of Rue Soufflot and Rue St Jacques); hence the name Jacobins, by which the Dominicans were known in Paris.

Case 11 traces the history of arms which, it appears, were first used in the Crusades as a means of identifying mail-clad knights. Incidentally, three of the eleven windows of this room retain their original heraldic motifs: the ermine of Brittany in the macle of the Rohans.

Case 12 shows the first use, in the thirteenth century, of a new writing material imported overland from China: paper. Formerly records had been committed to papyrus, parchment or even, for ephemerae, to wax tablets.

C.G.P.   E

Cases 13 and 14 record the Hundred Years War, beginning with a letter from the English King, Edward III, challenging Philippe of Valois to a duel, the prize to be nothing less than the kingdom of France.

Case 15 contains the only drawing from life of Joan of Arc, doodled in the margin of the register of the Council of Parlement recounting the deliverance of Orléans. Perhaps one may doubt whether the warrior-saint had quite so weak a chin as the registrar has given her here, but still, this is a peep into the fifteenth century for which one is grateful.

Case 25 traces the development of writing and the first appearance of the vernacular in official documents (1034). Some of the spelling (*toz ceaus* for *tous ceux*) might have interested Bernard Shaw and doubtless made life easy for the University students referred to in a document in the next case. After yet another of the numerous disputes between guards employed by the Abbot of St Germain des Prés and University students on the Pré aux Clercs, the Abbot is found to have been at fault, and he cedes to the king half of the proceeds from the Foire St Germain, held on what is now Rue Mabillon. Also in this case is a sixteenth-century miniature depicting the church of St Germain des Prés with its original three Romanesque towers.

Case 27 contains the charter whereby St Louis founded the Sorbonne and an interesting book with drawings (1387) showing occupations whereby poor students paid for their keep: waking the household for Mass, cleaning the chicken-run, stacking books in the library.

Case 28, devoted to Paris, contains an agreement (1210) between the merchants of Paris and Rouen regarding the measurement of salt: notable because it carries the first example of the city's seal.

We arrive in the former assembly-room of the Princess's apartments, hung with mythological paintings by Van Loo, Boucher and Restout: here the Rohans danced down the eighteenth century in a series of masked balls: for the Hôtel de Soubise was one of the gayest and most splendid of its day. The numbering of the cases now begins anew, on the theme: the Rise of Absolute Monarchy in the Sixteenth Century.

Cases III and IV—'The Religious Wars and the League'— are particularly relevant to this house, where François de Guise often entertained his niece, Mary Queen of Scots, and later rallied the Catholic nobles; again, after the assassination of François, his son Henri, the new Duc de Guise, twice (1563 and 1572) fortified the house as a military headquarters of the Catholic party; from here in 1588 he made himself master of Paris, only to fall into a trap and die, pierced by swords of the King's Guard. Despite this disaster a Guise might yet have come to the throne had not Henri IV considered Paris worth a Mass and later made religious tolerance the law of the land with his Edict of Nantes.

Case VI contains the decree of Parlement condemning Leonora Galigai (see p. 79) and a German engraving of her execution, as well as the first volume of the first Parisian newspaper, *Gazette de France*, founded by Dr Théophraste Renaudot.

Case VII again has a bearing on this house. François de Rohan and his brother Soubise, two ardent Protestants, were holding out in Brittany, with English help, against Louis XIII: a revolt which caused bloodshed for several years and can be said still to drag on to-day: rumour has it that the children of the Ducs de Rohan-Chabot do not learn a word of French before the age of seven: they speak only Breton! In the same case lies the most disastrous of French documents, fruit of that absurd catch-phrase: 'Differences of religion disfigure a great nation'—the Revocation of the Edict of Nantes (1685).

Two documents are displayed bearing on the religious history of Paris: Vincent de Paul, who attended Louis XIII in his last hours, receives from the King a sum of money to ransom French slaves in Algeria; and Sister Louise de la Miséricorde (Louise de La Vallière) writes on behalf of her Carmelite convent.

Case XI contains documents relating to John Law's Bank, and four bank-notes—presently we shall be passing Law's former office, No. 43 Rue Quincampoix.

The next room, despite the bed, was in fact a reception room. The Princess, after passing the night in her small bedroom adjoining, came here for her levee, flaunting her charms behind the gilt balustrade like a filly in a racecourse paddock, while admirers and friends retailed the latest gossip and sought her patronage, perhaps for a cousin in need of an army commission, for a penniless poet, for a child prodigy named Mozart.

Next is the Princess's **oval salon**, a masterpiece of Boffrand and Natoire, who painted the scenes from the Story of Psyche;

then the Princess's bedroom, decorated chiefly by Boucher and Van Loo, where documents illustrating France's foreign policy are on display; and the **Salle du Dais**, with the monogram R.S. still visible on the cornice. Here are exhibits relating to the French Revolution: a model of the Bastille, the chess set used by the royal family imprisoned in the Temple, the Dauphin's game of lotto, a letter of Louis XVI pleading for three days' stay of execution 'so as to prepare his soul': 'désirerai' changed to 'demanderai'—a weak man trying to be strong. Here too are the album of samples of clothes in Marie Antoinette's wardrobe—each morning she put a pin-prick beside the dress that caught her fancy for that day—and the ungrammatical, misspelled note pricked out at top speed with a pin when she was a prisoner in the Temple and Rougeville promised to rescue her: '*Je suis garde a vue je ne parle persone je me fie a vous je viendrai.*'

Here too is a letter from a French pharmacist named Parmentier concerning the cultivation of a South American vegetable unknown in France which he had eaten while a prisoner of Frederick the Great. Marie Antoinette patronised Parmentier and wore potato flowers in her hair at an official reception, while the King gave him a hundred acres near Paris to grow for the first time in France a vegetable which had been discovered 250 years earlier.

The next room is devoted to Napoleon: the love affairs and victories finally punctured by the coldly clinical letter of the English surgeons who conducted the official autopsy: 'On a superficial view the body appeared very fat.' Alas for the glories of Marengo and Austerlitz, Eckmühl and Wagram.

So much for the more notable items on display; hidden in this and adjoining houses are several million other records which the student is free to consult—maps and plans alone number 100,000—all being swelled by an annual tide of decrees, registers and other papers running into thousands. The past threatens to become well-nigh unmanageable.

By turning right when we leave the Hôtel de Soubise we cross Rue des Archives, and glancing north can see a robust fourteenth-century gateway belonging to an earlier house— the **Hôtel de Clisson**—generously integrated into his plans by Delamair. This is the last outpost of grandeur in the 3rd arrondissement: now we leave the palaces and enter working-class Paris.

Rue Rambuteau; Rue du Temple—because it led north to

the now vanished house of the Knights Templars: indeed, al
this densely populated district is officially Quartier du Temple;
then Rue St Merri—behind the shuttered windows artisans are
hammering copper and tin, making buckles and buttons,
feathers and artificial flowers. Wholesalers abound here, selling gloves in bundles by the gross—not those hand-made,
web-fine wisps of lace for smart shops in Rue de Castiglione
but heavy, gauntlet-sized gloves reinforced at the tips with
metal, for men working cranes, or handling steel ingots.

This is a closed, village-like world, where everyone knows
everyone else in the local bar or bistro; a thrifty world, where,
if a housewife needs only one egg, she buys one egg and no
more; and, in some of the streets, a shady world, where it may
be indiscreet to stare at the tattooed arm of a barman: if the
tattoo shows five points, as found on dice, that means he has
spent time in solitary confinement: 'all alone between four
walls.' Colonies of Spaniards, Poles, Turks and North
Africans speak a patois French enriched with *argot*. The word
derives from a certain Ragot, leader of a gang of beggar-
robbers under François I, when such gangs had their own laws
and special language, clustered around the various Cours des
Miracles, where, at the end of a day in well-to-do Paris the
beggars laid aside their acting and returned to their natural
condition—the blind seeing, the lame walking. Present-day
argot, as piquant as Cockney rhyming slang, is well worth
getting to know. Face: *la poire*; eyes: *les mirettes*; ears: *les
feuilles*; dog: *le clebs*; sun: *le bourguignon*; to be rich: *être
plein aux as*; to run away: *jouer des flûtes*; to eat: *se remplir le
buffet*; and so on.

Hereabouts you can find any number of betting cafés and
the central state pawnshop, but scarcely one bank—capitalists
in the 3rd arrondissement evidently stuff their money into
mattresses. And yet streets such as Rue de Venise and Rue des
Lombards were once the home of money-lenders, changers
and owners of those rudimentary banks which had begun to
be established in the sixteenth century by Italians, despite
opposition from some theologians, who considered an interest
rate of up to 8% contrary to God and His law.

But these bankers were not theoretical economists and
when, at the death of Louis XIV, trade in France came almost
to a standstill, no one could propose a sure remedy. It was
then that John Law of Lauriston appeared on the scene. The
son of a Scottish goldsmith-banker, he had had to leave

Britain after killing a rival in a duel over a pretty girl. Good-looking, charming, intelligent but somewhat impetuous, Law saw that the best means of stimulating the flow of commerce was to replace gold and silver in all commercial transactions by something less cumbersome and insecure, in short, by bank-notes. 'My secret,' he confided one day to the Abbé Dubois, 'is to make gold out of paper.'

In 1716 a state bank was established, with Law as managing-director, and proved an immediate success. In the following year Law set up the Compagnie des Indes Occidentales, with himself as leading director, and it was natural for him to choose an office in this district, where trading in shares was usually conducted: to be precise, in the next street, **Rue Quincampoix**, at No. 43. The Company was granted the monopoly of trade with Louisiana and absolute control of the internal affairs of the colony, both for twenty-five years. Law backed the Company, and public confidence in Law made the shares soar. No one knew very much about Louisiana—one writer declared it to be an island—but they believed its mountains were full of gold and silver, lumps of which the natives readily exchanged for knives or looking-glasses. In fact it was something of a swamp, where convict-settlers were ravaged by yellow fever.

The boom continued a full year. It became necessary to enclose each end of Rue Quincampoix by gates and to restrict dealings to the hours of daylight, so that the inhabitants of the neighbourhood could sleep. At eight each morning the gates were opened to the roll of drums and all who could afford them rushed to buy 500-*livre* shares at a price of up to 200,000 *livres*. Servants, grown richer overnight than their masters, swaggered about in coach-and-four. And then the huge bubble began to tremble. Confidence dwindled. Finally alarm verged on panic. The Regent's doctor, Chirac, on his way to see a female patient, passed through Rue Quincampoix and learned that the price of Louisiana stock was dropping. He could think of nothing else, and even while holding the lady's pulse was heard to exclaim, '*Mon Dieu, elle baisse, elle baisse*,' much to the consternation of the patient and her family.

Inflation and uncertainty caused a run on Law's bank. 'I will compel confidence,' snapped Law, and decreed the successive devaluation of both money and shares, almost by half. The result, naturally, was to shatter confidence. Law had to resign as finance minister, and an edict of 10th October,

1720, decreed that the use of gold and silver would be resumed in all commercial transactions.

Law retreated to Italy. Absolutely honest, he had paid the penalty of being in advance of his age. 'Do not forget,' he said towards the end of his life, 'that the introduction of credit has brought about more changes among the powers of Europe than the discovery of the Indies.' And one great permanent monument remained. In 1719 Law had ordered a new town to be founded on a wide bend of the Mississippi River, just over a hundred miles from its mouth, and called it after his patron—New Orleans.

Rue aux Ours is a deformation of Rue aux Oües—that is, Rue aux Oies, after the roasters of geese who lived here in the Middle Ages. It leads to Rue St Martin, once the great Roman road to the northern provinces. At the corner of Rue Réaumur is the church of **St Nicolas des Champs**, 250 years a-building: the façade, most of the clock tower and the seven first bays of the nave are flamboyant Gothic, the rest largely Renaissance. The south portal was built from a design found among the papers of Philibert Delorme. The eighteenth century has left its usual imprint: white windows and fluted Doric columns in the last bays of the choir. Medemoiselle de Scudéry, the tenth Muse as she was called, is buried here.

Opposite the church is one of the chief entrances to the **Sewers**. Visits to the sewers and the morgue were popular at the turn of the century: it was one way of familiarising oneself with sordidness and violence. Now, with such needs satisfied by tough films and Zola's imitators, I imagine that few people to-day make this particular descent to Avernus. The municipal authorities point out that the visit is not possible in winter or after storm and heavy rain; and for some odd reason members of artistic, literary or scientific societies pay half-price.[1]

Farther up Rue St Martin is the former priory of St Martin des Champs, which the Revolutionaries turned into a Science Museum under the name **Conservatoire des Arts et Métiers** (*open daily except Monday*, 1.30–5.30; *Sundays*, 10–5). It is worth looking into the **Refectory**, on the right side of the *cour d'honneur*, the work of Pierre de Montereau, who built the Sainte Chapelle. The scientifically-minded will find an odd assortment on display: magnetos and induction coils, plans of lime and cement works, Blériot's aeroplane, a statue of

[1] Visits at 2, 3, 4 and 5 p.m. every Thursday from 1st July to 15th October. Assembly-point: the statue of Lille, Place de la Concorde.

Zénobe Gramme (resounding name!) to whom we largely owe electric light and, in the gallery devoted to prevention of accidents, boiler-parts showing defects likely to cause explosions. Decidedly, for those with enough time there is much curious information to pick up in Paris.

A right turn along Rue du Vertbois brings us to Rue Volta, No. 3 of which is the oldest house in Paris, having been built by the mayor of St Martin in the Fields about 1292. It has four stories but, strangely enough, no cellar. The ground floor was divided into two shops, the entrances lying off the street on the side of the house. The shopkeeper stood in the street, where he could keep an eye on his display of goods, while urging shoppers to stop and buy. He shut up shop at dusk, for in those days it was forbidden to sell by candlelight, since this might deceive customers into buying shoddy articles or unfresh food.

The north end of Rue Volta becomes Passage du Pont aux Biches, which leads into Boulevard St Martin. Turning left we arrive at the **Porte St Martin** and the **Porte St Denis**, built in 1674 and 1671 respectively to commemorate victories of Louis XIV. In the form of Roman triumphal arches, they pierced the tree-lined ramparts (now vanished) with which the Sun King replaced the line of fortifications surrounding Paris.

The Porte St Denis is the more important, standing astride the Rue St Denis, said to have been first marked out by the track of the saint's footsteps when, after his martyrdom, he walked in quest of a burial place. Through this gate the kings of France made their first entrance into the capital, and through the same gate their bodies were drawn to burial at Saint Denis. So it was fitting that the final, daring attempt to save the French monarchy should have taken place within shadow of this gate: the exact spot was the first intersection to the right looking down Rue de Cléry.

It was a foggy January morning in 1793 when Louis XVI set out on his last journey, from the Temple prison to the scaffold. To the rolling of drums his carriage passed down the boulevards between ghoulish crowds, guarded by the Marseillais battalion, a company of mounted police and two field batteries. As the cortège passed the Porte St Denis a powerful voice rang out, calling, 'To my side, all who would save the king.' A tall man ran towards the king's carriage, flourishing his hat in one hand, a sword in the other. Half a dozen daredevils followed him into the massed pikes and bayonets, most of them to be cut down at once by the guards. The procession was halted, the alarm given. The tall man—Jean, Baron de Batz—threw a quick, anxious look over his shoulder: where were the five hundred armed followers who had sworn to follow him? Unknown to Batz the list had fallen overnight into the hands of the Convention, and all but thirty had been arrested while leaving their homes. For a few moments longer the tall man's sword flashed, and frightened guards used their sabres on the crowd. Blood was shed, women screamed, bodies fell sprawling. Then, seeing the game was up, Batz cut a way out and escaped on a fast horse hidden beyond the Gate. He lived to make another daring but vain attempt at rescue, this time on behalf of the Queen.

CHAPTER ELEVEN

Faubourg Saint Germain

❧

*The Invalides – Church of St Louis – Napoleon's Tomb – Rue
de Grenelle – Rue du Bac – St Sulpice – Luxembourg Gardens
– Fontaine de l'Observatoire*

AFTER Notre Dame, the Invalides is perhaps the most important foundation in Paris: important as a work of art, for
the ideas it embodies, as Louis XIV's most munificent gift to
his capital city and as a monument to absolute monarchy.
(*The cour d'honneur and galleries are open daily*, 7–7.)

The forecourt, entered from the Place des Invalides, immediately sets a mood: flower-beds and prettily-made guns
which, ignited with a taper, might or might not fire cannon-
balls: we are back in the days when scarlet-clad soldiers
marched to flag and drum and the cavalry charge of a gallant
general could turn defeat into victory, when war depended on
character, not on machines. The façade, which extends like a
battle-line—it is over an eighth of a mile in length—is decorated with masks, helmets and breastplates. Each of the attic
windows is in the form of a trophy and each is different. In
the centre double Ionic pilasters support an arch and bas-
relief of Louis XIV in Roman dress on horseback, between
Justice and Prudence. The bas-relief replaces an original by
Coustou, who also fashioned the huge statues of Mars and
Minerva flanking the entrance.

How, in the *grand siècle*, might an absolute monarch attain
to glory? He could rule virtuously, maintain a splendid court,
beget handsome children. St Louis had done no less. But since
the Renaissance, at the back of every educated Frenchman's
mind lurked the Roman emperors. *They* had won glory by
feats of arms, by subduing, by extending an empire. If Louis
XIV wears Roman dress in this bas-relief, it is not as panto-
mime. Already he had won the beginnings of glory in a war
against Spain; more campaigns lay in store. But glory cost
dear in bloodshed and wounds. What of the soldiers, maimed
or grown old in his service—were they to continue to drift, as

in the past, until some abbey or priory, taking pity, gave them
a job ringing bells or sweeping the church? By no means.
Such conditions would be base, dishonourable, inglorious.
And so, in 1670, with one magnificent gesture, Louis XIV
asserted the royal virtue of mercy, decreeing that a great
hostel—more than a hostel, a palace—be built for the King's
soldiers, wounded or veterans, who now became, in effect,
members of the royal household. That this was the King's intention is shown by the status of doctors, surgeons and
apothecaries of the Invalides: they were appointed by the
King and enjoyed the same privileges as those in attendance at
Versailles.

The dome, although it belongs properly to the chapel
behind, seems to crown the long façade. This is no accident.
The dome represents the absolute, quasi-divine monarchy
which the soldiers have served and which now, in their old
age, protects them.

The central gateway leads to the *cour d'honneur*—only one
of fifteen closed courtyards in this minor township which, in
its heyday sheltered no less than 7,000 old soldiers. The attic
windows are noteworthy, particularly the fifth on the right
of the left-hand pavilion, as you enter. This takes the form of
a wolf, its head half-hidden by palms and its paws supporting
the *œil de bœuf*: in short, a wolf that watches (*loup voit*),
recalling the part played in the planning of the Invalides by
Michel de Louvois, Under-Secretary for War, reorganiser
of the Army and a staunch benefactor of the rank-and-file.
An oblique reference only: not for Louvois to intrude on the
monarch's display.

On the side opposite the entrance is the door of the **church of
St Louis** (*open daily except Tuesdays and holidays*, 10–12.15,
1.30–5, *or* 5.30 *in summer*); above is a bronze statue of
Napoleon which originally surmounted the Vendôme column.[1]
The church interior is decorated with captured flags. In the
crypt are buried governors of the Invalides, famous soldiers,
including Leclerc, and one woman: Marie de Sombreuil.
Aged only eighteen, during the Revolution she saved the life
of her father (Governor of the Invalides) by throwing herself
over his prostrate body and beseeching the executioners to
put up their swords.

[1] This is Seurre's statue, dating from 1833. On the Vendôme column
it replaced an enormous fleur-de-lis, which Royalists had substituted for
Chaudet's original statue, later melted down (see p. 20).

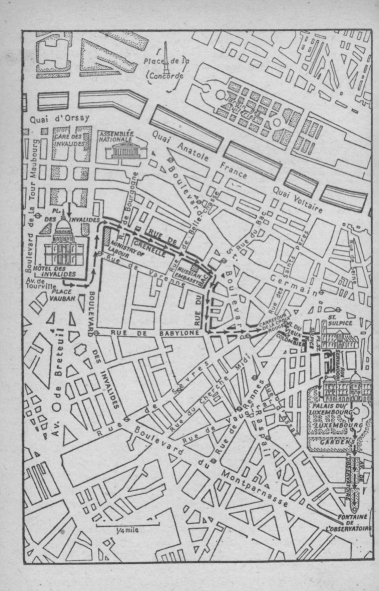

Place de la Concorde

Quai d'Orsay

GARE DES INVALIDES

ASSEMBLÉE NATIONALE

Quai Anatole France

Quai Voltaire

Boulevard de la Tour Maubourg

Boulevard

Boulevard

de Bourgogne

PL. DES INVALIDES

RUE DE GRENELLE

R. de la Classe

Rue du Bac

R. de Belle-Classe

St.

Rue des Saints Pères

Rue de Seine

HÔTEL DES INVALIDES

MINISTRY OF LABOUR

Rue de Varenne

RUSSIAN EMBASSY

Boulevard

Germain

Av. de Tourville

PLACE VAUBAN

RUE DU

Rue de Rennes

CARREFOUR DE LA CROIX ROUGE

R. DU VIEUX COLOMBIER

ST. SULPICE

BOULEVARD

RUE DE BABYLONE

R. DU BAC

ST. SULPICE

PL. ST.

DES

Rue de Sèvres

Rue du Cherche Midi

Rue du

RUE

PALAIS DU LUXEMBOURG

INVALIDES

Rue de Vaugirard

Rue de Rennes

R. de Rennes

R. d'Assas

LUXEMBOURG GARDENS

Av. O de Breteuil

Rue de

Boulevard

du

Boulevard du Raspail

Montparnasse

AV. DE L'OBSERVATOIRE

FONTAINE DE L'OBSERVATOIRE

1/4 mile

So far the architect has been Libéral Bruant; now, turning right and again right, we pass through the Corridor de Metz into another courtyard and the **church of the Dome** (*open daily*, 9.30–5, *or* 5.30 *in summer*), the work of Jules Hardouin-Mansart, who was responsible for the Place Vendôme and the Palace of Versailles. Begun in 1677, the year after Bruant's work was finished, the domed structure was added to the church of St Louis as a chapel royal. The statues in niches on the ground floor are of St Louis and Charlemagne, by Coustou and Coysevox; those on the first cornice represent four of the cardinal virtues.

With St Peter's of Rome and St Paul's of London, this is one of the memorable domes of Europe. Seen from the south like five spurts of a single fountain the columns of the portico soar in a continuous line through the drum and ribs of the dome to meet in the lantern and form, in the obelisk, a single jet. The gilt trophies, garlands and helmets trumpet the theme of military glory across to the Arc de Triomphe. Each of the helmets conceals a window, which explains the flood of light which meets the visitor when he enters the chapel.

A painting on the cupola shows St Louis offering his sword to Christ: war—even against Spain or Holland—is still some-thing of a crusade. But St Louis and Louis XIV are here eclipsed by the man who carried the theme of military glory to its logical conclusion and thereby fell. The chapel is the burial place of the first Napoleon.

He lies amid warriors and members of his family. If we stand at the entrance and read clockwise, beginning at the high altar, the six chapels contain the tomb of Marshal Foch, by Landowski; the tomb of Vauban; the tomb of Napoleon's brother Joseph, King of Naples; the tombs of another brother Jérôme, and Napoleon's son, the King of Rome; the tomb of Turenne; and the heart of La Tour d'Auvergne.

Walls, chapels, cupolas and floor are richly ornamented, setting off, by contrast, the plain and simple open crypt with its pavement of laurels in mosaic on which stands Visconti's red porphyry tomb. Here lies the body of Napoleon, wearing the green uniform of a *chasseur de la Garde*, his heart in a silver urn at his feet, which point in the direction opposite to the chapel entrance. Beside him are coins bearing his image and his personal plate. Twelve colossal figures of Victory surround the tomb and a statue stands nearby, to remind us of the man as he was on his coronation day: a nineteenth-

century work by Simart. Stairs lead down to the crypt, which
is entered between tombs of Napoleon's two favourite
generals—Duroc and Bertrand, by a door cast from bronze of
cannon captured at Austerlitz, surmounted by the famous
directive from Napoleon's will.

The directive was obeyed. In the eyes of Frenchmen,
Napoleon was too great for the Panthéon. The Invalides was
clearly the right spot: often he had come here to pass his
veterans in review; two streets away, in the École Militaire,
he had learned the art of war; and nearby flows the river.

A moving building. Pensioners linger still in one or two of
the courtyards. But most of the rooms are occupied by the
Ministry of War. I like to imagine that where old soldiers recalled a sabre-charge, electronic brains are now ready to chart
the path of guided missiles. A solemn building and, believe it
or not, one with numerous progeny—half a world away.
Travel through Central and South America and, on the outskirts of almost every capital city, the chances are that you
will see an immense and magnificent modern skyscraper, perhaps a dozen or twenty stories high: superior to all but a few
buildings in the entire country. Ask what it is and the people
will tell you: the military hospital. Even dictators have been
schoolboys once.

Leaving the Chapel of the Dome we turn left at Place Vauban and again left up Boulevard des Invalides, as far as **Rue de
Grenelle**. Grenelle derives from *garanella*, the little warren,
for it used to lead to a game reserve noted for quail and hares,
outside the city walls. When the Invalides went up on this
waste ground, speculators hurried to buy. Between 1690 and
1790 two hundred large houses were built, of which fifty
remain to-day. The Marais quickly became *démodé* as family
after family crossed the river; the district between Rue des
Saints Pères, the Seine, Boulevard des Invalides and Rue de
Varenne became the Noble Faubourg, a title it retains to-day.

A quiet district, where high walls enclose gardens the size of
a small park (there was plenty of land available), with few bus
routes and even fewer cinemas, revealing its grandeur quietly,
in a carved key-stone or a door-knocker worthy of Cellini.
No. 127 Rue de Grenelle, at the corner, was built in 1770 as
the town house of the Duc du Châtelet, guillotined under the
Terror. The property was requisitioned and is now, most
anomalously, the Ministry of Labour. A *porte cochère*, a
gravel drive, a courtyard facing the street, the main façade

behind, overlooking lawn and trees—this is the usual plan in
the Faubourg. Opposite stands the **Hôtel de Chanac de
Pompadour**, built twenty years earlier by Delamair, architect
of the Hôtel de Rohan and Soubise in the Marais, and now the
Swiss Embassy.

At No. 115 is a plaque erected by one of her admirers to
Adrienne Lecouvreur, who died nearby in 1730 and was buried
secretly by night under the pavement at the corner of Rue de
Grenelle and Rue de Bourgogne, by three friends, including
her lover, Maréchal de Saxe, while Voltaire thundered a
tirade against the curé of St Sulpice for refusing the traged-
ienne a place in his cemetery.

No. 101 is the **Hôtel de Rothelin**, a fine example of late
Louis XIV domestic architecture by Lassurance; No. 116 the
former Hôtel de Villars, now the *mairie* of the 7th arrondissement. Particularly beautiful are No. 87, the **Hôtel de Bauffre-
mont**, with a curved façade, and No. 85, the **Hôtel d'Avaray**,
where Horatio Walpole lived as British ambassador. No. 102,
the **Hôtel de Maillebois**, was built by Delisle Mansart about
1724 and let to the Duc de Saint Simon, who was well placed
to gather the final piquant anecdotes for his *Memoirs*. No. 79,
the **Grand Hôtel d'Estrées**, was built in 1713 by Robert de
Cotte; the Tsar stayed here when he laid the foundation-stone
of the Pont Alexandre III. That was in 1896, when French was
spoken by all Russian gentlefolk and French capital financed
Russian railways; now the hammer and sickle show it to be
the Russian Embassy.

These are only a few of the houses in one of the Faubourg's
four main streets. Their beauty makes one catch one's breath.
Unlike the houses of the Marais, their history is fairly calm.
There has been no memorable violence here, and now there is
no shouting, no flashiness, only an air of dignity and quiet
distinction. Happy houses, and so there is no story.

The architecture is pure eighteenth century. The nineteenth
century added almost nothing: the noblesse continued to live
here, biding their time, waiting for the noisy plutocrats of the
Second Empire to burn themselves out, and here many of
them continue to live to-day. Not many own an entire house,
for these change hands at anything up to four million new
francs apiece, but even half a floor provides a spacious apartment. The Faubourg Saint Germain is still the best address in
Paris. In the stretch of Rue de Grenelle between numbers
134 and 69 live the Comtes des Nétumières, d'Oilliamson, de

Moustier and de Sercey; the Duc de Caraman and the
Vicomte de Curel; the Duc de Blacas, Monsieur André Jean
de Talancé and the Marquis d'Ayguesuives. This is more than
a random list of names woven into French history; all happen
to be members of the most exclusive club in the world, the
Jockey.

Le Jockey was founded in 1834 by Lord Henry Seymour for
the encouragement of the improvement of racehorses in
France; and—though this was not written into the constitu-
tion—for the promotion of all that was chic and *racé* among
the French nobility. It was the Jockey which made Paris such
an agreeable place to Edward VII, and to-day it sets the social
tone of the capital. Qualifications for admission—again un-
written—are character, wit, *tournure* and a title five or six
hundred years old. At a vote, which is secret, at least a hundred
members must ballot, and one adverse ballot out of six is
sufficient to blackball a candidate. There is a handful of foreign
members, including the Duke of Edinburgh and the Earl of
Hardwicke.

The noblesse of the Faubourg, whether members of the
Jockey or not, shun the public eye; their photographs are not
to be found in gossip columns, *Paris Match* or *Jours de
France*; and yet they form one of the most powerful forces in
Paris. Because their money comes largely from estates, they
have kept a sense of reality and responsibility; they have
adapted themselves to an age of commerce and science; their
names are to be found at the head of banks, insurance com-
panies, textile firms. They still take the lead in Paris, though
more often than not they let others steal the prestige. And
because they have adapted themselves, it would be a mistake
to think they have lowered their standards or changed their
political minds. On the contrary, few invitations are more
prized than one to the Manoir du Coeur Volant, for at Coeur
Volant lives the Comte de Paris.

This title dates back to 665, when the prefect of Paris (a
Roman office) took the name of Comte. Hugh Capet was
Comte de Paris and Duc de France; proclaimed king in 987,
he united the county of Paris with the crown. The present
Comte—for royalists, the legitimate King of France—is a
direct descendant through Louis-Philippe of the House of
Orléans, but his choice of title asserts an even older tradition
and the geographical fact that the lord of that city lying
slightly north of centre thereby holds all France in his grip.

Where there is a court, acknowledged or not, there is etiquette. The noble Faubourg holds to its standards: it still matters to choose the appropriate one of thirty-six possible formulas for ending a letter, to have wedding invitations printed by L'Oeuvre des Orphelins d'Auteuil, to know just which afternoon a grey topper will be suitable for Longchamp. It is for a society aware of such nuances that artists and artisans give their best.

We turn right down **Rue du Bac**, so named because it led to the ferry which transported stone for the construction of the Tuileries. The ferry was replaced in 1689 by the Pont Royal: this direct link with the Right Bank did much to increase the Faubourg's popularity, especially under the Regency, when the Court lived in the Tuileries.

No. 97 Rue du Bac, the **Hôtel de Ségur**, provides a glimpse of the sort of people who have lived in the Faubourg. It was built about 1720; Vicomte Pierre de Ségur was the owner in 1795, a brigadier-general who led the life of a man-about-town and wrote plays. In 1809 it belonged to the Prince of Salm Dyck, landowner and botanist, and his wife, Constance Marie de Théis, formerly married to a certain Pipelet de Leury, member of the Academy of Surgeons. Constance Marie wrote poems, letters and reviews which won her the titles 'Reason's Muse' and 'Feminine Boileau'. The house was rented in 1821 by Albert Gallatin, American minister, in 1829 by the Marquis de la Châtaigneraye, poet and expert in heraldry, and in 1854 by Marshal Vaillant, Minister of War. The careers are revealing: up to the First World War diehards admitted only three occupations fit for a gentleman: landowner, army officer and engineer (its status seems to date from Napoleon). Literature of course, in Paris, has long been a law unto itself: an Academician, for instance, takes precedence over everyone but a prince, duke or bishop.

Nos. 118 and 120 are the **Hôtel de Clermont Tonnerre**, where Chateaubriand spent the last ten years of his life, walking every afternoon about three o'clock to visit Madame Récamier in the Abbaye aux Bois, Rue de Sèvres. There, in her drawing-room hung with white silk, he read her the manuscript of *Mémoires d'Outre-Tombe* and she would soothe his moods of anger and depression. Their tender relationship seems to have been one of the few Platonic love affairs in the history of Paris.

No. 128 is the Seminary of Foreign Missions, founded in

1663 to train missionaries for Persia by Jean Duval de
Clamecy, whose droll title, Bishop of Babylon, is commemorated in the next street.

We turn left along Rue de Babylone and the beginning of its
successor, Rue de Sèvres. The first large building is the
Magasin du Bon Marché, a pioneer department store, founded
in the reign of Louis Philippe to offer the new middle classes a
limited range of ready-made articles and ready-to-wear
clothes, just as to-day chain-stores, Monoprix, Prisunic, etc.,
have begun to offer people even less well-off inexpensive, mass-
produced goods. The Bon Marché is the best place in Paris to
buy linen and scarves, other than luxury scarves. Farther
along the wife of the founder of the Bon Marché, Madame
Boucicaut, is commemorated by a monument.

At the Carrefour de la Croix Rouge we leave the noble Faubourg, forking right down Rue du Vieux Colombier (after a
dovecote belonging to St Germain des Prés). In this street
Boileau had an apartment where Racine, Molière, La Fontaine
and a neglected poet called Chapelle met three times a week to
read their latest works and take supper, each paying his share
of the bill. The tradition of drama was continued by Jacques
Copeau, who founded the small theatre at No. 21 just before
the First World War.

The shops of **Place St Sulpice** display missals, amices, albs,
monstrances, pyxes, thuribles and, of course, the kind of
statue and holy-picture known the world over as *art St
Sulpice*. On the south side of the square stands the former
seminary, founded n 1645 and in 1906, when Church and
State were separated, assigned to the Ministry of Finance.
The centre of the square is enlivened by Visconti's fountain,
with statues of bishop-preachers: Bossuet, Fénelon, Massillon
and Fléchier.

The foundation-stone of the **church of St Sulpice** was laid in
1646 by Anne of Austria. Paris builds its churches slowly, and
it was finished only in 1788, with the help of a lottery (St Roch
and the Panthéon also owe their completion to lotteries).
Servandoni's design for the towers was judged to clash with
his own façade and the architect Maclaurin was commissioned
to build two very different towers. These were unpopular also
and twenty-eight years later Chalgrin was asked to replace
them. The Revolution interrupted this work; so the left-hand
tower is by Chalgrin, the right-hand tower, fifteen feet lower,
by Maclaurin: the pair likened by Victor Hugo to 'clarinets'.

The interior is notable for the shells which serve as holy-water stoups (a present to François I from the Venetian Republic), for its organ, for Delacroix's frescoes in the first chapel on the right and for the Lady Chapel, decorated by Van Loo, Lemoyne and Pigalle.

Rue Servandoni, formerly called Rue des Fossoyeurs, Street of the Grave-Diggers, leads to the Luxembourg Gardens. At No. 15 Condorcet, outlawed and hunted by the Convention, was hidden by Madame Vernet, widow of the artist, and here, while head after head was thrust into 'the little window' and toppled over into the straw, Condorcet wrote *Sketch of the Progress of the Human Spirit*. Condorcet, like Tchekov, seems to have grown optimistic in proportion to his own disasters: he continued to believe in progress even while taking poison to escape the scaffold.

No. 14 is an old house decorated with bas-reliefs, one of which depicts Servandoni showing his plans for St Sulpice. At No. 12 lodged M. d'Artagnan of the King's Musketeers—the original of Dumas's hero—when he first came to Paris. This is Dumas country, for Athos lived in the street to the west, Rue Férou, Aramis in Rue de Vaugirard and Porthos in Rue du Vieux Colombier.

Crossing the Luxembourg Gardens we come to **Avenue de l'Observatoire**, its flower-beds and lawns decorated with vases and marble groups of Morning, Noon, Evening and Night. We have left Faubourg St Germain well behind; the young men walking among the chestnuts are probably students from the Sorbonne or nearby technical schools; and we take this long green peninsula, the Luxembourg Palace Avenue, because it is the pleasantest way of approaching the extremely interesting south-east corner of Paris and also because it leads to the **Fontaine de l'Observatoire**. Davioud designed the fountain in 1875; the Four Quarters of the Globe, carrying a sphere, are by Carpeaux, the sea-horses and turtles by Frémiet. This Parisian sculptor of animals sometimes nodded (as in 'Gorilla Carrying Off a Woman', for instance) but here his taste is faultless. After Coysevox, Coustou and Le Lorrain one might have thought that the horse had had its artistic day, but here is something new: untamed, whinnying, curved-necked creatures, with the power of the ocean in their flanks. Sometimes they seem to be prancing across the parapet, at other times to be rearing up, shy and mistrustful of their own reflections in the pool beneath.

CHAPTER TWELVE

South-East Paris

⁂

Observatory – Port Royal – Val de Grâce – Gobelins Tapestry-works – St Médard – Square Scipion – Saltpêtrière – Jardin des Plantes – Île St Louis

THE south-east corner of Paris, a medley of former religious establishments and buildings erected for the State, bears the unmistakable stamp of Louis XIV. In 1670 the King considered that his victories in Germany and Holland (those commemorated by the Porte St Denis) had made France safe from invasion and decided to pull down the ramparts surrounding Paris. The south-east suburbs, comprising the Faubourgs St Michel, St Jacques, St Médard, St Marcel and St Victor, were now made part of the city. Building continued from the end of the seventeenth to the first part of the nineteenth century, but in clusters. This was never a fashionable district and therefore lacks the unity of the Marais or the Faubourg St Germain. Nevertheless in it are scattered a number of curious buildings and places of historic interest.

The **Observatory** is a graceful mark of recognition accorded the stars by the Sun King. Claude Perrault designed the building, begun in the same year as his Louvre colonnade, and containing neither iron, for fear of magnetism, nor wood, for fear of fire. The four sides face the cardinal points of the compass, and the latitude of the south side is the recognised latitude of Paris. A line bisecting the building from north to south is the recognised meridian of Paris, so that here, over a mile from Notre Dame, an astronomer would claim we were standing in the precise centre of the city. This sort of thing does not make for trust in astronomers. A terraced roof permits celestial observations, but these are now conducted in a new observatory in the Alps. However, with due regard for tradition, a speaking clock has been installed here, and can be heard on dialling ODE 84.00.

The first director was an Italian, Cassini, and the directorship remained in his family for four generations so that until

the Revolution the Cassinis can be said to have enjoyed a royal
monopoly of all planets, stars, meteors, asteroids and galaxies.
The statue in front of the building is not a Cassini but Le
Verrier, who discovered Neptune: indeed there was talk of his
name being given to the planet, an idea received with little
enthusiasm outside France. Tucked away in deep cellars at a
constant temperature are the meteorological instruments; in
the main part of the building are older instruments which can
be seen on the first Saturday of each month at 2.30 by visitors
who have obtained the director's permission.

Rue du Faubourg St Jacques leads to Boulevard de Port
Royal. At numbers 121–5 was the former abbey of **Port
Royal**, established from the mother-house in 1626. Mother
Angélique Arnauld, the great reformer whose portrait by
Champaigne hangs in the Louvre, lies under the flagstones of
the chapel choir. It was she who designed the white scapular
with red cross, she who encouraged the nuns in Jansenist
opinions. The abbey was suppressed in 1664, but the principal
buildings still stand.

At **25 Rue Henri Barbusse** is the site of Paris's first cathedral
and first episcopal palace—though you would scarcely know
it now. At the end of the courtyard is a modern Gothic-style
chapel containing a staircase which leads down to a Roman
crypt. Here, according to a sixth-century tradition, St Denis
first installed himself when he arrived in Paris—it was a
quarry then—and here he was arrested by the Roman prefect.
The quarry became a place of pilgrimage and finally, in the
seventeenth century, a convent. To see the remains of the
convent it is necessary to turn along Rue du Val de Grâce into
Rue St Jacques.

At **284 Rue St Jacques**, fifteen yards off the street, stands a
door flanked with columns: plain and undistinguished, as be-
fitted the entrance to the strict Carmel of the Incarnation, yet
rich in memories, for it was this doorway that separated, and
kept apart, an absolute monarch from his mistress. Louise de
La Baume Le Blanc was a loving and lovable young girl with
blue eyes, ash-blonde hair and a slight limp which added to
her charm. In 1662 at the age of twenty she became the mistress
of Louis XIV, who gave her the title of Duchesse de La
Vallière. She adored the king and bore him four children. Six
years later she was supplanted by Madame de Montespan, a
stupid, ambitious, badly-groomed woman, who did not really
love the king. For a while Louise was used to mask the new

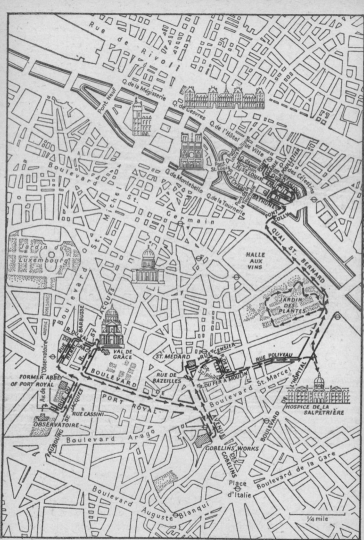

affair. Twice she tried to leave the court and enter a convent, but each time the King went in person to bring her back.

In 1674 after a serious illness she succeeded in persuading the king to allow her to enter the Carmel of the Incarnation, known for the holiness of its nuns. On the eve of her departure she was obliged to dine with the triumphant Montespan; next morning, wearing a gold dress and accompanied by her children, she climbed into a carriage at Versailles and drove off. The king was seen to weep bitterly.

At this doorway Louise de La Vallière kissed her children good-bye, then walked into the convent and threw herself at the feet of the Mother Superior. '*Ma mère*,' she cried, 'I have always misused my will so badly, from now on I put it into your hands—for ever.' A year later she took the veil as Sister Louise de la Miséricorde; her friend Bossuet preached and all the court were there to shed a silent tear. Mademoiselle de Scudéry said she never wept so much in her life. For thirty-six years Sister Louise was sacristan in the Carmel—and an admirable nun. She received visits from the queen and from Madame de Montespan, who had been replaced in the king's affections by Madame de Maintenon. But neither of these mistresses had La Vallière's warmth and sincerity: there were days when the king regretted letting her go.

Farther up the street, at 269 and 69 bis, stood a convent of English Benedictine nuns, established in 1640. One room and part of the chapel remain. James II was buried here in 1701, but his body was lost at the Revolution; for the mob it was enough that he had been a king: the Kings of Judah on the façade of Notre Dame were smashed pell-mell with the busts of the Bourbons. At the turn of the century, aptly enough, this convent became a **Schola Cantorum**, under the composer Vincent d'Indy.

Benedictine nuns were also established at **Val de Grâce**, as one might guess from the statues (modern replacements) of St Benedict and his sister, St Scholastica, flanking the doorway. (*Open daily except during the services*, 9–5.) The monogram A.L. on the church and adjoining wings announced that they were built by Anne of Austria in thanksgiving for the birth of Louis XIV. The queen had been childless during twenty-two years of marriage and when, on 5th September, 1638, she was at last delivered of a son (with two teeth) the event was regarded as something of a miracle. The cornice is inscribed 'Jesu Nascenti, Virginique Matri' and the decorations of the

interior refer to the birth of Christ, in allusion to that of
Louis XIV. The miraculous child himself laid the foundation-
stone at the age of seven; not only of the church, one feels,
but also, given the extravagant fuss, of his quasi-divine status.

The church imitates the Gesù at Rome and the dome St
Peter's—and it is perhaps one of the most beautiful domes in
France. The fresco in the cupola by Mignard—**The Glorifica-
tion of the Blessed**—shows Anne, led by St Louis and St Anne,
offering God a model of her church; the Queen's portrait also
hangs on the right of the choir: a pathetic rather than pretty
face, with sad, pouchy eyes.

The convent, now a military hospital, can be seen by going
along the covered passageway at the end of the courtyard on
the right of the church. (*Open Tuesday, Thursday and Saturday*,
12.30–5.) Again on the right is another passage leading to a
fine stone staircase and to the cloister. The cloister opens on
to a garden and fountain. Here Anne of Austria used to with-
draw, first from court intrigues before she established herself
by giving birth to an heir, and again in later life. Her apartment is at the north-east corner, entered by an Ionic porch
decorated with a pelican.

Rue St Jacques brings us back to Boulevard de Port Royal,
from which runs Avenue des Gobelins. Here, at No. 42, is the
Gobelins tapestry-works (*open Wednesday, Thursday and
Friday*, 2–4). A good plan is to visit the museum first and trace
the history of the institution, from the time when the Gobelins,
dyers of Flemish origin, settled by the Bièvre, a small stream,
now covered over, said (but recent analysis has dispelled the
myth) to contain alkaline properties useful in dyeing. In a
house belonging to the Gobelins Henri IV installed two
Flemish tapestry-weavers; this establishment Louis XIV,
through his minister Colbert, transformed into 'The Royal
Workshops for making Furniture and Tapestry for the
Crown.' Its first directors were Le Brun (his statue stands in
the Cour d'Antin) and the Mignard responsible for the Val de
Grâce fresco.

We are allowed to visit the workshops, watch tapestries
being made and marvel at human patience, for each worker's
daily quota is an area little larger than a postage-stamp.
During the Second World War a group led by Jean Lurçat
experimented with dyes, wools and new designs. They decided
to return to the simpler methods used by early weavers, with
a 'palette' of less than a hundred colours compared with the

20,000 in use when Fragonard and Boucher were designing tapestry. Contemporary tapestries, which have been strongly influenced by the simple, bold design of French advertising posters, are exhibited in **La Demeure**, 20 Rue Cambacérès.

The high standard of Gobelins tapestries to-day speaks well for State patronage. Here, if anywhere, you might expect a folksy, round-the-maypole morris dance; instead, modern methods and up-to-date designs, with the result that wherever a cold glass and steel building is erected, whether in Rio or Beirut, Gobelins tapestries are likely to be commissioned for its walls.

The Avenue des Gobelins and Rue de Bazeilles lead to the **church of St Médard**, which is intimately connected with the Jansenist movement that flourished nearby in Port Royal. In the reign of Louis XV it seems that this church was served by a very austere Jansenist named François de Pâris, who died at the age of thirty-six still a deacon, for humility deterred him from taking Holy Orders. At his own wish he was buried with the poor, not in the church, but in the churchyard, now the little square on the south side of St Médard.

Pious parishioners came to pray at his tomb. Their numbers grew with their fervour, which soon became hysterical. By 1729, two years after the death of deacon Pâris, there were eight hundred determined convulsionists in the parish, divided into several sects: jumpers, mewers, barkers and so on. Some would howl all night, while others leaped about like little frogs. Sister Rose sipped the air with a spoon and lived on that for forty days; some swallowed burning coals, another swallowed a New Testament bound in calf. For five years the convulsionists continued their misguided devotions in this little square. Finally they were removed by the police, whereupon a wag affixed the following notice:

De par le Roi, defense à Dieu
De faire miracle en ce lieu

—just another skirmish in the war between emotional religion, championed by the Jansenists, and reasonable religion, represented by the King and the Jesuits. Despite the royal prohibition, convulsions continued in private until 1762, when the Jesuits were expelled from France. After that they ceased. And throughout the history of Paris a strong irrational undercurrent can be detected, rising to the surface now in astrology, now in gambling, now in religion: the *convulsion-*

naires of St Médard are perhaps its most extraordinary as well as its most pitiful manifestation.

The church itself is once again Gothic turning into Renaissance—we are coming to think of this as a typically Parisian style. St Médard was Bishop of Saint-Quentin and adviser to the Merovingian kings. The weather on his feast-day (8th June) is believed to set the pattern for the whole summer, like St Swithin's Day (another bishop-statesman) in England.

Rue Censier and Rue de la Clef lead to **Square Scipion**. No. 13 is now the central bakery of the Paris hospitals, but by going into the courtyard you discover a fine Renaissance façade in stone and brick, with an arcade surmounted by terra-cotta medallions, two of soldiers, two of women. Unusual materials, unusual motifs—and this is because the house was built by an Italian. Indeed, the medallions are attributed to one of the della Robbia family.

Scipio Sardini was a Tuscan who came to France in the suite of Catherine de Médicis. Starting from scratch as a banker, he amassed a huge fortune which prompted this quip: 'He used to be a sardine; now he's a big whale; that's how France fattens little Italian fish.' The third medallion from the left may be a portrait of Sardini's wife, Isabelle de Limeuil. This seductive and amoral young woman was one of Catherine de Médicis's 'flying squad', entrusted to use all her feminine charms to elicit secrets from political rivals. Isabelle's most memorable feat was to win the heart of the Huguenot Prince de Condé and obtain from him the port of Le Havre, which the Huguenots had delivered from the English. In 1567 Isabelle retired from the secret service by marrying Sardini, much to the chagrin of Ronsard, who loved her; so at least he said, for in that age 'douce mâitresse' could mean almost anything.

Sardini became Henri III's banker and died in 1609. His house declined from banking to baking in 1656.

Rue du Fer à Moulin and Rue Poliveau lead to the **Salpêtrière**. The name and part of the original buildings date from Louis XIII, who in his timid way decided that the powder-factory in the Arsenal constituted a danger to a fast-developing section of Paris and moved it out here, to the country. Part of the original powder-factory still exists in the low houses to the north of the entrance.

Again it was Louis XIV who made the building his own with a large and magnificent gesture. In 1656 he decreed that homes

be established for some of Paris's 50,000 poor and workless.
The Salpêtrière was to be a hospital for poor women, and
Scipio Sardini's old house would supply bread both to the
Salpêtrière and to the men's hospice, the Bicêtre. In 1684
King Louis set aside part of the Salpêtrière for prostitutes
and incorrigibly criminal women: they were to sleep on straw
and eat only bread, water and soup. Another section was
reserved for the insane.

To-day the Salpêtrière is still a home for elderly or insane
women, and it is curious to learn that one of its courtyards is
named 'Cour de Manon Lescaut', after the Abbé Prévost's
heroine, who for a time was imprisoned here. A statue to the
left of the gateway commemorates Dr Charcot the hypnotist
and serves as a reminder that many advances in psychiatry
have been achieved in this hospital: one of Louis XIV's lasting
achievements and an extraordinarily liberal and progressive
foundation for the seventeenth century.

Boulevard de l'Hôpital leads to Place Valhubert and the
Jardin des Plantes (*open daily from* 8, *or* 7 *in summer, until
dusk*). This was originally a garden of medicinal herbs founded
in 1626 by Louis XIII. He was fussy about his health and lived
in the age of herbals. Exotic plants from the New World and
Asia were here cultivated, studied and classified; lessons given
in botany, chemistry and anatomy. Near the entrance is a
statue of Lamarck, a pioneer in the field of evolution, who
held a professorship here (at the present day there are twenty-
one professorial chairs of science), while the left-hand
avenue of lime-trees commemorates Buffon, greatest director
of the Gardens, whose statue was put up while he was still
alive. The parterre to the right, between the central avenue
and the Allée Cuvier, contains 11,000 species of plants,
systematically classified. In addition, there are fine displays
of peonies, roses, gladioli and dahlias. Of the galleries (*open
daily except Tuesday*, 1.30–5) the most important are the
mineralogical, geological and palaeontological collections, all
among the most complete of their kind.

To the north of the Gardens lie the labyrinth and the zoo.
On the slopes of the labyrinth stands a fine cedar of Lebanon
over two hundred years old and on the summit a belvedere
with a sundial bearing this charming motto: *Horas non
numero nisi serenas:* I count only the sunny hours.

The **zoo** (*open daily*, 9–5, *or* 7 *in summer*) dates from the
Revolution. The first director planned to take over the

Versailles menagerie, but this was found to be sadly depleted:
one zebra, one bubal and one rhinoceros. However, in 1793
all wild animals exhibited in travelling fairs were ordered into
the zoo, which owes its origin to these ex-circus performers:
chiefly monkeys, seals, bears, leopards and lions. *A propos* of
lions, Daubenton, professor of mineralogy at that period,
being a good republican would not admit that there was such
a thing as a king of animals. I wonder how Daubenton would
have welcomed the most sensational arrival of all at the zoo,
Mehmet Ali's gift to Charles X of a giraffe (a precursor, as it
were, of the obelisk he presented four years later). Nothing
like it had been seen before and for years songs, caricatures,
even hair-styles were all *à la girafe*.

To-day the zoo contains all the expected animals and many
unexpected reptiles—reptiles being its strong point. Across the
river in the Bois de Boulogne is a slightly larger zoo, the
Jardin d'Acclimatation (*open daily*, 9–5, *or* 7 *in summer*), run
by a private company. Competition seems to keep the animals
in both zoos sleek and in good fettle.

Quai St Bernard leads to Pont Sully and the Île St Louis. In
1360, as part of Paris's defences, the island was divided into
two small islets lined with poplars and willows, both belonging to Notre Dame. The islets were often used for settling
disputes, notably that between the gallant dog of Montargis
and the Chevalier Macaire, whom the dog had insisted on
recognising as the murderer of his master and attacking
whenever it met him. In the presence of Charles V and his
court the dog sank its teeth in the Chevalier's throat and
obliged him to confess. The islands were also used by washer-
women for drying their linen, by bathers and by fishermen.

Louis XIII joined the islands and arranged for building to
start. By 1664 the Île St Louis had become a fashionable
residential quarter, an annex of the Marais. One of the
prettiest streets is **Quai de Béthune**, formerly called Quai des
Balcons because, at Le Vau's suggestion, all the riverside
houses on the island were designed to have wrought-iron
balconies. Nos. 16 and 18 belonged to the Duc de Richelieu,
great-grandnephew of the Cardinal, bane of Madame de
Pompadour but gallant soldier and indefatigable lover. Inscriptions in this street show that many of the houses were
built for financiers and for magistrates, presumably because
it lay convenient to the Palais de Justice.

Rue Poulletier follows the line of the canal which once

divided the island, and leads into Rue St Louis en l'Île. No. 2 is the **Hôtel Lambert**, designed by Le Vau, decorated by Lebrun and Lesueur. Voltaire lived here for a short time with his 'Emilie': the mathematical and stony-hearted Marquise du Châtelet. About the time of the Revolution, the paintings and decorations were dispersed and are now in the Louvre and Luxembourg. The house, which is closed to the public, has belonged since 1842 to the Czartoryska family, who used to entertain Chopin and Delacroix here.

Le Vau, Lebrun and Lesueur are also responsible for the even more magnificent **Hôtel de Lauzun**, 17 Quai d'Anjou. This house is the property of the City of Paris, which lends it for frequent lecture-visits.[1] It is worth joining one of these to see the original splendour of the seventeenth-century rooms. Walls and ceilings, stairways and halls are astir with gods, goddesses and galumphing heroes; no wonder Lauzun's life was a crescendo of almost Olympian adventures.

From the outside the house evokes another adventurer, this time of the mind. Here, in 1849, Charles Baudelaire took three rooms on the top floor. His friend, Théophile Gautier, also lived in the house; their Hashish-Eaters' Club met in the large second-story salon. A small island in the centre of the city, yet cut off from others: it was perhaps an obvious choice for Baudelaire. The balconies that figure in so many of his poems are doubtless those very balconies we see to-day; certainly his conception of Paris has become partly ours. Baudelaire saw that the modern city was different from the ancient: instead of joining, it divided. 'Multitude, solitude: identical terms, and interchangeable by the active and fertile poet.' He evolved a mystique of the city in which the masses became an absolute: 'What men call love is a very small, restricted, feeble thing compared with this ineffable orgy, this divine prostitution of the soul giving itself entire, all its poetry and all its charity, to the unexpected as it comes along, to the stranger as he passes.'

'The unexpected'—it was precisely this quality which set the city apart from the routine of nature and his own crippled and therefore predictable soul. 'The appearance of a city changes more quickly than the human heart'—he was thinking doubtless of Haussmann's rebuilding. To-day the city changes very much more slowly, and harbours few of the ragged beggars in

[1] Details from Ministère des Affaires Culturelles, Service des Visites-Conférences, 3 Rue de Valois (Tel.: GUT 05-41).

whom Baudelaire saw a picture of his own misery. Yet the basic flux and insecurity of urban life, and, above all, its loneliness which Baudelaire first put into words—these are still true of Paris and any large city.

The Île St Louis is still one of the loneliest places in Paris, and rather sad in the way of provincial towns. If you ask in a shop for, say, a roll of film, quite likely it will be out of stock, and the shopkeeper will say, 'You'll have to go to Paris for that.' So to Paris let us go, by the Pont Marie (named not from Notre Dame but after its builder), an old seventeenth-century bridge which once rang to the precise military tread of Richelieu and Lauzun, to the dragging, drugged steps of Baudelaire.

CHAPTER THIRTEEN

Revolution

✦

Place de la Bastille – July Column – Hôtel de Sully – Hôtel de Sens – St Gerçais St Protais – Statue of Etienne Marcel – Hôtel de Ville – Tour St Jacques – Conciergerie – Square du Vert Galant

THE **Place de la Bastille** is the site of three revolutions, of which the first and most important has least visible commemoration. Part of the ground-plan of the **Bastille** prison is marked on the pavement in an outline of dark stones. Oblong in shape, it was set with high walls and eight towers. By going into the little Square Henri Galli, between the end of Rue du Petit Musc and Pont Sully, we can see the foundation of one of these towers, which gives an idea of their diameter and thickness. This was called the **Tower of Liberty,** because prisoners there had the right to walk in the prison court or governor's garden.

The Bastille St Antoine, to give it its full name, was built in 1370 to defend the eastern entrance to Paris, and also the royal palace, which stood nearby. Richelieu turned it into a state prison. Generally no criminals condemned by the law-courts were shut up here; only those arrested on the strength of a *lettre de cachet*—an arbitrary order of exile or imprisonment signed with the king's seal.

Voltaire was sent to the Bastille at the age of twenty-three for some malicious verses—he actually finished his play *Oedipe* in captivity—and again nine years later for daring to challenge one of the Rohan family to a duel. No disgrace attended either jailing. The Bastille, in short, was for irritating offenders: dangerous ones were sent to the dungeon of Vincennes. Books as well as their authors were imprisoned in the Bastille—the *Encyclopédie*, for instance—and released when considered harmless.

Prisoners in the Bastille were well looked after. They could furnish their rooms and keep a servant. Cardinal Louis de Rohan even threw a dinner-party for twenty guests. Indeed,

the Bastille was fast becoming a luxury the State could ill afford. Some years before its fall it was already under sentence of demolition. One project called for the destruction of seven towers, the eighth to be left standing in a dilapidated state. A pedestal formed of chains and bolts from the dungeons and gates was to bear a statue of Louis XVI in the attitude of a liberator, pointing with outstretched hand towards the remaining tower in ruins.

The Bastille was stormed not because it was the symbol of autocratic government, but because 125 barrels of gunpowder lay within its walls. On the morning of 14th July, stirred by Desmoulins's speech two days earlier, a crowd of several hundred malcontents took up arms, only to find themselves short of powder. At 11 a.m. they fired a few shots at the Bastille, whereupon a short parley took place with the governor, the Marquis de Launay. At 1.30 the firing was resumed, then again at four. Shortly afterwards the assault began against the main gate at what is now No. 5 Rue St Antoine: 633 revolutionaries (of whom only 200 were Parisians) against thirty-two Swiss soldiers and eighty-two French pensioners. In the assault eighty revolutionaries were killed, and only one of the garrison—a soldier named Fortuné. Launay was forced to release the prisoners, then cut to pieces with half a dozen of the Swiss garrison.

Who were the prisoners? Four forgers, a hopeless young rake and two madmen—one, an old Englishman named Whyte, was paraded in an open carriage. Whyte could make neither head nor tail of his triumphal drive and begged to be taken back to his dungeon.

That summer and autumn the Bastille was demolished. Some of the stones were used to complete the Pont de la Concorde; others, with metal from the dungeon locks, were made into models of the prison, inkstands, boxes and toys. These had a ready sale all over France. The patriot Palloy had a set of dominoes made from variegated marbles of the fortress which he offered to the young Dauphin 'to inspire in him a horror of tyranny.' The key of the main gate was presented by Lafayette to George Washington and is now at Mount Vernon.

As we have seen, a small part of the Bastille remained standing. And so, even after the King's head fell, did part of the old social order. The Revolution of 1789 had to be refought in 1830—against the same enemies, in the same streets of the same city. Charles X, an émigré and bigot, had sought to restore the old order, supported by nobles back from exile, ultra-royalists who had 'learned nothing and forgotten nothing'. In 1830 he suspended freedom of the Press and dissolved the Chamber. The successors of the first Revolutionaries again took up arms, raised the tricolour and the barricades, from which they fought for three days: immortalised by Delacroix's painting in the Louvre. Finally Charles X withdrew the offending edicts. But it was too late. 615 Parisians had died and Charles X had to go. This second successful uprising of the Paris populace is commemorated by the July Column of the Place de la Bastille. The shaft is in three parts, commemorating the three Glorious Days; the lion symbolises the month: July; the four cocks: France. A staircase of 238 steps leads to the top of the Column and a view over eastern Paris. (*Open daily except Tuesday*, 10–4; *later in spring and summer*.)

The Paris insurgents thought they were making a revolution; but the politicians wrested control and established a bourgeois monarchy. Louis Philippe, the citizen king, lacking the prestige of legitimacy, satisfied neither Right nor Left, and here in 1848 the Paris mob, in its third Revolution, burned his throne, beside the column the King had erected. One of the mob's chief barricades stood near the junction of the square with Rue St Antoine. Those who fell in the fighting were buried beside the column and their names added to the inscription.

In 1848 the mob was the new proletariat of an industrialised city. Impatient for justice, they immediately introduced universal suffrage—and thereby signed the death-warrant of the social revolution for which they had fought, for by universal suffrage Paris handed over its right to govern to the provinces, and the provinces elected Louis Napoleon. So of the three revolutions commemorated in this square, the first issued in Napoleon's Empire, the second in the July Monarchy, the third in the Second Empire. None achieved its ideal.

Rue St Antoine leads out of the Place de la Bastille. No. 62 is the seventeenth-century Hôtel de Sully, bought by Henri IV's minister in his old age. Designed by Jean du Cerceau, it is remarkable for the richness of its decoration: the elaborate dormers, for instance, with carved scrolls, friezes and masks. Eight statues represent the Elements and Seasons; the statue of Water is said to have served Ingres as a model for his painting 'La Source'. These nymphs remind us that Sully in his old age renounced sobriety: wearing an extraordinary bonnet he would dance the pavan with street girls and parade the Place des Vosges in clothes a century out of date, encrusted with diamonds and gold necklaces.

Rue du Prévôt leads to Rue du Figuier, named after a fig-tree which stood at the end of the street in front of the Hôtel de Sens, and which Queen Margot had removed because it hampered her carriage. This house was built at the end of the fifteenth century for the Archbishops of Sens (until 1622 Paris was only a bishopric, subject to Sens). It is earlier than Cluny by only a decade, yet is much more severe, almost a fortress. The Archbishop who built it, Tristan de Salazar, came of a military family and himself fought gallantly, lance in hand, beside Louis XII at Genoa.

The licentious Margot was fifty-two when she came to live here, so fat there were some doors she could not pass through, bald and with such a bad complexion she hid it in powder, thus starting a new fashion in France. Here—seldom alone— she used to sleep between black satin sheets in order to show off the admirable whiteness of her skin.

One morning as she was returning from Mass, her page and favourite Julien was shot dead at her carriage door, in a fit of jealousy, by Vermond, a former lover. Vermond was arrested while Margot screamed furiously, 'Kill him, someone. Here's my garters, strangle him.' She swore that she would neither eat nor drink until she had her revenge. Two days later Vermond was beheaded, in Margot's presence, opposite the house. But the queen conceived such a horror of the place that she soon moved to the other side of Paris and never returned.

If we walk west along Rue de l'Hôtel de Ville, we enter part of the Marais, the fashionable district of the seventeenth century. At the corner of Rue des Nonnains d'Hyères is a stone bas-relief depicting a knife-grinder. We turn up Rue des Nonnains d'Hyères to Rue de Jouy. No. 7 is the Hôtel d'Aumont, built by Le Vau in 1648. The wrought-iron bal-conies on the garden front (by François Mansart) are decor-ated with the monogram A.D. (Antoine d'Aumont, duke and governor of Paris). The house stayed in the Aumont family a hundred years; the fifth Aumont, finding that the Marais had become démodé, sold the house and bought one of Gabriel's two new palaces on the Place de la Concorde. The garden here is well worth a visit.

68 Rue François Miron is the Hôtel de Beauvais. Owing to shortage of space, the main façade faces directly on to the street—unusual in Paris. The façade is much spoiled, and the best feature of the building is the staircase. In 1763 the second floor facing the street was let to a German family: an idle father, his daughter aged ten and his son, aged seven, the breadwinner. The boy, Wolfgang Amadeus Mozart, had a notable success at Versailles but was disappointed when Madame de Pompadour, to whom he was introduced, did not kiss him.

Place St Gervais is notable for its elm-tree, successor to the original elm beneath which justice used to be administered. (*Attendre sous l'orme* is still a proverbial expression for waiting till Doomsday.) The elm reappears on the first-floor wrought-iron window-rails of 2 to 14 Rue François Miron. The flamboyant Gothic church of St Gervais St Protais, with classical façade, has fine stained glass and a pleasant view from its garden (entrance by the sacristy). The Chanteurs de St Gervais sing unaccompanied plain-song in this church on important feasts.

Under the Revolution, when the Paris churches were re-dedicated to the cult of Reason, St Gervais St Protais was notorious for its orgies. Reason was a woman chosen from the sansculottes; the tabernacle from a high altar was her footstool; a gun's crew, pipe in mouth, provided acolytes. The market-women arrived with heaped baskets, and the whole church smelled of herrings; the clink of drinking-cups accompanied the eating of salted fish. There was dancing in the lady-chapel, lit by smoky candle-ends. Then the crowd sang their way down to the Place de Grève, to warm their hands at a fire of altar-rails and choir-stalls.

The churches, besides being desecrated, were renamed. St Étienne du Mont became the Temple of Filial Piety, St Eustache the Temple of Agriculture, while this church became the Temple of Youth, *À la Jeunesse*. For beliefs particular to only one culture were held to be erroneous: only what was common to all men must be true—and promoted. Chinese, savages and Frenchmen alike delighted in children, reverenced their parents and tilled the soil: these objects then were worthy of esteem. But such a cult of generalities, like Robespierre's cult of the Supreme Being, was too vague to last and under the Directory degenerated into a cult of *La Patrie*: nationalism.

The change of names which took place at the Revolution was not confined to churches. The months of the year were changed (only *thermidor* has survived in the phrase Lobster Thermidor), and the days of the week were numbered. Street names were garbled. A traveller in Paris told a coachman to drive him to Rue St Denis. 'No more saints,' the coachman corrected. 'Then drive me to Rue Denis.' 'De is aristocratic— we've abolished it.' 'Then drive me to Rue Nis!' As for names of people, one Léonard Sauvage preferred to be known as Physitrophyme, i.e., nurtured by Nature; a patriotic woman changed her name from Louise to Raison; an architect called Château became Chaumière. Among particular civilisations only the Roman was wholeheartedly admired: Desmoulins, for instance, named his son Horace.

Let us turn now to the garden on the south side of the Hôtel de Ville. The equestrian statue depicts **Etienne Marcel**, leader of Paris's first revolution. Since Marcel was hacked to death for trying to deliver the keys of Paris to the English during the Hundred Years' War, it might at first sight seem surprising to find a statue to him at all, let alone in such a conspicuous place.

We have to remember that Paris never had a charter, only certain privileges, granted by kings, to such groups as water-merchants, butchers, drapers, and, occasionally, to the bourgeoisie as a whole. In 1192 the definition of a Parisian was economic, not political: he was a man free to unload wine and keep it in his cellar long enough to sell at a good profit. The first municipal authority dates from the reign of St Louis, who in 1246 allowed the bourgeois to elect four officers and a provost, with powers to police the port, fix the price of food, make streets and erect public buildings.

The provost's power grew. The provost stood for Paris; the king stood for all France; often their interests clashed. The provost and his officers were accustomed to meet in a fortress-gateway belonging to the king; it was Etienne Marcel who, in 1357, gave them their own offices in a large house which he bought on the site of the present Hôtel de Ville. Marcel continually but unsuccessfully tried to limit royal power and create the vestiges of parliamentary government. The following year, while the king, Jean le Bon, was a prisoner in England, Marcel led three thousand revolutionaries into the royal palace on the Cité and murdered the dauphin's two favourite ministers. Marcel put his own red and green cap on the dauphin's head, and himself wore the dauphin's cap of cloth of gold, in which he showed himself triumphantly to the people.

That was in February; in March the dauphin slipped out of Paris; in July Marcel tried to ally himself with the English. But treason stuck in Parisian throats; his supporters refused to follow him, Marcel was cut down by an axe and on 4th August the dauphin was master of Paris. The Crown had learned its lesson. The old palace on the Cité was abandoned, and a new, stronger palace was built close to the impregnable Bastille.

The statue of Marcel means this: in the history of France not Parliament but Paris, and only Paris, has been the one effective check on the central government. And Marcel's action in the royal palace was curiously paralleled in 1789 when the mayor of Paris, at the Hôtel de Ville, gave Louis XVI the republican cockade to wear in his hat and thereby show that he accepted the principles of the Revolution.

The present **Hôtel de Ville** is a modern replica of the sixteenth-century town hall burned down by the Communards in 1871. Statues on its walls depict 136 famous citizens; the interior, which can be visited on Mondays at 10.30 a.m., is decorated with paintings worth seeing for their extraordinary subject-matter. Physical and Intellectual Exercises, for instance; Hymn of the Earth to the Sun; Meteorology and Electricity; Songs of the Banks of the Seine; Victor Hugo dedicating his lyre to Paris!

Allegorical nonsense, perhaps, but there is no nonsense about the work done in these bombastic rooms. The Hôtel de Ville is the centre of power in Paris, and the power is in the hands of one man, the Prefect of the Seine Department. There is no mayor and the *conseil municipal*, elected by the Parisians, talks freely without being heeded. It is the Prefect, appointed by decree on the advice of the Minister of the Interior, who manages all the services of the city. Roughly, he possesses all the powers of the ordinary departmental Prefect plus the powers of a mayor. In times of weak Government, the Prefect can become—and once was, in the thirties—virtual ruler of France.

The municipal authority of the Hôtel de Ville is divided into nine principal directorates: finance, technical services, personnel, social affairs, commerce and industry, architecture and town planning, general administration, departmental affairs, and municipal affairs. Since the twelfth century Paris has been subject to town planning: no changes could be made in alignment, no repairs carried out save with municipal—and, ultimately, royal—approval. The palatial buildings of Paris, the space, the vistas—these we owe to the predominant role played by the State; but the unity of style, the absence of jarring notes—these we owe to the Hôtel de Ville. Just after the war, when housing was desperately needed, an enterprising firm erected a block of flats eight stories high. When the Hôtel de Ville at once had the top two stories pulled down, protests were few and half-hearted. The sky-line of central Paris is sacrosanct.

The Hôtel de Ville makes the rules; the Prefect of Police, based on the Cité, sees that they are obeyed. He, like the Prefect of the Seine, owes allegiance only to the Minister of the Interior. He has under his orders no less than 18,000 uniformed police, 2,000 plain-clothes detectives, 2,000 men of the Garde Républicaine and an undisclosed number of Special Branch investigators, to keep a check on political suspects. No one envies him his difficult job. Paris has a tradition of revolution, and he who rules the streets of Paris rules France.

Perhaps the most dramatic event in the Hôtel de Ville was the fall of Maximilien de Robespierre: he who believed in a pure Republic where men are equal, and all equally good. In the summer of 1794 the Terror had been taking its toll of heads for over a year, growing more ruthless as the danger of foreign invasion increased. Under the terrible Law of Prairial (June 1794) the Public Prosecutor, Fouquier-Tinville, saw to it that 1,351 heads fell in one month in Paris alone. But June 1794 was also the month which removed the threat of invasion. The need for terror at home was gone. And the need for a terrorist.

On 27th July, 1794 Robespierre was denounced in the Convention and put under arrest. His friends managed to rescue him and hurry him to the Hôtel de Ville. Here they made urgent plans to call out the working people of Paris against the Convention. The Hôtel de Ville, symbolising Paris, would rescue the Revolution from a treacherous France. A call-to-arms was drawn up: the document can still be seen in the Carnavalet museum. Robespierre read the call, reluctantly picked up his pen and began to sign. Two letters only—'Ro' then he stopped. He never signed the order which would also have been his reprieve from death: a lawyer to the last, he believed it illegal.

Presently men of the Convention burst in and a musket was fired, smashing Robespierre's jaw. Blood from the Incorruptible's mouth dripped on the still unsigned order. Robespierre was dragged to the Tuileries, where he lay for hours, bleeding, mocked by his former comrades, on a table which can still be seen in the Archives Nationales. Next evening in the Square of the Revolution his bandaged head, its broken jaw sagging, was held aloft by the executioner, while drums rolled and the people cheered. So the Terror ended; the square was renamed Place de la Concorde, and fulfilment given at last to Louis XVI's dying words: 'May my blood consolidate the happiness of France.'

Between the Hôtel de Ville and the river lies the **Place de Grève**. Here public executions used to take place, notably that of the Protestant leader, the Comte de Montgomery, who earlier had accidentally caused the death of Henri II, and Ravaillac, assassin of Henri IV; here, too, the unemployed used to gather, often indignantly, in the hope of being offered casual work. In this way the word *grève*, meaning 'beach', acquired its secondary meaning of 'strike'.

Following the river downstream we glimpse to the right a Gothic tower, the **Tour St Jacques**, only remains of a church destroyed at the Revolution. The tower has always had a list towards science: Pascal used it to verify barometric experiments, the Revolution turned it into a shot-tower; now it is a meteorological station and so cannot be visited.

We cross the Pont au Change, which was the route of the tumbrels, to the **Conciergerie**: that is, the lower floor of the northern frontage of the Palais de Justice. (*Open daily except Tuesday*, 10–12, 1.30–5, *or* 6 *in summer*.) The concierge was governor of the king's residence: he had a right to two chickens a day and ashes from the king's chimney. But this door by which we enter was not his door: it did not exist even during the Revolution, and the tumbrels arrived and left by the wrought-iron gateway of the Palais de Justice, already visited in Chapter II.

The first rooms we enter are the fourteenth-century **Salle des Gardes** and **Salle des Gens d'Armes**, which lead into the **Galerie des Prisonniers**, its windows looking on to the courtyard where Charlotte Corday, Madame Roland and other women prisoners were allowed to walk and talk. Near the end of the Galerie des Prisonniers is the original door of **Marie Antoinette's cell**. The queen had said that whatever indignities her oppressors might inflict they would never force her to bend her head. The challenge was taken up and the door cut transversely in half, the upper part of the doorway being barred so that the queen had to stoop in leaving her cell.

Louis XVI, heard and condemned by the Revolutionary Tribunal, had been dead some six months when Marie Antoinette was separated from her son and brought to the Conciergerie in the summer of 1793. The trial of the Austrian woman took place in the court above the prison before five judges and fifteen jurors, while, in the north of France, the last French army fought to stem the Austrian troops, ten days' march from Paris. The trial coincided with the most momentous days in French history, when the success or failure of the Revolution hung in the balance.

The queen's auburn hair was ashen, though she was only thirty-eight. Her pale cheeks were painted red. She wore black in mourning for her husband, a little lace scarf and a great white linen cap. She held her head high, never flinching an instant, while the hollow-cheeked, pock-marked, beetle-browed public prosecutor, Fouquier-Tinville, questioned her and his witnesses. Among them was Hébert, neat and powdered, who put forward his fixed idea of incest between the widow Capet and her son. This grotesque charge almost turned the court in favour of the accused; when Robespierre heard of it at the dinner table he broke a plate in his anger.

On the first day the court sat thirteen hours, with only one short break; on the second day seventeen hours. Still the queen's spirit held. The judges and jury were asked: Had there been relations between the Executive and the foreign enemies of the State, and promises of aid to facilitate the advance of their armies? If so, was the widow Capet proved to have been privy to that plan? The judges put on their nodding black plumes. On each count she was found guilty.

She was hurried back to this cell, where the prison maid who looked after her (and worshipped her) gave her a little soup and vermicelli. She wrote a last unfaltering letter giving instructions as to her children's upbringing—sensible, loving instructions. The constitutional priest sent to absolve her she dismissed with a curt word. Then, stooping, she was let out into the long dark corridors and the courtyard where a tumbrel waited. She who had ridden through life in a golden carriage drawn by white thoroughbreds was now hauled to the scaffold, under a murky drizzle, by two plodding cart-horses.

Continuing along Quai de l'Horloge we arrive at the tip of the island, a garden which shows the original level of the ground before it was built on. It is named **Square du Vert Galant**, a reference to Henri IV's love-making. The **statue of Henri IV** is of great importance. Formerly lay statues had represented donors, like that of Charles V in the Louvre, which was made for the doorway of a royal church. But this statue, the original of which was erected by Henri IV's son, Louis XIII, shows a triumphant monarch in isolated glory—worthy of respect in himself, not for what he gave nor as God's representative on earth. And respect he received. From the time of the death of the Grand Dauphin, Parisians used to carry their petitions of complaint to the foot of this statue and in 1789 they forced those who passed in carriages (including the Duc d'Orléans) to get out and kneel before one whom they considered the people's King.

In 1792 the bronze was melted down to make cannon, and this new statue, cast in 1818, was made to replace it from the bronze of destroyed statues, including that of Napoleon in the Place Vendôme. The man who cast it was a fervent Bonapartist; in Henri IV's right arm he secretly placed a small statue of his idol, and in the belly of the horse a heap of Bonapartist writings and songs. In Paris no hero is revered for long, but, on the other hand, no Revolution is ever quite complete.

CHAPTER FOURTEEN

Official Paris

✦

Pont Neuf – Hôtel de la Monnaie – Hôtel de l'Institut de France – École des Beaux Arts – Palais de la Légion d'Honneur – Palais Bourbon – Tuileries Gardens – Arc du Carrousel – Musée du Jeu de Paume

OFFICIAL Paris stands along and near the Left Bank, opposite and conveniently near Royal Paris—the Louvre and Tuileries. The **Pont Neuf** is the link: over-ponderous, perhaps, were it not for the fine row of masks running above the arches and the semi-circular projections, formerly occupied by stalls, among them that of Tabarin the mountebank. Until the disappearance of the stalls in 1854 the Pont Neuf was one of the most animated spots in Paris and inspired generations of artists, notably the etcher Jacques Callot.

The **Hôtel de la Monnaie**, or Mint, is a Louis XVI building, with a double staircase and Great Hall, now a numismatic museum. The pioneer of French coinage is St Eloi (or Eligius). This seventh-century bishop, statesman and goldsmith was the first to stamp the name of Paris on coins; he also enamelled chalices and reliquaries, made crowns and engraved them. He was as tolerant as he was gifted: he taught Parisians to treat their foreign slaves as friends: so well was the lesson learned that Clovis II married an Anglo-Saxon slave: the first union of a French king with an Englishwoman.

Inflation, with its paper money, means that designers of coins turn their attention more and more to medals and plaquettes. The best of these justify a short visit to the museum (*open daily, except Saturday and Sunday*, 11–5). French coins even to-day strike me as being remarkably faithful to the Revolution. The one-franc piece, for instance. On the reverse: Liberté, Egalité, Fraternité; on the obverse, République Française and La Belle France scattering seed before a rising sun. The cap she wears is the Phrygian cap, chosen as a revolutionary emblem by Citizen Jullian at the Café Procope on the grounds that the shepherd Paris, traditionally believed

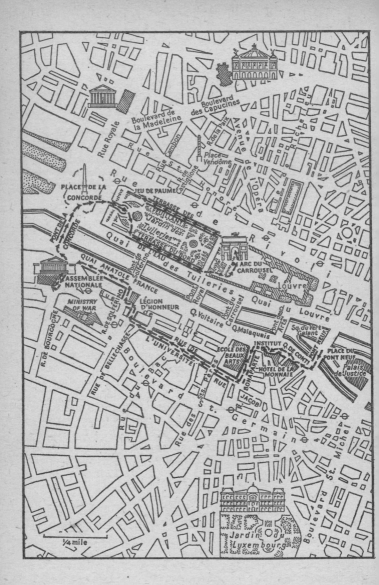

to be the city's founder, wore this particular head-dress. Later the Phrygian cap was given by the Romans to freed slaves, so it has a double connotation: back to nature and emancipation.

The next important building is the **Hôtel de l'Institut de France**, home of the Académie Française and four other learned bodies which together comprise the Institut. (*Open all day Saturday to those with written authorisation from the Director of Administrative Services of the Institut*.) It stands on the site of the Tour de Nesle, scene of the love affairs of Margaret and Blanche of Burgundy, familiar to readers of Dumas and Druon. The present seventeenth-century building originated as a college founded under the terms of Mazarin's will for the four new provinces (Alsace was one) which he had united to France. Mazarin's coat of arms is carved at the base of the dome. The Institut, established just after the Revolution, was transferred here by Napoleon.

Its dome has become the symbol of the **Académie Française**. This body was founded in 1635 by Richelieu, who for reasons of state wanted French to become a universal language, as Latin had been. The Académie's original function was to keep French stable and clear. It also divided words into groups which we should describe to-day as 'U' and 'non-U' and spent much time in unctuous literary flattery. In the reign of Louis XIV it once proposed as a subject for discussion, 'Which of the King's virtues is most admirable?' It rejected both Racine and Boileau until Louis XIV insisted on their admission, and never elected Molière. Despite such gaffes the Académie has always been an important and influential body, the only institution in Paris comparable to the English Parliament. It meets every Thursday, bringing together men of letters, historians and scientists on a basis of equality with men of action and important figures in the State. A permanent committee of members is at work modernising the official dictionary of the language. André Maurois used to recall that when he left to serve with the army in 1939 the word under discussion was *agresseur*. When he returned after the German surrender, the Académie had progressed to *ardeur*.

Election as one of the forty immortals entails canvassing all the Academicians and, if successful, the purchase of a bottle-green uniform, hand-tailored and hand-embroidered with green palms, and a filigreed sword. Thus dressed, the new member makes a speech eulogising his predecessor, to which the Director replies, praising the new member. These speeches are pompous and very dull, though that by Jean Cocteau was a recent exception.

The Institut also houses the Académie des Beaux Arts, an elderly body which exercises a paramount and sometimes paralysing influence over its youthful neighbour, the École des Beaux Arts. The École des Beaux Arts stands on the site of a convent of Augustinians, installed here by the eccentric Queen Margot. Day and night these poor canons were obliged to chant praises to, of all people, the patriarch Jacob, accompanied by modern music composed according to Queen Margot's directives. The queen dismissed the canons after four years, saying they sang out of tune, but the cult echoes still in the name Rue Jacob.

The entrance to the School is in Rue Bonaparte. Its origins go back to the Revolution, when Alexandre Lenoir (he who so gallantly saved the funeral effigy of Richelieu) collected some 1,200 pieces of sculpture in what was then an abandoned monastery. Lenoir's own statue stands in the first courtyard between the columns of a chapel doorway (by Jean Goujon and Philibert Delorme) removed from the Château d'Anet.

The façade looking on to the courtyard, by Dubon, is considered one of the best works of nineteenth-century architecture. To the right is the charming Court of the Mulberry Tree, decorated with sculptures by winners of the Grands Prix de Rome. These prizes, whose origins date back to 1666, are awarded annually to students of painting, sculpture and architecture, every second year to engravers and etchers, every third year to medallists and engravers of gems. They have exerted immense influence by taking almost every French artist of exceptional promise to the Villa Médicis in Rome, there at a formative age to sketch the work of antique and Renaissance masters. As long as the Grands Prix de Rome are awarded, French art is likely to remain predominantly classical.

The liveliest month here is June, at the end of the academic year, when students build a pavilion in the school quadrangle for their annual costume dance and parade the streets all night, raiding cafés and ragging the police. Dance or no dance, the Beaux Arts students always seem to me the gayest in Paris, following their vocation in a city which stimulates and encourages art.

Rue Bonaparte leads into Rue Jacob, one of the pleasantest old streets on the Left Bank, which becomes Rue de

l'Université. Both streets have a strong literary flavour—
Sterne, for instance, stayed at 14 Rue Jacob on his Sentimental
Journey and at 15 Rue de l'Université the *Revue des Deux
Mondes* has its office. Many of the houses in Rue de l'Uni-
versité are fine examples of seventeenth and eighteenth-
century domestic architecture.

Rue de Bellechasse leads to the nineteenth-century **Palais de
la Légion d'Honneur.**[1] Of the original palace only the bas-
reliefs remain. Its builder, Salm Kirburg, a German prince,
was guillotined: the palace was then offered as a lottery prize
and won by a wig-maker's apprentice, who here presently
gave a fête costing over a million *livres*, the theme being the
triumph of the jonquil, his favourite flower. The walls were
covered and the tables decorated with jonquils; the scent of
jonquils was so overpowering that some of the guests felt ill.
But the former wig-maker's apprentice had his one evening of
rapture. Then, some weeks later, he was sentenced for forgery,
disappeared and was never heard of again.

Since 1804 the palace has been the chancellory of the Légion
d'Honneur, an Order founded by Napoleon to reward civil
and military services. It is the only Order of France, and consists of the five classes of grand cross (limited to eighty), grand
officer (200), commander (1,000) officer (4,000) and *chevalier*
or knight, in which the number is unlimited. Normally twenty
years of military, naval or civil service is a condition of
eligibility. A *chevalier* can be recognised by a red ribbon
running from his buttonhole to the edge of the lapel, an
officer by a small red rosette.

Following the river downstream you arrive at the **Palais
Bourbon,** seat of the **Assemblée Nationale.** The entrance is on
the south side, but in order to be admitted you must write at
least three weeks beforehand to MM. les Questeurs de
l'Assemblée Nationale for an invitation card.

The palace became the meeting-place of the Council of Five
Hundred in 1796, and has been used as the House of Parliament only since 1815. The library and Salle du Trône are
decorated with paintings by Delacroix. The present assembly-
room, dating from 1828, is shaped like a half-moon. Deputies
address the Chamber from a tribune decorated with a bas-
relief of Fame and History. Directly opposite the tribune sit
the Ministers.

[1] There is a small museum at 2 Rue de Bellechasse. Open Sunday,
Thursday and Saturday, 2-5.

Debates are conducted with passion, often with bitterness and sometimes with blows. Party politics, as other countries know them, are alien to the French temperament. Every speaker in the Assemblée is first and foremost an individual; the national gift for clarity of thought, by serving to emphasise the differences between himself and everyone else in the hall, makes compromise and party loyalty difficult if not impossible. Moreover, politically the Frenchman is a perverse creature, one moment idolising a hero, the next moment tearing him down: hence the heart-breaking series of political catastrophes in the decade before de Gaulle came to power.

Part of the trouble with French politics is that there is no tradition of political service among the upper and upper-middle class, whose attitude seems to be that politics are best left to the climbers. Until more public-spirited Frenchmen, particularly those of independent means, enter the Chamber, crisis will follow crisis. But bad politics make good entertainment: anyone who wants to understand Paris would do well to spend an hour here in the visitors' gallery, an hour in the Law Courts and an hour in a Latin Quarter café.

The Pont de la Concorde takes us across to the Right Bank where, skirting the Place de la Concorde, we enter the garden and walk along the south side, the Terrasse du Bord de l'Eau, passing on the way Maillol's statue, 'Reclining Woman'. The clay soil hereabouts was originally used in tile-kilns, hence the name **Tuileries**. This was the first garden to continue the style of a palace into the open air and provide a larger stage and more impressive background for its social life. Its designer, Le Nôtre, applied the laws of perspective rediscovered at the Renaissance, lining his *allées* with the lopped trees, the 'clipped and trimmed nature' which so surprised Horace Walpole. Parisians were free to walk in the gardens, where they felt in touch with the monarch, and discussed society news and foreign affairs. Here Louis XIII as a boy was taught to build fortresses, here the Dauphin (Louis XVII) worked with his little rake and hoe guarded by two grenadiers, here Marcel Proust used to bowl his hoop. Did he know, I wonder, that under the Empire and Restoration in this very garden a *pâtissière* named Madeleine sold certain cakes made of flour, sugar, butter and eggs, which ever since have borne her name?

The Tuileries, still primarily a children's playground, lead to the **Place du Carrousel**, named from a great equestrian display given in June 1662, to celebrate the birth of Louis XIV's first child. *Le roi soleil* was dressed as Emperor of the Romans, with a cockade of red plumes. Princes of the blood led brigades of Persians, Americans, Turks, and Indians each with its own colours. The cavalcade crossed Paris twice to the sound of trumpets and drums. Louis XIV rode particularly well that day, for watching him was Louise de La Vallière.

Rome has seldom been absent from Parisian minds. She reappears in the **Arc de Triomphe du Carrousel** erected by Napoleon to commemorate the victories of 1805, and modelled on the arch of Septimus Severus in Rome. A tragic irony attends this imitation: both emperors erected their arches to commemorate victories in the east; to both Nemesis came from Britain—Septimus dying in York, worn out by the Scots.

In the chariot on top of the Arch the architects planned to place Napoleon's statue. 'What statue do you mean?' replied the Emperor angrily. 'I have never intended or given orders that a statue of me should form the principal subject of a monument erected by me and at my expense to the glory of the army I have the honour to command.' The chariot remained empty. To-day the statuary contains an allegorical figure, thought perhaps to represent the Restoration of the Bourbons.

Returning along the north side of the Tuileries we are walking in the **Terrasse des Feuillants**, named after a Benedictine monastery which in 1791 was the meeting-place of the Club des Feuillants, moderate republicans such as Lavoisier the chemist and André Chénier, in opposition to the extremist Club des Cordeliers across the river. The whole idea of a club for men only was an importation from England, totally foreign to Parisian tradition. Without the gentle restraint of women, members gave voice to their most brutal and violent impulses. But for the Clubs there might have been no Terror.

Farther along on the same side is the **Jeu de Paume**, a nineteenth-century tennis court, housing the Impressionists (*open daily except Tuesday*, 10–5). A good introduction to the group is provided by Fantin-Latour's **The Studio at the Batignolles**, painted in 1870. The artist seated at his easel is Manet, a Parisian bourgeois, oldest of the group and the most traditional. Behind Manet, hands crossed, is Renoir, son of a Limoges tailor, poor but irrepressibly gay, sensuous, always enjoying life. Next to him is Zola, who wrote favourable reviews of the Impressionists but angered them with his

novel *L'Oeuvre*, in which the hero, a composite portrait of
Manet and Cézanne, ends in utter failure, a suicide. The
tallest figure is Bazille, well-to-do, a loyal and true friend (at
one time he was supporting both Renoir and Monet). To the
right stands the stocky Norman grocer's son, Claude Monet,
belligerent, impoverished, painter of fugitive impressions, he
who most deserves the epithet 'Impressionist', which actually
originated in a journalist's remark about Monet's 'Impression
of Sunrise.'

What we do not see in Fantin-Latour's painting is the
hostile public which for twenty years jeered at their work. To
take only one example. A play in the year of their third show
(1877) brought on stage an Impressionist painter whose
works could be contemplated in the normal way and also
upside-down; a landscape with a white cloud, for instance,
became, if turned around, a seascape with a sailing boat. And
the audience roared with laughter.

Manet's **Le Déjeuner sur l'Herbe** is an attempt to paint the
female nude outdoors in a contemporary setting. The composition is actually a copy of a Raphael, for Manet seems to
have been uninventive in this respect. What chiefly interested
him was colour, and certainly his colours here are more vivid,
say, than in an Ingres or Corot. But to me the painting is un-
satisfying, because psychologically unsound. What was
acceptable in Raphael's Arcadian scene jars in the precise context of the Second Empire.

Manet's professed aim was to strip painting of its intellectual and literary content, but curiously enough 'Le
Déjeuner' and another early work, **Olympia**, both fall short of
this revolutionary goal. For 'Olympia' could almost serve as
an illustration to the poem which inspired it: *Femme aux Îles*,
by one Zacharie Astruc. In 'Olympia' Manet again sets off his
nude by a clothed figure, the Negress, and also by the black
cat, the slipper, bracelet, black velvet ribbon and hairbow. It
comes as no surprise to learn that this painting, which
shocked Napoleon III, was a favourite with Baudelaire.

In **Foyer de la Danse** Degas achieves a striking contrast between the marble pilasters and thick arch, and his light,
tremulous ballerinas. Degas, like Manet, was an intellectual.
He liked the precise, disciplined movement of ballerinas and
racehorses, which he observed for hours on the spot but
painted in the studio. 'You need natural life,' he explained to
his colleagues, 'whereas I need artificial life.'

Degas was thinking particularly of Monet who, with Renoir, visited La Grenouillère, a bathing place on the Seine, in 1869. There the two friends painted a number of studies of light on river-water, using rapid strokes, dots and commas to depict the vibrations of light and water. The technique has become more perfect in Monet's **Regatta at Argenteuil**, another popular bathing place. Like Paris itself, we can say that Impressionist painting was born from the Seine.

The unsatisfactory nature of the term 'Impressionist' becomes apparent in Paul Cézanne's **Dr Gachet's House**, in such striking contrast to Monet's river-scene. Whereas the stolid Norman sought the aery and ephemeral, Cézanne, a Provençal also in reaction against his environment, wanted 'to make out of impressions something solid and durable like the art of museums.' And he makes something strong as a fortress from this house of a doctor-friend of the group, whom we shall speak of again when we come to van Gogh.

Renoir's **Le Moulin de la Galette** was painted in 1876 when the artist was living in Montmartre. Here is a scene exactly suited to Impressionist technique: sunlight and shadow, movement, quick glances, half-smiles. The models are sprinkled with spots of light falling through the foliage, faces are suddenly glimpsed in the crowd. As for the all-pervasive blue, this is not an effect intended by Renoir, but due to the fading of his pigments.

In his **Girls at the Piano** Renoir again chooses a fugitive moment well suited to Impressionism: a hesitant, faltering piano-practice: we seem to feel the notes passing from eye and lip to tremulous fingers, almost to hear them. The seated girl has the rounded chin, wide mouth and 'cat face' which hallmark a Renoir.

It is curious how, even as a youth of sixteen, Renoir was painting this kind of face. His boss at the porcelain works had to plead with him to give his Marie Antoinette a longer, more regal nose. Later, in middle age, Renoir met a Burgundian girl of nineteen who exactly embodied his canons of beauty. He married her. Monsieur Jean Renoir goes so far as to claim that his father was painting portraits of his future wife for almost thirty years before he met her.

Monet's **Gare St Lazare** makes poetry out of wisps of smoke. He is not interested in the engine or carriages, the track or signals (still awkward novelties, which, however, excited Zola)—only in the ephemeral light effects. Monet knew Turner's 'Rain, Steam and Speed', but found Turner too romantic. Pissarro summed up the Impressionists' attitude to the English painter: Turner had no understanding of the analysis of shadow, which he used as a mere absence of light, whereas it was precisely the colours of shadows that the Impressionists sought to paint.

The Red Roofs is, to my mind, a more interesting picture than the tree-lined roads by which Pissarro is usually known. It was part of the Impressionist philosophy that an artist should put out of his head any prior knowledge of what his subject was and paint only what he saw. Here the red tiles seem to grow on the trees, like fruit fed from the red soil.

Pissarro transmitted the ideas of Impressionism to younger painters like Gauguin and Cézanne. The **Still-Life with Soup-Tureen** shows Cézanne in perhaps his greatest role: as painter of fruit and homely objects. These assume an astonishing three-dimensional quality; as the painter once told a friend: 'See in nature the cylinder, the sphere, the cone . . .'

Gauguin painted his **Breton Landscape: The Mill** in the year after his return from Tahiti. Painters carry their light with them. As Canaletto drenched London in clear Venetian sunshine, so Gauguin exoticises grey and granite Brittany. These oranges and reds are not colours we see in Britanny: doubtless Gauguin would have replied, 'Don't you wish you did!'

Van Gogh's **Portrait of Dr Gachet** was painted in the last year of the artist's life. The doctor, a heart specialist and amateur etcher, was a close friend and patron of the Impressionists and had offered to look after van Gogh in his madness. He was a gay, cordial man, but van Gogh, describing this portrait, maintains that he wears 'the distressed expression typical of our times'.

The painting of **Dr Gachet's Garden** is of particular interest. The agave rears up like hostile barbed wire, the colour of the roof is Provençal, not Île-de-France (where the garden actually was), and the tree, which we know to have been a yew, becomes a sinuous cypress—such as van Gogh had painted so often in Arles. Here, then, is a remarkable projection of a visionary world so obsessive that the real world is all but effaced.

Gauguin's **Women of Tahiti** and **Vairumati** (the Tahitian Venus) are among the rare examples in French galleries of Gauguin's mature style. The symbolism of the bird in the second picture Gauguin describes in a letter: 'a strange white bird holding in its claws a lizard, representing the uselessness of vain words.' Gauguin defined his mature style like this: 'Don't copy too much from nature. Art is an abstraction; derive it from nature by indulging in dreams in the presence of nature'—a creed which would have shocked the first Impressionists. They were in revolt and demanded a return to sense impressions. But sense impressions were soon found to be not enough: art must do more than capture the fugitive, it must become a way to certainty and absolute truth. And so the whole drift of painting in this museum is towards the metaphysical. Van Gogh was crushed by the task of evolving a personal metaphysic, even Gauguin ended by borrowing one from a more primitive culture.

The Douanier Rousseau, though a much-lesser figure, also dreams of a primitive world and feeds his dreams in the glass-houses of the Jardin des Plantes. The Snake Charmer has a menacing quality worthy of Kafka, but like K. and his pursuers seems to me to lack authenticity, the throb of real life, and so usually pleases more at first sight than after long study.

Finally, Renoir's The Bathers, painted in old age, when the brush had to be attached to his wrist; crippled by rheumatism. 'I look at a nude,' said Renoir, 'there are myriads of tiny tints. I must find the ones that will make the flesh on my canvas live and quiver.' Here he has achieved what perhaps was in Manet's mind: a return to nature. These women seem to grow like flowers out of the soil. A denial of clothes, of the city, of the contemporary: but also a finding of an age-old, perhaps eternal link—for Renoir's generation was much influenced by the theory of evolution. It is curious that Renoir and Gauguin should have both found their culmination in the painting of the female nude, while Pissarro, Cézanne and van Gogh all devoted their artistic lives to Mother Earth. But a philosophy based exclusively on sense impressions could hardly arrive at any other goals.

So much for a few of the Impressionist paintings in the Jeu de Paume. Their successors we shall see later in the Musée d'Art Moderne.

CHAPTER FIFTEEN

The Louvre: Sculpture

❧

*St Germain l'Auxerrois – Louvre Colonnade – Salle des Caria-
tides – Greek and Roman Antiquities – Winged Victory –
Galerie d'Apollon – Medieval, Renaissance and Eighteenth-
century Sculpture*

THE church of St Germain l'Auxerrois was founded about 560
by St Germain of Paris in honour of his namesake, a bishop
of Auxerre who made two journeys to Britain to combat
Pelagianism. It is now a Gothic building of the thirteenth to
sixteenth centuries and for long served as parish church to the
Louvre. When Catherine de Médicis incited Charles IX to
order the Massacre of St Bartholomew, it was the three silver
bells in the small south tower of his church which, at two in
the morning, gave the signal for bloodshed. As though to
efface this memory, the chimes in the modern Gothic-style
belfry between the church and the adjoining *mairie* twice a
day, at 11 a.m. and 4 p.m., ring out a gay carillon: Rameau's
'Tambourine', the 'Marche de Turenne' and an old chanson
by Chapuis. When I first heard these innocent, ingenuous
and child-like chimes, my head reeled for a moment, so unexpected were they here under the flamboyant Gothic porch,
beside the fifteenth-century statue of St Mary the Egyptian, a
slim figure wearing her long tresses like a hair-shirt and carrying three loaves. Paris has always had a particular affection
for penitent women saints: this Mary atoned for seventeen years of revelry by forty-eight years as a hermit in the
desert.

St Germain l'Auxerrois used to be the artists' church.
Coysevox and Coustou, Soufflot and Gabriel, Chardin and
Boucher, who had grace-and-favour apartments in the
Louvre, are buried here and on the second Sunday of every
month Mass is said for departed poets. Fittingly, the interior
is of great artistic interest, first for the Renaissance stained
glass in the transepts, then for the curious eighteenth-century
'improvements' to the choir-arches. The piers have been

transformed into fluted columns, the capitals heightened and garlands added.

In the left aisle is a sixteenth-century French triptych, in which carving and painting are ingeniously combined; in the south transept is a holy-water stoup—three children with upraised arms—designed by Lamartine's wife, née Miss Marian Eliza Birch, daughter of an English army officer. Finally, on the left of the nave is the churchwardens' pew, a flourishing fanfare, with canopy all in carved wood, designed by Lebrun and Perrault, whose **colonnade** we meet as soon as we leave the church.

The construction of the colonnade makes a curious story. Louis XIV, having completed the Cour Carrée and wishing to give the royal palace a splendid east façade, summoned from Rome the greatest living architect. Bernini duly arrived, was fêted like a prince and drew up plans which called for stone from Italian and Egyptian quarries and for statues soaring above the line of the façade, such as he had used to good effect in the piazza of St Peter's. Louis XIV realised that Bernini's display of tormented baroque would never harmonise with the severe work of Lescot and Le Vau. And what of the Gothic church immediately opposite? Bernini, however, refused to modify his plans by so much as a single declamatory gesture, and he was too important to offend. So nothing was said, the foundation-stone of the eastern façade was laid with due pomp and while Bernini, thanked and congratulated, was escorted back to Rome, Louis XIV quietly told his minister, Colbert, to find a suitable French architect.

Colbert's right-hand man was a lawyer, civil servant and writer named Charles Perrault, a delightful fellow, leader of the 'moderns' against the defenders of the 'classics', Boileau and Racine, and later, in his seventieth year, to publish France's most famous collection of *Fairy Tales*. Now Charles had a younger brother, Claude, by profession a doctor (Boileau in one of his verses calls him an 'assassin', but then Boileau was no friend to the Perraults). Claude dabbled in art and archaeology but had never designed a building before he submitted his plans for the Louvre. The highly original colonnade was accepted partly thanks to his brother's influence and partly because the leading French architect, Le Vau, was beginning to be employed at Versailles. Claude Perrault thereafter designed other buildings, but continued his

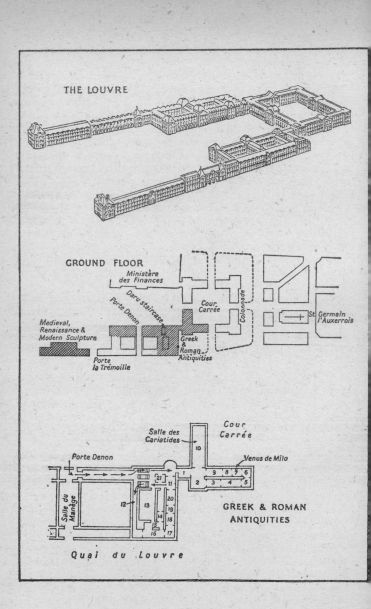

THE LOUVRE

GROUND FLOOR

Ministère
des Finances

Daru staircase

Porte Denon

Medieval,
Renaissance &
Modern Sculpture

Porte
la Trémoille

Greek
&
Roman
Antiquities

Cour
Carrée

Colonnade

St. Germain
l'Auxerrois

Salle des
Cariatides

Cour
Carrée

Porte Denon

10

Venus de Milo

9 8 7
1
2 3 4 5 6

Salle du
Manège

12

13

3

11

14

20

19

18

15

16 17

GREEK & ROMAN
ANTIQUITIES

Quai du Louvre

interest in science, and died of a disease contracted while dissecting a camel.

Perrault had the idea of imposing on a storied building the façade of a Roman temple. This elegant piece of classicism is a far cry from the Renaissance style of most of the Louvre, yet harmonises all the same because so restrained and sober. The colonnade not only proved that French architects were the equal of the best Italians but powerfully influenced subsequent Paris architecture. Incidentally, two modifications to Perrault's original design were made under Napoleon: the niches between the columns were replaced by windows, and a bas-relief of Victory distributing crowns placed over the main entrance.

We enter the Louvre by the Porte Denon, turn left and, staying on the ground floor, eventually arrive at Room 1 of **Greek and Roman Antiquities.** Here is sculpture dating from the seventh to fifth centuries B.C.: rigid, tight figures such as had been fashioned almost unchangingly in Egypt and the Near East for three millennia, mummified by taboo and inertia. (Notice the traces of paint on the **Maiden's** hair and the **Rider's** eyes, reminding us that Greek statues were originally polychrome.) And then, in Room 2, within a mere hundred years the mummy-bands are being unwound, and the figures walk free from a dusty tomb into the sunlit present: this is perhaps one of the decisive moments in Western civilisation without which Paris and everything in it would never have been. I am thinking particularly of the two **metopes from the Temple of Zeus** at Olympia, one showing a marvellously gentle Athena accepting the birds of Lake Stymphale killed by Heracles, the other depicting Heracles and the Cretan bull: probably the best rendering of a bull in Greek art. How successfully the turn of the head is conveyed, how decorative and yet how natural is the raised swinging tail, how convincing the powerful body ready for attack!

Also in Room 2 is part of the **Parthenon frieze**, showing the procession of Athenian girls filing up to the Acropolis to offer Athena the veil they have woven. This treatment of drapery we shall find reappearing with very slight changes in Jean Goujon's 'Deposition' two thousand years later.

After these original works, three rooms of antique replicas of statues by Phidias, Polycletus and Praxiteles. In this wing of the palace lived the queens of France, and Room 7, where the **Venus de Milo** now stands, was Anne of Austria's gold-fitted bathroom. The Venus, slightly larger than life, consists of

five pieces of marble. The work belongs to the second century
B.C. but its purity of style suggests that it may be a copy of a
fourth-century statue. The arms and also the lobes of the
pierced ears are missing. It is uncertain whether the goddess
once held some attribute of victory, a shield, a melon (a
punning reference to Melos) or an apple. I like to believe it
was an apple, the prize awarded by Paris when he preferred
the love of a beautiful woman to military glory or the sover-
eignty of Asia. Until at least the fourteenth century the city of
Paris was believed to have been founded by her Greek namesake, and if that is pure legend, it is nonetheless appropriate
that the most famous work of art in a city that has long held
love in high esteem should be this statue of Venus.

Found in 1820 by a peasant in the Island of Melos, the
statue was offered for 25,000 francs to the French consul, who
hesitated to spend so much for his Government. Finally it was
the account given to the Marquis de la Rivière at Constantinople by Dumont d'Urville (not yet a famous explorer but a
young lieutenant on board the man-of-war *La Chevrette*) of
the marvellous statue he had seen during his voyage, which
secured the Melian Venus for Paris.

Rooms 8 and 9 contain statues by Lysippus: the slim, light
body and rather small head are characteristics of his style.
Lysippus was court sculptor to Alexander the Great, and it
was the bloody dismemberment of Alexander's empire which
inspired the violent, pathetic sculpture to be found in Room
10 (the Salle des Cariatides): no longer laurel-crowned
victors in the games but plain men struggling and enduring.

From here the rather labyrinthine route recrosses Room 1,
passes through a rotunda, turns left into Room 11, then right,
up a stairway and left into Room 12, which contains important
Graeco-Roman frescoes.

Room 16 was already under Louis XIV furnished with
classical works of the royal collection. To-day it contains
statues of **Augustus**, or **Octavius**, nephew and adopted son of
Julius Caesar, and of **Agrippa**, who knew Gaul as Augustus's
special emissary; also a splendid basalt head of **Livia**, Augustus's wife and mother of Tiberius, said to have been a marvel
of beauty, dignity, intelligence and tact.

The series of vivid, uncompromising Roman portraits continues into Room 20, which contains a **bas-relief of Mithras**,
the bull-killer (on the reverse Mithras and the Sun eat the
bull's flesh sacramentally), and a statue thought to represent

Julian the Apostate, commander of the Roman armies protecting Gaul against the Germans and proclaimed Emperor in this very city. A left turn brings one to the great Daru staircase, on the landing of which stands the Winged Victory. In 1863 over a hundred fragments of Parian marble were discovered on the island of Samothrace. When put together, they were found to compose a winged female striding forward, drapery wind-swept. The wings and posture are those given by the Greeks to their symbolic figures of Victory. This particular Victory was presumably intended to stand like a figurehead on the stone prow of a galley found near the statue. In 1950 the right hand of the statue was discovered (to be seen in a case on the right of the landing) and seems to have been raised in a gesture of triumph. The other hand may have held a rudder or an ornament of a ship's prow.

It is surely one of the lightest, most ethereal of statues. The lines of the body are difficult to discover: a moment or two pass before we realise that it is the right leg which advances. We recognise powerful movement, not specifically human movement, but something more elemental. The early Greeks had imagined spirits—nereids and naiads—in the sea and air, and had given them a quasi-human shape, a life, a name. And now in the full flush of sophisticated art—the Victory dates probably from the end of the third century B.C.—the sculptor seems to be dissolving just such a personification back into its constituent parts—air and water. In a century or two—we feel it—Victory will be no longer a goddess but a mere word.

The staircase leads to a splendid pair of seventeenth-century wrought-iron gates, which seem chiselled rather than forged: the entrance to the Galerie d'Apollon. This hall, because encumbered by only a few small museum objects, provides a glimpse of the Louvre as it really was: a house, immense perhaps, but a house to be lived in. The architect was Le Vau, the painter Le Brun, who took as his theme Apollo, the Sun God, emblem of the young Louis XIV, and his procession of Seasons, Months, Hours and Elements. This kind of allegory, which to us seems so artificial, then had at least three advantages to recommend it: it allowed the artist to draw on and improve the figures—particularly the nudes—of Graeco-Roman art; it perpetuated Rome, considered the masterpiece of civilisation; and, above all, it glorified the King. The kind of glory then admired was no part of the Christian tradition, which reserves its nimbus for saints; it became feasible only by drawing on pre-Christian values and imagery.

The hall itself is a triumph, a salvo carrying through three centuries. Severe pilasters and blind doors restrain the gilt stucco ceiling figures and florid frames that set off Le Brun's canvases (the central panel, 'Apollo killing the Python,' was added by Delacroix). One feels that, just as animals adapt their pelt or plumes to a new environment, a king who lived here could hardly help but be imbued with glory.

On display are the crown jewels and personal valuables of the French kings. The first case contains jade, lapis lazuli, jasper, amethyst and amber vases, the best the property of Louis XIV, who had a passion for precious stones. The second contains **Napoleon's crown**, modelled on that of Charlemagne, and the **crown of Louis XV**, the only royal crown extant and even so its jewels are imitation. Real jewels, however, can be seen in the fourth case, the most valuable being the 137-carat Regent diamond sold by Thomas Pitt to Philippe d'Orléans in 1717. Among other notable works are objects from the treasury of Saint Denis (Case 6), the **Virgin of Jeanne d'Evreux**, a gilt statue of the first half of the fourteenth century (Case 7) and the **treasure of the Order of the Holy Spirit** (Case 9).

If we retrace our steps down the Daru staircase, and walk west, we come to the Porte La Trémoille, entrance to the **Department of Sculpture**. The first room contains Romanesque sculpture, all of it provincial, and it may come as a surprise that Paris, arch-borrower from Rome, seems to owe nothing at all to Byzantium.

Room 2 brings us to the Gothic in which Paris is so rich. At the end of the room, on either side of the door, are statues of **Charles V** and **Jeanne de Bourbon**, a fourteenth-century work from a now demolished church attributed to André Beauneveu. Room 3 contains the deeply moving **Tomb of Philippe Pot**, the *grand sénéchal* of Burgundy, who died in 1493. As we might guess, these eight weeping figures, cowled in grief, are too emotional to have come from Paris: they belong to the abbey-church of Cîteaux. The artist was probably Antoine le Moiturier, about whom little is known except that he found it difficult to obtain commissions.

Rooms 4 and 5 display French sculpture as it was immediately before the influence of Italian Renaissance art: notably the **Tomb of Louis de Poncher and his wife,** formerly in the church of St Germain l'Auxerrois. From the rood-screen of the same church comes the **Deposition of Christ and the Four Evangelists**, by Jean Goujon, whose sculptural decorations and bas-reliefs we have already seen in the Cour Carrée and the Carnavalet. This work, dating from 1545, un-ashamedly transfers the long, stiffly-pleated drapery of Athena's worshippers to a Christian context.

The statue in the centre of the room is the **Diana and Stag** from the Château d'Anet, sometimes attributed to Goujon but more probably an Italian work, though David d'Angers, in the nineteenth century, took one look at it and exclaimed, 'That's Greek, not Italian!'—so closely did the Renaissance, both in Italy and France, manage to identify its vision with that of the past. The fusion of cultures is even more evident in **The Three Graces**, commissioned by the Florentine Catherine de Médicis, executed by a Parisian, Germain Pilon, to hold the heart of the most Christian king, Henri II: the whole to stand in the Church of the Célestins!

It was Henri II who acquired, from a Florentine refugee, the two **Slaves** destined for the tomb of Julius II, which are the glory of the next room. They were completed in 1520, when Michelangelo was forty-five, and according to him they symbolise the liberal arts, made prisoners of death by the dis-appearance of the great pope, their protector. The monkey lurking behind one of the figures remains unexplained.

In the same room is the bas-relief in bronze of the **Nymph of Fontainebleau**, by Michelangelo's disciple, Benvenuto Cellini. This work is of the utmost importance in the history of French sculpture and we happen to know the story behind it.

Benvenuto Cellini swaggered on to the French scene in 1540: 'spirited, proud, lively,' says Vasari, 'very quick to act and terrifyingly passionate, a man who knew only too well how to speak his mind to princes.' He was conceited—each circumstance of his life appeared to him a miracle—and he believed that a genius like himself was not bound by the laws. He was forty years old and already the most famous gold-smith of his day.

Cellini was summoned to Fontainebleau by François I. After kissing the king's knee, he produced a cup and basin, of which the king said, 'I doubt whether the ancients can have seen a piece so beautiful as this.' According to Cellini, the king was 'vastly pleased' by his arrival. But two annoyances soon ruffled the Italian: the court was always on the move, with a suite of never less than 12,000 horse, and he was offered only 300 crowns a year. Cellini rode off in a huff and was finally given 700 crowns a year, the salary Leonardo had received.

Cellini asked for the Hôtel de Nesle, one of the largest houses in Paris. He got it—though the provost had to be turned out—and began to design the Nymph, described thus in his *Autobiography*: 'In the lunette above I placed a female figure lying in an attitude of noble grace; she rested her left arm on a stag's neck, this animal being one of the King's emblems. On one side I worked little fawns in half-relief, with some wild boars and other game in lower relief; on the other side were hounds and hunting dogs of various breeds, such as may be seen in that fair forest where the fountain springs.'

After studying both this design and a model of a fountain with Mars, the King laid his hand upon Cellini's shoulder, saying: '*Mon ami*, I don't know which has the greater pleasure, the prince who finds a man after his own heart, or the artist who finds a prince willing to furnish him with means for carrying out his great ideas.' Cellini, well aware that François genuinely liked him, took advantage of the fact to evict a manufacturer of saltpetre from a wing of the Hôtel de Nesle, declaring that he wanted the apartment for his workmen: with his own hands he flung the poor man's furniture into the street. Shortly afterwards he evicted a second lodger, whereupon Madame d'Etampes, the King's mistress, 'had the insolence to tell the King: "I believe that devil will sack Paris one of these days."' This lodger brought a lawsuit, claiming Cellini had stolen some of his property. When he found the suit turning against him, Cellini attacked the plaintiff with a dagger.

Meanwhile, he was at work on his first venture into statuary, the bronze Nymph before us. As model he engaged a poor girl of fifteen. 'Since she was somewhat savage in her ways and spare of speech, quick of movement, with a look of sullenness about her eyes, I nicknamed her Scorzone, her real name being Jeanne.' Cellini got Jeanne with child and with typical perversity named the infant Costanza. 'This was the first child I ever had, so far as I remember. I settled money enough upon the girl for dowry to satisfy an aunt of hers, under whose tutelage I placed her, and from that time forwards I had nothing more to do with her.' However, every succeeding generation of French artists has had to reckon with Cellini's sullen Jeanne, for this was the style of Italian art—elegant, refined, mannerist—which finally won the acceptance of Parisian society.

Cellini continued intolerable. A protégé of Madame d'Etampes—a perfumer—tried to install himself in the tennis-court at Nesle. Cellini 'made a daily attack with stones, pikes and arquebuses, firing, however, without ammunition;' frightening the perfumer out of the house and almost out of his wits. Finally in 1545, for domestic reasons, Cellini returned to Italy, where he was to produce in 'Perseus' a masterpiece of sculpture. With characteristic recklessness, he left the land of his adoption before he had properly squared accounts with the King. He was stopped and obliged to hand over three pieces of silver plate and some bullion. So ended a lively episode in Franco-Italian artistic relations.

Room 10 is particularly interesting, for it contains works of sober French classicism, notably a **head of Henri IV** by Mathieu Jacquet, and three works of French baroque by Puget. Whereas Coysevox, the Coustous and Girardon were in favour at court, Puget, a pupil of Bernini, led a solitary life apart, in Rome or the South of France, though Colbert did commission him to carve the prows of the royal galleys. He devoted every minute and every ounce of energy to his art. At sixty, after completing his masterpiece, **Milo of Crotona attacked by a Lion**, he declared: 'I am kept alive by undertaking great works, I seem to swim when I work at them, and the block of marble, however large, trembles before me.'

But Puget remains an exotic in Paris or Versailles. The main French tradition is seen in Room 11, particularly in such a work as Coysevox's **Marie Adélaide de Savoie**, who (Cellini's influence again) is posing as Diana. And Diana reappears in the sculpture of the eighteenth-century master, Jean Antoine Houdon. His work is in the **Salle Houdon**, at the north-west corner of the Cour Carrée, on the first floor (the nearest staircase is the Escalier Henri IV).

Houdon's works include a bronze **Diana** and a plaster bust of **Madame Houdon**. Houdon may be called master of the smile. He was the first French sculptor to succeed in the United States. Lafayette, Benjamin Franklin and Paul Jones sat for him. On the recommendation of Jefferson he was chosen by the State of Virginia to execute the statue of General Washington for the cupola of the Capitol at Richmond. There is a bronze copy of this work in London, outside the National Gallery.

The Louvre authorities hope one day to continue the display of French sculpture, which now ends with Houdon, to embrace the whole of the eighteenth and nineteenth centuries. For the later period we need feel no sense of loss: it is already well represented in the city's gardens and squares, on its bridges and public buildings, while Rodin has his own museum. These modern sculptors, even the most original, were nurtured in the Louvre among the works we have just seen. From Carpeaux to Bourdelle, with barely an exception, they came here to study Greek friezes and Roman portraits, Goujon and Pilon and Coysevox. Kipling put his finger on this extraordinary continuity when he wrote of Paris:

'First to follow truth and last to leave old truths behind.'

Detail from 'The Sense of Taste' : 'La Dame à la Licorne' tapestry, in the Musée Cluny

The domes of Paris
top left Church of the Sorbonne, 1629   *top right* The Invalides,
1735   *bottom left* The Panthéon, 1790   *bottom right* Sacré
Coeur, 1890

right Nymphs on the Fontaine des Innocents, by Goujon

The Seine
top left Notre Dame from the east   *top right* Part of the Pont
Neuf   *bottom* The Quai de la Tournelle

The Louvre
top left 'Napoleon' by David   *top right* David, a self-portrait
bottom The Galerie d'Apollon

top left The Vendôme Column
top right The July Column in the Place de la Bastille
bottom A fountain in the Place de la Concorde

top 'The Horses of Apollo', by Robert Le Lorrain, in a courtyard of the Hôtel de Rohan
bottom left 'Fame', by Coysevox, at the entrance to the Tuileries
bottom right 'Sea-horse', by Frémiet; part of the Fontaine de l'Observatoire

In the Bois

CHAPTER SIXTEEN

Montmartre

❧

Montmartre Cemetery – Rue Lepic – Montmartre Vineyard –
Place du Tertre – St Pierre de Montmartre – Sacré Coeur –
Place Pigalle

THERE are three Montmartres: the place itself, the myth and
the place trying to live up to the myth. The first is a pleasant,
largely self-contained cluster of streets, tumbledown houses,
gardens and cafés on a wind-swept hill with sudden surprising
views; the second is a Bohemian world of unrecognised
geniuses and good-hearted can-can dancers, a village where
everyone plays amusing practical jokes and sings half the
night, the cafés extend limitless credit and wine flows like
water; the third is an artificial, self-conscious world where, for
a fee, street-'artists' sketch the portrait of a passer-by in five
minutes and certain cabarets stage 'brawls' by 'apache dancers',
with blood in the form of red ink. Merely because this
spurious world exists, there is no reason why we should not
enjoy the place itself, in its unselfconscious aspects, and the
myth. Both are well worth getting to know.

Montmartre probably means the Hill of Mercury: of all the
Roman gods he who was pre-eminently honoured by Parisians.
Mercury was inventor of the arts, lord of travel and patron of
many trades, including Celtic smiths and weavers. St Martin
said that Mercury was the most difficult Roman god to out-
law. He was finally routed by Michael the archangel, who,
however, retained many mercurial virtues, hence the fervent
devotion to Michael during the early Middle Ages. To-day
Mercury and Michael reign jointly on the hill of Montmartre,
whose name evokes a school of painting and a basilica.

A convenient way of approaching Montmartre is to take a
No. 30 bus to Place Clichy, then walk a little way along
Boulevard de Clichy into Rue Caulaincourt and so to the
cemetery. By the year 1780 forty generations of Parisians had
found an anonymous grave in the Innocents, which at last
could hold no more. After the Revolution it was decreed that

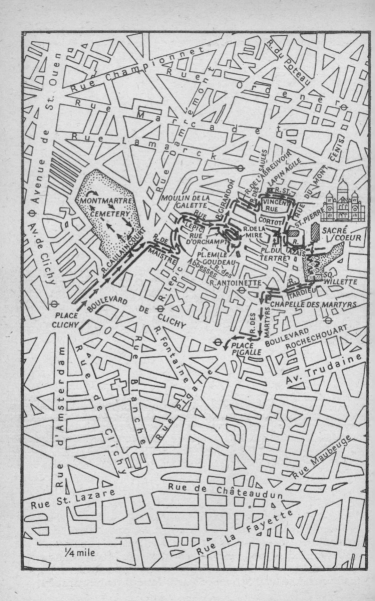

Parisian dead should be laid farther afield, here in **Montmartre cemetery** and in the much larger Père Lachaise. Among the monuments is a fine figure of Cavaignac, brother of the head of state in 1848, by Rude. Here also are the tombs of Gambetta, Greuze, Berlioz (buried between his two wives), Delibes, Offenbach, the Goncourt brothers, Alfred de Vigny, Henri Murger, Marie Duplessis, who played *la Dame aux Camélias*, Dumas the younger and the physicist Ampère. Below the bridge a stele bearing a sarcastic mask is inscribed 'Arrigo Beyle Milanese': the tomb of Stendhal.

The best time to see this or any French cemetery is All Souls' Day, 2nd November, when black-clad tearful groups, the young supporting the old, widows in extraordinary hats swathed in black veiling, come to lay wreaths on carefully-tended graves. Then one realises the cohesion of the French family. In other cities of the world you hear the complaint, 'To-day there is no security; if only I felt more secure!' but seldom in Paris. The reason would seem to be that security is the obverse of responsibility, and most Parisians still possess a very strong sense of family responsibility.

Rue de Maistre leads to **Rue Lepic**, in the lower section of which a busy market is held every weekday morning, overflowing on to the pavements. On the third floor of No. 54 Vincent van Gogh lived with his brother Théo in 1886. Farther along is the **Moulin de la Galette**, a seventeenth-century wooden mill, which has belonged to the Debray family since 1640. Formerly the Butte was covered with windmills, and Montmartre was a village of flour-millers. Tasso wrote in 1570 that the two things which most struck him about Paris were the windows of Notre Dame and the windmills at Montmartre. Donkeys carried up corn, in the morning and took down flour in the evening. By the time Renoir came to live in the village, in 1876, most of the mills had disappeared and this particular one had become an open-air dance-hall.

Rue de la Mire leads to Place Émile Goudeau. Here (13 Rue Ravignan), in a tumbledown laundry-house called the **'Bateau Lavoir'** because it swayed unsteadily like a boat, Picasso, Modigliani and Max Jacob worked together and here the Cubist movement may be said to have been born. That marked the end of Montmartre as a village of painters of genius, for Picasso and his followers moved to Montparnasse, and it was Montparnasse which between the wars fostered the highly cosmopolitan School of Paris. Montmartre had stood for village life, the familiar, the humble; in Montparnasse artists sought the cosmopolitan, the intellectual, the recherché.

Rue d'Orchampt leads by way of Rue Girardon to Rue de l'Abreuvoir, which runs down towards the Château des Brouillards, a white house among trees where Gérard de Nerval lived. Rue Cortot is another pretty old street: at No. 20 Gabrielle d'Estrées lived from 1590 to 1599.

If we turn back now, up Rue des Saules, we shall find at the corner of this street and Rue St Vincent, on the site of the former property of Aristide Bruant (one of the great *chanson- niers*, inventor of songs in Parisian slang), the little **vineyard of Montmartre**, encircled by an iron fence. The 3,250 Thomery vines are stripped every autumn in a municipal festival to yield a white wine with a reputation for making you 'leap like a goat'. This wine, profits from which go to charity, can be had at most of the bar-restaurants on the Butte, perhaps the best being at No. 4 Rue des Saules: the **Lapin Agile**. Here, seated on wooden benches, you can sip brandied cherries and take part in old French songs.

Beaumarchais declared that in France everything ends in songs. Often on the Butte or around Pigalle you hear the sound of an accordion and customers singing: these are the bistros to visit, for people break into spontaneous com- munity singing only in a sincere and friendly atmosphere. The new songs, like the old, are quick, witty, malicious and full of feeling: yes, frankly sentimental. Parisians, who exclude sentiment from their painting, architecture and drama, be- come delightfully sentimental in their songs. Here is part of a recent example, 'Mademoiselle de Paris', words by Henri Contet, music by Paul Durand:

> On l'appell' Mad'moisell' de Paris
> Et sa vie c'est un p'tit peu la notre
> Son royaum' c'est la rue d'Rivoli
> Son destin, c'est d'habiller les autres.
>
> On dit q'elle est petite main
> Et s'il est vrai qu'ell' n'est pas grande
> Que de bouquets et de guirlandes
> A-t-ell' semés sur nos chemins.
>
> Elle chante un air de son faubourg
> Ell' rêve à des serments d'amour
> Ell' pleure plus souvent qu' à son tour
> —Mad'moisell' de Paris.

Mais le cœur d'une enfant de Paris
C'est pareil aux bouquets de violettes
On l'attache au corsage un sam'di
Le dimanche on le perd à la fête.

Adieu guinguette, adieu garçon,
La voilà seule avec sa peine
Et recommence la semaine
Et recommence la chanson. . . .

And so on. The words give only a faint idea of its charm.

Young singers crowd forward with their latest songs, but those of the recent past are not to be disdained. The best of them remain vigorous and relevant, on gramophone records. I am thinking in particular of the Compagnons de la Chanson singing 'Le Prisonnier de la Tour' and 'Mes Jeunes Années', and Edith Piaf singing—well, anything at all, but particularly 'Milord'. Piaf was a legend in her own lifetime, and the truth about her tormented life had to wait until she died in 1963; then it was revealed in a moving biography by her sister.

Side by side with the sentimental song flourish the more roguish lyrics of *chansonniers* like Jean Marsac, Pierre Destailles and Fernand Reynaud, as well as anonymous bawdy —sometimes exceedingly bawdy—ballads, part of the Parisian tradition ever since Villon serenaded his Grosse Margot. These too can be heard in certain bistros on the Butte, or just beneath, around Pigalle.

Rue St Vincent, another picturesque, wind-swept street, leads to Rue du Mont Cenis, from where we can glance down the unspoiled Rue St Rustique before arriving in the centre of Montmartre, the now heavily commercialised **Place du Tertre** with its *mairie* of the Commune Libre de Vieux Montmartre, inscribed—is it possible?—Gaieté, Art, Bonté. Here we are face to face with the myth of Montmartre.

To understand the myth, first a word about how Montmartre became a centre of artists. About 1830 Montmartre was a country village, outside Paris, difficult of access because Haussmann's wide streets had not yet been designed, pretty and inexpensive. Alphonse Karr and Gavarni were the first artists to come and live here. Henri Murger's *Scènes de la Vie de Bohème* and the artistic cabaret 'Le Chat Noir' gave the rest of Paris a glimpse of unconventional, gay village life in which for an occasional evening they tried to join. But Montmartre remained a centre of serious painting, attracting,

as we have seen, Renoir and van Gogh, as well as Toulouse
Lautrec, and producing two native artists in Suzanne Valadon
and her son Utrillo.

In the easy days before the First World War there came to
live on the Butte a group of gay young men-about-town, poets
and writers, headed by Carco and MacOrlan. They lived for
camaraderie, wine, music and rather schoolboyish practical
jokes. Dorgelès, for instance, would put up in the Paris
streets barriers and signs in big letters: 'Street Closed', with
red lanterns which he would light at dusk. If Carco forgot to
keep an appointment, La Vassière would break the pane of a
fire-alarm telephone and give Carco's address. Carco would
be reminded of his appointment by the arrival of a fire bri-
gade.

The very poor—the struggling journalist and out-of-work
artist—lived with the others and paid their shares in songs. At
'Marie's' unframed Utrillos were nailed crazily up and down
the walls—payment given by the painter for a round of drinks.
A blissful Peter-Pan world, where living was cheap, and no
one needed to grow up. Also a very unparisian world, hence
perhaps its fascination for certain Parisians.

The Montmartre of serious painters and gay, foolish and
unconventional poets was a fatal casualty of the First World
War. But such was the evocative power of reminiscences
which Carco and MacOrlan continued to publish through the
twenties and thirties, that many people continued to believe in
its existence. They flocked to the little narrow streets and
'artistic cabarets' to try and recapture the heart-ache of first
love, the illusions of youth and the artistic spirit. Montmartre was the village 'over the rainbow', and so, for many, it
still remains.

For others, Montmartre is a series of copies of Utrillo
paintings. Those blank-faced houses, the gardens with gaps
in the wall revealing clusters of nettles, brambles and rubble,
the domes of the Sacré Coeur—here, as seldom elsewhere in
Paris, the painter's vision seems to condition all we see. Part
of the explanation may be this. Montmartre stands on quarries of plaster of Paris, and this is used to whitewash the housefronts. To depict those housefronts Utrillo actually mixed
plaster of Paris into his paint: like a potter or sculptor
fashioning from local clay.

Just east of Place du Tertre lies the **church of St Pierre de
Montmartre**. Its façade suggests an eighteenth-century build-

ing, but in fact most of the fabric is early Gothic, older even
than Notre Dame, and Dante is known to have worshipped
here. It contains four Roman columns, perhaps from the
temple of Mercury. These are, with the Roman walls next to
the Cluny, the oldest standing witnesses to the city's past.
Notice the carving of Luxury on one of the capitals: a pig-
headed man riding a buck backwards. The prettiest part of the
whole building is perhaps the exterior of the apse.

St Pierre stands on the site of one of the earliest churches in
Paris, erected to commemorate the martyrdom of St Denis.
St Denis and his companions Eleutherius and Rusticus are
said to have been beheaded at the foot of the hill; and St
Denis to have walked, holding his head in his hands, as far as
the town which bears his name, in search of a burial place.
'Think, madame,' said a certain pious abbé to an eighteenth-
century lady, 'a distance of seven kilometres!' 'Peut-être,'
drawled the lady, who had a streak of Parisian irony, 'mais ce
n'est que le premier pas qui coûte.' So the hill has always been
holy, and some would even derive the name from Mons
Martyrum.

It was natural, therefore, that when in 1874 the National
Assembly decreed the building of a church as a votive offering
of repentance after the excesses of the Commune, this historic
and prominent site should have been chosen. The dedication
is interesting. It was in 1670 that the French Visitandine, St
Marguerite Marie Alacoque, was told, in a vision, to spread
devotion to the Sacred Heart. This assertion that divine
charity was the physical love of a real person did much to
rout Jansenism, but to-day we have lost the language of
symbols, and on some the imagery may jar.

The same may be said of the building itself. The basilica of
the Sacré Coeur was inspired by the church of St Front, Péri-
gueux. Its ancestry is impeccable, but is not slavish imitation
of the twelfth century somehow a mark of decadence? In
mitigation we should remember that this was a difficult period.
Continuity had been broken at the Revolution; everywhere
artists were trying to link their thin wires with high-voltage
cables of the past. But which past? At the turn of the century
we have the Byzantine in Westminster Cathedral, Gothic in
St Patrick's, New York and here Romanesque.

Three million Frenchmen contributed to the building fund,
so the basilica can truly claim to be a national shrine. The
Butte was riddled with gypsum quarries, wells and caves, so

that deep shafts filled with masonry had to be sunk a hundred feet down into the crumbling, sandy hill. The Romanesque, we know, is not a Parisian style: too many excrescences and bumps—anything but *net*; but Paris reclaimed this gangling design by building in white stone. The white stone was a stroke of genius, for it makes the church *pure*. Sometimes in summer, from a distance, it seems part of the haze and shimmer.

The statue above the main portal depicts the Sacred Heart. The façade is decorated with bas-reliefs of Christ and the Woman of Samaria, and Mary Magdalen at the house of Simon. The dome, which can be visited, provides views both of the basilica interior and of Paris, but the city can be seen almost as well from Square Willette, south of the basilica.

Rue Tardieu leads to Rue Antoinette. At No. 9, now a convent, is the old **chapel of the Martyrs** (*can be visited daily except Thursday* 10–12, 3–5), where in 1534, Ignatius de Loyola, Francis Xavier, four other Spaniards and a Savoyard priest bound themselves into a company which was to become the Society of Jesus. If this is really the spot where St Denis was martyred, what an astonishing continuity of cross-fertilisation within the countries of Christendom: St Denis—an Athenian; Paris, the new centre of learning, attracting Spaniards who would later make their headquarters in Rome, and one of whom would be first to preach the Gospel in India, Indonesia and Japan.

Rue des Martyrs leads down to **Place Pigalle** and the Métro. Pigalle has become synonymous with the strip-tease cabarets and dance-halls of this district, so that it may come as a surprise to find that it was named after the highly respectable sculptor Jean Baptiste Pigalle, whose most famous work, 'Voltaire in the nude', stands in the Institut. Pigalle is buried in the little churchyard of St Pierre, with Bougainville, who discovered bougainvillaea.

Perhaps it is only now, arriving at the bottom of the hill, that we notice something missing. For a moment we pause, wondering what it can be; then we understand. The wind has dropped. Up on the hill there was a delightful breeze, the breeze that turned the windmills and ground the flour of Paris. The air was light and exhilarating; perhaps it is that air which the poets and painters sought, as others seek the waters of Evian or Vichy.

CHAPTER SEVENTEEN

The West

꿎

*Bois de Boulogne – Bagatelle – Avenue Foch – Arc de Triomphe
– Avenue Marceau – Palais d'Art Moderne*

BETWEEN 1860 and 1914 Paris was given her boulevards, her
avenues, her trees and her favourite park. The western arrondissements became fashionable. From 1914 to 1947 Paris was
too poor to erect new houses or important buildings, but her
values, ideas and moods have been accurately preserved by the
painters of the period. So a walk from the **Bois de Boulogne** to
the Musée National d'Art Moderne should reveal something
of the growth of fashionable modern Paris.

A 43 bus sets us down near the Porte de Bagatelle, from
where we can walk up to the **Parc de Bagatelle** (*open daily*
8.30–7.30) and cross the Bois eastwards, eventually arriving
at the Porte Dauphine.

A half-ruined house on the site of the Bagatelle was bought
for a song by the Comte d'Artois. When his sister-in-law,
Marie Antoinette, teased him about his purchase, d'Artois
wagered he would put up an entirely new house in three
months. Bélanger drew the plans in twenty-four hours and
completed the present Bagatelle in sixty-four days, but he
was able to use the foundations of the older structure. Later
the Bagatelle became the property of Sir Richard Wallace,
who gave London his collection of French furniture and Paris
his rose-garden, as well as a hundred drinking fountains. To-
day the roses and the 139 varieties of water-lily are amongst
the park's chief attractions.

Crossing the Allée de la Reine Marguerite we enter a more
deserted part of the Bois: trees and glades which recall that
under the Merovingian kings this was the Forêt du Rouvre
('rouvre' being old French for oak). In 1308 some of the wood-
cutters went on pilgrimage to the shrine of Notre Dame de
Boulogne, and on their return built a chapel called Notre
Dame de Boulogne le Petit, hence the present name. Under
the Valois kings the wood was preserved as a hunting-ground:

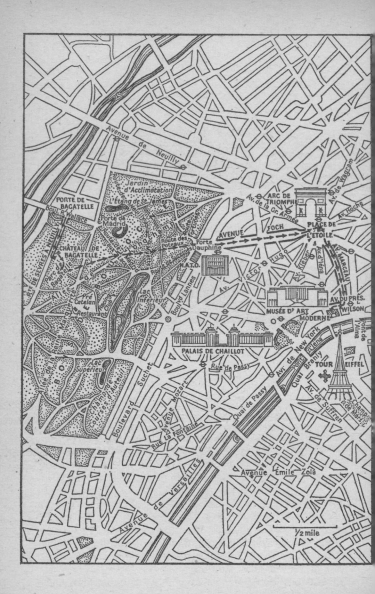

the royal passion for hunting explains why, half an hour's run from Paris, you can be in such beautiful forests as Rambouillet, Fontainebleau, Chantilly and St Germain.

In 1815 British and Russian troops bivouacked in the Bois burned down the oaks, which were later replaced by horse-chestnuts, sycamores and acacias, when Napoleon III designed the present park. In his youth Louis Napoleon laid out the Duke of Hamilton's garden at Brodick Castle in Scotland, and the Duke said of him in a letter: 'He's a marvellous landscape-gardener, and if ever he lost his job, I would gladly take him on as head-gardener.' When he came to power Napoleon III laid out the Bois de Vincennes, created the park on the Buttes Chaumont and, in co-operation with Haussmann, laid out the Bois de Boulogne on the lines of his beloved Hyde Park. Two lakes were dug, to resemble the Serpentine, and a pond surrounded by woods (it lies to our left) called **L'Etang de St James**. The Bois also offers good sporting facilities: tennis and swimming at the Racing Club, clay-pigeon shooting, polo at the Bagatelle, and two crack racecourses: **Auteuil** for steeplechases and **Longchamp** for flat races. The Grand Prix in June is every bit as colourful as a Dufy aquarelle and modish as a fashion-show at Maggy Rouff.

At the Porte Dauphine we can see to the south the back of **N.A.T.O. headquarters**, built in 1957. We can either walk up Avenue Foch to the Arc de Triomphe, or take the Métro to Étoile station. The **Avenue Foch**, a hundred and ten yards wide, is the broadest and one of the most imposing streets in Paris, one of twelve designed by Haussmann to radiate from the Étoile. Haussmann was only forty-four when Napoleon III appointed him Prefect of the Seine and handed him a plan of the city marked with the chief improvements he wanted made: a tall, broad-shouldered, bull-necked Alsatian with big eyes, nose and jaw, and a *barbe à collier*. He could shoot, swim, dance, fence, play the 'cello and organ. By training he was a lawyer, not an architect—'the legal style,' he says in his rather dry, cold *Memoirs*, 'if it lacks eloquence, encourages the very salutary habit of precision, to which the drafting of my prefectorial ordinances bears witness.' He was hard-working, strong-willed, full of audacity and cunning, capable of pitting expedient against expedient, setting trap for trap. Above all, he was incorruptible.

Haussmann's chief task was to enlarge the main thorough-

fares, and where this was impracticable, to drive new ones. A
Gavarni cartoon shows a working-class woman pointing to a
lady wearing a wide crinoline: '*C'est pour ces Madames-là
qu'on élargit les rues de Paris!*' Not so far from the truth.
Modern traffic and the horde of visitors brought by the new
railways simply could not move through largely medieval
streets.

Haussmann avoided orthodox American town-planning in
which straight streets cross each other monotonously at right-
angles; instead he planned Paris like a park: avenues adorned
with monuments, radiating from circuses. If Paris could not
have cloistered green squares like London, at least she could
be given greenery and so know the rhythm of the seasons.
Haussmann planted no less than 75,000 trees, many of them
horse-chestnuts and catalpas. This planning of air and light
and greenery came from the Emperor; but it was Haussmann
who saw that Paris must have piped water and drains. Hundreds of miles of underground drains were constructed. As
one wag put it: 'The sewers of Paris are so fine that something
really great should happen in them . . .'

Haussmann foresaw accurately that the population of Paris
(1,800,000 in 1865) would grow during the succeeding fifty
years to a maximum of about three million. Three-story
houses were replaced by six-story apartment blocks, still the
usual feature of residential Paris. Much had to be sacrificed,
but Haussmann, a Protestant, was not over-sentimental about
the past. He understood the period he lived in. When so many
people looked with dismay on the growth of transport, towns,
wealth and industrialism, Haussmann measured the problem
dispassionately, saw what needed to be done and did it. He can
be accused of vandalism only in his demolitions on the Cité
and the mutilation of the gardens of the Luxembourg.

Haussmann lacked a single first-rate architect: that is why
some of his most enterprising formal perspectives fail: the
Boulevard Malesherbes, for instance, which leads into the
feeble church of St Augustin. Other boulevards, especially
those leading to railway stations, and the avenues radiating
from the Étoile are successful precisely because the central
monument is worthy of the grand design.

Despite sneers at the 'Comptes Fantastiques de Haussmann', the Prefect did not enrich himself. He even demolished
Rue du Faubourg du Roule, his own birthplace. But seventeen years of power brought him many enemies, and those

enemies finally forced the Emperor to dismiss him. Three
years later, when Napoleon died, Haussmann did not attend
the funeral and never forgave his old chief. It seems a pity that
this partnership should have ended on a jarring note, for much
of Paris as we know it to-day is the product of these two men:
an Emperor who had dreamed in exile and a strong Prefect
capable of realising those dreams.

The Arc de Triomphe[1] will probably appear to us now in a
rather different light from that in which we first glimpsed it:
not a unique flash of Napoleonic genius, but the flower of a
long tradition. We have seen the Portes St Denis and St
Martin, erected by Louis XIV; even earlier Henri II was
hailed on his entry to Paris as the French Hercules with many
temporary triumphal arches, while the Pont Neuf was originally designed with a triumphal arch of three bays at each end,
before the more sober style carried the day.

Chalgrin took the Arch of Titus in Rome for his model, for
his scale the gigantic Colosseum. On top Rude wanted to place
a huge statue of France holding a torch and sword, accompanied by a lion. This idea was vetoed: instead we have
romantic bas-reliefs growing out of a classical structure. The
most famous is Rude's 'Departure of the Army' (facing the
Champs Elysées on the right). Next to it is 'The Triumph of
Napoleon in 1810'; on the other side are 'The Resistance of
the French in 1814' (right) and 'The Peace of 1815' (left).
Above are panels chiefly of battles, and a frieze showing the
departure and return of the French armies.

Under the arch a perpetual flame burns by the **tomb of an
unknown soldier** who fell in the 1914-18 war. Here Hugo's
body lay in state, he who has best hailed the arch:

Entre tes quatre pieds toute la ville abonde
Comme une fourmilière aux pieds d'un éléphant!

Above all, the arch is a monument to Napoleon, whose
hearse passed underneath on its return from St Helena in
1840. (The hundred stone pillars round the Arch are said to
represent the Hundred Days.) Napoleon III loved Paris as a
cosmopolitan, but the first Napoleon loved Paris far more,
with all the passion of a provincial. He wanted to make his
capital not only 'the most beautiful city there is, and the most

[1] The interior and the platform of the arch are open daily except
Tuesday, 10-4, 5 or 6, depending on the season.

beautiful there ever was, but also the most beautiful that ever could be.' In art, as he said to Goethe, he liked 'a decided style'; in architecture he allied a passion for order with prodigious imagination. He never planned buildings without specifying where the funds were to be found, often repeating that Louis XIV had been ruined by his architects.

As regards this arch and the Arc du Carrousel, Napoleon said that they were undertaken partly to encourage architecture and related arts. 'With these two arches I intend to nourish French sculpture for ten years.' He intended a third and fourth arch, one to Peace, the other to Religion. Napoleon's taste for the massive is shown in yet another plan (which reached only the stage of a plaster model, familiar to readers of *Les Misérables*): to erect in the Place de la Bastille an elephant 74 feet high, surmounted by a green howdah and discharging a jet of water through its trunk! A dream of India regained—the India Louis XV had lost for France.

I suggest we now take one of the wide avenues, that named after General Marceau, whose funeral is depicted on one of the arch's bas-reliefs. Here we are in the heart of fashionable residential Paris. It is curious how smart Parisians have gradually glided down-river over the centuries. From the Marais to Faubourg St Germain, thence to the eighth arrondissement (Proust, for instance, lived at 104 Boulevard Haussmann—but his apartment is not on view) and now to the sixteenth. Originally perhaps they were driven by the stench of the filthy streets, for the prevailing wind is westerly; more recently Passy has tempted them with plenty of building land, relatively high-lying, in sight of the river and near the fashionable Bois.

In Avenue Marceau and the adjoining streets most of the new buildings are of ferro-concrete. This mixture was invented by a French gardener, Mounier by name, to make flowerpots and garden furniture. It was the Perret brothers who first used it for blocks of flats and for the revolutionary Théâtre des Champs Elysées. The swinging curves and bold cantilevering possible with ferro-concrete are gradually softening the straight lines of Haussmann's avenues and boulevards.

Avenue Marceau is largely a street of apartments. Throughout Paris the apartment has now almost entirely superseded the private house. A well-to-do Parisian buys his apartment outright; it then becomes his property, to be sold at will.

Annexes usually include a maid's room at the top of the building and a private wine-cellar in part of the basement. Since Paris has no mews, private garages are rare: more often than not motor cars are left overnight in the street below. A concierge in a small ground-floor flat ensures that no unauthorised person enters the building. She also takes in parcels and letters when an occupant is away and, in general, acts as liaison with shopkeepers, cleaners and neighbours. A wrought-iron and glass outer door which is opened when the concierge presses a button and later closes automatically; a courtyard, usually treeless, and an asthmatic lift—these complete the picture.

Life in such surroundings in the years before the First War is familiar to us from Proust. A new image of Paris had lately been created by the Impressionists, by Verlaine, Rimbaud and Mallarmé. The world found the image attractive and once again came to school in Paris, as had happened twice before, in the age of Dante and in the reign of Louis XIV. Mirò from Spain, Modigliani from Italy, Chagall from R ssia; T. S. Eliot, 'possessed' (as he himself admits) by the sp it of Jules Laforgue; philosophers to study under Henri Bergson, scientists under the Curies and Maurice de Broglie. A happy, fruitful age: here and there in the wide avenue a tailor's window, a chocolatier or a particularly graceful balcony, provide echoes and reminders.

Avenue Marceau ends in Avenue du Président Wilson. Turning right we come to the **Palais d'Art Moderne**. The tall thin columns without capitals which support the portico are a hallmark of buildings erected for the 1937 Exhibition. The west wing is the **Musée National d'Art Moderne** (*open daily except Tuesday*, 10–5), an important but difficult collection of some 2,000 paintings, sculptures and tapestries ranging from Pierre Bonnard to artists still alive. Difficult because so much of the collection is art reflecting on itself, on its own first principles as Valéry does in his poems, and because in this quickly dissatisfied twentieth century one artist in his lifetime may practise as many as half a dozen widely different styles.

There is space to note only some of the outstanding paintings. Among the early rooms, that devoted to the Nabis is perhaps the most important. The Nabis (from the Hebrew word for Prophet) were attracted by Gauguin's advice to paint decoratively in flat, pure colours. Their war-cry was uttered by Maurice Denis: 'Any painting—before being a battle-horse, a nude woman, or some anecdote—is essentially a flat surface covered with colours arranged in a certain order.' **Pierre Bonnard** (1867–1947) started as a Nabi, but he soon tired of the arbitrary imposition of colour and pattern, and his main *œuvre* is Impressionist. Among Bonnard's most pleasing works are **The Beach at Low Tide** (1922) and **The Harbour of Trouville** (1938–46).

Suzanne Valadon (1865–1938) began life as a travelling acrobat, posed for Toulouse Lautrec and was Degas's favourite model. She too was influenced by the technique of Gauguin and his Pont Aven friends, though Degas also gave her advice. **The Blue Bedroom** (1923) is perhaps the best of her paintings, too often marred by crude colours and obvious contrasts.

Suzanne Valadon's son Maurice was born in Montmartre in 1883; in 1891 a Spanish artist, Miguel Utrillo, consented to make the child legitimate. **Maurice Utrillo** early developed into a confirmed drunkard and drug addict, spent many years in clinics and sanatoria, and his drinking bouts often ended in prison. His mother, to whom he was devoted (he usually signed Maurice Utrillo V—for Valadon), made him learn to paint as a form of therapy. He soon showed an uncanny feeling for the atmosphere of a particular street or building, painting hundreds of canvases with an amalgam of plaster, sand and glue. His best work, much of it painted from picture-postcards, extends from **The Garden of Montmagny** (1909) to **Rue du Mont Cenis** (1915). Thereafter Utrillo had nothing more to say. Imitators, however, sprang up and continued his work for him: there are probably more forgeries of Utrillo in existence than of any other modern painter.

Henri Matisse was born in le Cateau (Nord) in 1869, settled on the Riviera in 1914 and died in Nice in 1954: in short, yet another Northerner who fell in love with the southern sun.

His first painting in this museum is the extremely conservative **The Breton Weaver**, dated 1896, when he was making numerous copies in the Louvre from Champaigne, Poussin and Chardin. After being influenced by Impressionism and Cézanne, Matisse spent the summer of 1904 with Signac in the South of France. This led to the explosion of colour called Fauvism. **Southern Landscape, the Pink Wall**, is a Fauvist work in which the art of painting has been reduced to colour and a few other fundamentals, chiefly line and rhythm.

Luxury, decorative and calm, and **The Algerian Woman,**
vehement, black and incisive, very appropriately hang side-by-
side, for all his life Matisse was to oscillate between a longing
for classical simplicity and a taste for hectic colours.

The Painter and his Model is the last of a series of rather
monochromatic canvases with syncopated rhythm heralding
the calm, mature Riviera years when Matisse painted the
series of odalisks and still-lifes which are his main *œuvre*. Of
these **Odalisk in Red Trousers** (1922) inevitably invites comparison with the nudes of Ingres: where the classical painter
gives us a living, breathing woman, for Matisse she is merely
part of a pattern, neither more nor less important than her
ornaments.

The model for **Woman Reading against a Black Background**
(1939) was Princess Hélène Galitzine. With the blonde Lydia
Delectorskaya, Matisse's favourite model for the last twenty
years of his life, she also sat for **The Two Friends** (1941).
'Revelation has always come to me from the East,' said
Matisse, who was attracted not only to women of Russian
descent but to Russian icons, Persian miniatures and Islamic
textiles.

A useful commentary on the still-lifes which follow is a note
from one of Matisse's lectures when he ran his own art school
in Paris from 1906–10: 'It is nothing to copy the objects which
compose a still-life. What matters is to express the sensation
with which it inspired you, the emotion aroused by the whole,
the relationship between the objects represented, the specific
character of each, modified by relationship with the others, the
whole intertwined like a rope or like a serpent.' And again: 'I
seek only to apply colours which reflect what I feel.'

The Sadness of the King is one of two abstract works in cut-
out paper produced towards the end of his life: the hands are
said to have been inspired by those found in the prehistoric
caves of Ariège and the Haute-Garonne. 'There is no break,'
Matisse declared, 'between my old pictures and my cut-outs;
only with more formality, more abstraction, I arrive at a form
decanted to the essential.' 'You are going to simplify painting,' Gustave Moreau had predicted to his young pupil; at
the age of eighty-five Matisse was still simplifying.

The museum is inevitably dominated by its Picassos, though
far from representative of all the artist's different periods. The
first, **Portrait of Gustave Coquiot,** was painted in 1901. **Pablo
Picasso,** the son of a painter of flower-pieces and still-lifes,

was then aged twenty. His home was in Barcelona. In the six-teenth century he might have gone to study in Toledo, in the seventeenth to Rome, but in the second year of the twentieth century Paris was the world's art centre. And to Paris Picasso came, showing his works (painted on cardboard) at 6 Rue Laffitte. They caused little stir but brought Picasso the friend-ship of Max Jacob and of the influential critic who sat for this portrait.

At the end of 1901 Picasso entered his Blue Period, but there are no examples of this in the museum nor of his Pink and Negro Periods. In 1903 Picasso settled in Paris.

The next work, **The Glass** (1914) is a gouache and *papier collé* on cardboard. For the past few years Picasso had been working closely with Braque and Derain, painting the few articles to be found on a café table, plus the Spanish guitar. When Braque and Derain went off to war, Picasso enlarged his vocabulary, as we see from the next paintings. His work continued to be marked by a pronounced dualism: on the one hand a systematic development and exploitation of Cubism (for example, the **Still Life** of 1922), on the other hand, representation of the human face and figure by traditional means (for example, engravings and lithographs, chiefly for books—Picasso has illustrated close on a hundred *éditions de luxe*, notably Ovid's *Metamorphoses* and Buffon's *Natural History*).

The Milliner's Workshop (1926), painted in a narrow range of greys and an interwoven pattern of curves, was inspired by the view from his studio window in Rue La Boétie, and re-minds us that many of Picasso's best works depict the Paris scene (notably Notre Dame and Square du Vert Galant).

Woman's Torso (1929) reveals yet another new interest—sculpture—and a growing lordliness towards the female form, which Picasso now takes to pieces and puts together at will. In the still-lifes and nudes of the thirties the artist is at last fulfilling Rimbaud's astonishingly accurate prophecy: 'We will free painting from its old habit of copying and give it supremacy . . . Objects will no longer be reproduced; instead, feelings will be expressed through the medium of lines, colours and designs, taken from the external world but simplified or controlled . . .'

Portrait of Nush Eluard (1941) is a rare naturalistic work, for during the war years Picasso was obsessed with the Seated Woman in which he redistributed facial features. Nush

Eluard was the wife of the famous surrealist poet, a friend of Picasso since the mid-thirties. Picasso wrote surrealist poetry himself but as a painter he was never a surrealist. What he borrowed was the concept of 'metamorphosis'—anything can develop from anything, as in a fairy tale.

If Picasso was saved from surrealism by innate *joie de vivre* and acceptance of life, he was saved from expressionism by his unfailing confidence as a draughtsman. The important Aubade (1942) shows how profoundly he can impose a personal vision while still respecting the integrity of his subject. Two figures are defined entirely by straight lines and curves, among a network of vertical, horizontal and diagonal lines all intersecting at sharp angles. They attract all the light in the picture, making an immense prism: and this prism can be taken as a symbol of the love uniting the two figures.

The Rocking Chair (1943) is another work which gives us the emotion attaching to the subject as well as the subject itself. The curve of the rockers is emphasised against a square tiled floor which extends more than half-way up the canvas. And slowly we come to recognise this as the distinctive feeling of being in a rocking chair: swinging forward so that the floor comes up to meet us.

One of the best of the later Picassos is The Enamel Pan (1945). In contrast with the wine and fruit which distinguished his still-lifes of the twenties, the darkness and austerity of the war years are here evoked by a candle-end, an empty jug and a rather tinny saucepan.

'The painter,' Picasso has said, 'makes paintings in the urgent need to discharge his own emotions and visions.' These, then, are personal paintings, to be understood in the light of Picasso's own character. And whatever else it may be, that character is, from first to last, Spanish. Spanish in its eternally unsatisfied striving, Spanish in its humour, Spanish in its exhibitionism. In Paris as a young man Picasso attended balls dressed as a matador; lately, marrying again at the age of eighty, he dressed up as a high priest, and made his young bride prostrate herself publicly in homage before him. A harlequin delighting in masks and mime: hence the profusion of new moods and styles: hardly has one canvas been finished before another is started to deny it. As a graphologist said of Picasso's handwriting in 1942: 'He loves intensely and kills what he loves.' Perhaps Picasso's dichotomy (or multiplicity) goes deeper than that: anyway, a score of paintings are here to be questioned and perhaps to provide an answer.

Georges Braque, the son of a house-painter, was born in 1886 at Argenteuil, a bathing-place near Paris frequented by Impressionists like Manet and Renoir. He was deeply influenced by Cézanne, for a time sought release in the Fauve movement, then, with Picasso, carried Cézanne's constructivist principles a stage further. From the experiments of Braque and Picasso Cubism was born.

Le Guéridon (1911) is an early Cubist canvas. The subject, a round table on a pedestal, is represented by geometric shapes which heighten the sense of mass. But this highly intellectual way of painting did not suit Braque. He continued to search for a style which would satisfy his unusual sensitiveness towards texture. **Still-Life with Playing Cards** (1913) is one of the first *papiers collés*. Three strips of wallpaper imitating the grain of woodwork are linked by a few charcoal strokes. Here Braque is not so much undermining the conventional dignity of 'fine painting' as reasserting the importance of humble objects and the pleasures of touch.

The still-lifes of the twenties show Braque painting and re-painting a repertoire of simple objects mainly in greys and browns that suggest a primeval humus. Emotion and intellect are now in perfect balance. 'I am not a revolutionary,' Braque used to say. 'I do not exalt an idea.' And again, 'A picture is finished when it has effaced the idea behind it.'

The Duet (1937) is one of Braque's rare figure-paintings. 'No one,' said his friend Apollinaire, 'is less concerned than he with psychology, and I fancy a stone moves him as much as a face.' I think we can go further and say that in Braque's canvases the human figure brings disruption into a peaceful world.

The Salon (1944) is Braque's first painting to render a full and natural expression of the space contained within the four walls of a room, an experiment carried still further in **The Billiard Table**, painted the same year. 'Always beware of your own preconceptions' was one of Braque's maxims; and proves it by turning upside-down our notion of perfect flatness.

If Picasso's development follows a curve from acceptance to refusal, Rouault's takes an exactly opposite line. Born in 1871, **Georges Rouault** was apprenticed to a maker of stained glass: this early training shows itself in the dark, thick lines by which he articulates the human body. Later he studied with

Matisse under Gustave Moreau, whose disciple he became. A friend of Huysmans and Léon Bloy, he protested violently and indignantly against the skin-deep Catholicism of his day: indeed, as **The Mirror** (1906) shows, against the human condition itself.

If we compare **The Apprentice**, a self-portrait dating from 1925, with the next canvas, **The Holy Face** (1933), we begin to understand Rouault's religious outlook: an almost Byzantine hierarchism, in which God counts for everything and man for almost nothing. **Homo Homini Lupus** (1939-45) continues the pessimistic social protest, with a ray of hope in the star in the top corner.

Finally, in **Passion** (1949) Rouault seems to have arrived at serenity and a measure of tenderness. It is a lovely, deeply-felt work that succeeds in making Christ both humble and dignified. It has recently served as model for a provincial church window.

Russian art has traditionally sought to depict the invisible. **Marc Chagall** (*b.* 1887) is not only a Russian but a Jew whose religious upbringing stressed the irrational and miraculous. For instance, in his home town of Vitebsk, if a horse was stolen, a holy rabbi would be asked in all seriousness to perform a miracle to secure its return. Chagall's world always has projections into the past and future, while miracle is just around the corner.

In 1910 Chagall came to Paris, where, he says, he was born a second time. Instead of sacrificing his private vision, he used Cubist technique to give it greater authority. **A la Russie, aux ânes et aux autres** dates from 1911: a woman flies towards a cow that she is going to milk and loses her head in the clouds. 'Metaphor!' joyfully exclaimed Chagall's friend Apollinaire, who also wrote: 'Chagall is a gifted colourist who flies away on the wings of his mystical, pagan imagination; his art is very sensual.'

Double Portrait with a Glass of Wine (1917) shows Chagall on the shoulders of his adored wife, Bella, whom he had married two years previously, drinking a toast to life, while their daughter Ida hovers above.

In later canvases Chagall's favourite symbols reappear—cows, cocks, flying fish, huge eyes, lovers. For most people they will have little precise meaning: what matters are the shimmering colours, the dynamic movement, the reminder that miracles can happen even in ultra-rational Paris.

All these masters have their followers in the younger generation. But perhaps the strongest influence at work to-day in Paris is the abstract art of the Russian, **Wassily Kandinsky** (1866–1944). Kandinsky's work and that of his disciples hang on the first floor.

A few abstract artists attempt to unearth the archetypal forms common to all created things, whether crystals, metals or living cells. But, more often, the abstract artist substitutes for the disharmony and unintelligibility of the visible world a harmony and unity of his own creation. He claims to express the colour and shape of his own soul. Whereas the relationship between a figurative painter and his audience is one of friendship, with his subject as a common interest, the relationship between an abstract painter and his audience is much more direct and intimate, like passionate love. Explanatory remarks by a third person therefore become irrelevant.

Among the gifted younger painters in this museum are Yves Brayer (*b*. 1907), Gustave Singier (*b*. 1909) and Bernard Buffet (*b*. 1928), whose cage motifs seem to have a strong appeal for those who live in cities.

The sculptors include Rodin's successor, Antoine Bourdelle —a particularly fine head of **Anatole France**; Aristide Maillol (1861–1944); Pablo Gargallo (1881–1935)—a delicate **Harlequin Playing the Flute**; and Jacob Epstein—a bronze head of **Sir Winston Churchill**.

In addition to the permanent collection, frequent temporary exhibitions of modern artists are held in this museum: details are to be found in *Le Monde*, *Le Figaro* or *Une Semaine de Paris*.

CHAPTER EIGHTEEN

Exhibition Paris and the Musée Rodin

✥

Palais de Chaillot – Pont d'Iéna – Tour Eiffel – Champ de Mars – École Militaire – Palais de l'UNESCO – Musée Rodin

PARIS is something of a mannequin. She loves dressing up and being admired—in short, she loves exhibitions. The **Palais de Chaillot**, for example, was built for the 1937 exhibition to replace an earlier hall, the Trocadéro, a fantastic conglomeration of water tower, minarets and steam-driven organ, showpiece of the 1878 exhibition. Across the Seine soars the Eiffel Tower, built for the 1889 exhibition. Up-river stand the **Grand Palais** and **Petit Palais**, cast-iron and glass memorials to the 1900 exhibition; their form recalls the First Universal Exhibition, an English not a French affair, held in the Crystal Palace in 1851. There France took second place. Four years later France held her first great display, attended by Queen Victoria and Prince Albert, at which England took second place.

The nineteenth century had much to exhibit: electric light, refrigeration, aniline dyes, the telephone. It was found that standards could be raised appreciably by international competition; makers of chocolate, flannel, pastilles, liniment strove for gold and silver medals, pictures of which were proudly displayed on box or wrapping. The days are gone when it was better for a product to be old than new, but lists of awards at Paris exhibitions can still be found, for instance on the labels of Chocolat Mounier.

Exhibition halls, in their old age, tend to harden into museums. The Palais de Chaillot has become four, of which the ethnographic **Musée de l'Homme** (*open daily except Tuesday*, 10–5) is quite outstanding. Although they have nothing to do with Paris, the exhibits—a carved tom-tom, the royal throne of Dahomey, the Tortoise of Quirigua, mummies of Peruvian women—take on an added exoticism in so civilised a city. Some are on the gruesome side; perhaps that is why this alone among Paris museums boasts a bar.

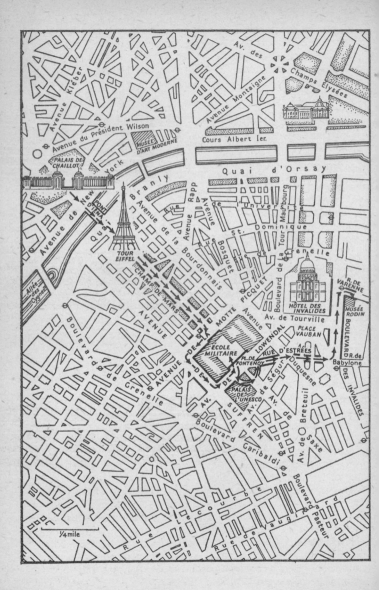

From the large central terrace of the Palais de Chaillot there is an excellent view across to the Champ de Mars and the École Militaire—the route we are going to follow. This palace, its garden and its view, appear to be a calm backwater withdrawn from shops and traffic, where the only sound is the roller-skates of well-dressed children from Passy playing tag on the concrete paths. Yet this district of exhibitions is neither a backwater nor a diversion: it is the outward sign of a profound, perennial Parisian ambition. Since at least the time of Richelieu Paris has aspired to be the capital of Europe. The first Napoleon saw the continent as an empire, the third as a group of united states, and those nineteenth-century exhibitions were a direct claim to leadership. Now the idea of a United States of Europe is again much in the air, and if the complexity of modern inventions makes the ordinary exhibition, intelligible to laymen, a thing of the past, Paris herself has now become the exhibition, witness the care lavished on drama and music festivals, on *Son et Lumière* and parades, on preserving the highest standards of architecture and statuary. Paris has long been eager for the spiritual hegemony of Europe. And I doubt whether her motives are wholly selfish. Paris feels a sense of mission towards her neighbours. Going one better than the adage 'Good Americans, when they die, go to Paris', her *arrière-pensée* seems to be this: When good Europeans are eventually born, they will be born in Paris.

How and in what way? By a moment of exaltation, a sudden vision of what Paris has given Europe, perhaps at a café table in Place St Germain des Prés, or perhaps crossing the Pont d'Iéna, as we do now, with its view of the curving Seine. The eagles on the pillars show that the bridge was built by the first Napoleon, and the by now familiar equestrian theme appears in the groups of Arab, Gallic, Greek and Roman horse-tamers. Once again Paris makes her claim to be the new Rome! The island down-stream is the **Allée des Cygnes**. The swans were first settled there by Louis XIV, and the statue at the far end is a small-scale bronze copy of Bartholdi's **Liberty Enlightening the World**, the original of which was presented by France to the United States.

Bartholdi's huge statue would never have got farther than the drawing-board but for a highly original interior iron framework constructed by a certain Gustave Eiffel. Eiffel had inaugurated the new Iron Age at the age of twenty-nine by spanning the Garonne with a metal viaduct 500 yards long. That viaduct linked the era of wooden and stone constructions to our twentieth-century steel and ferro-concrete structures.

Eiffel was a bridge-builder, inventor and engineer: in later life he confessed he was jealous of the 'flag-staff' as he called it, which, built as a curiosity from 1887 to 1889, perpetuated his name. For long the Tour Eiffel was simply the world's highest building. Now other new inventions have given it a function: it transmits radio and television programmes, and communicates with ships in the Atlantic. Even so, it would surely have been dismantled long ago had not it fitted in with the Paris scene. Scorned though it may be by some, the Tower has this of the Parisian spirit: it is an astonishingly light construction, almost bodiless. Moreover its legs have a vigorous spring and it soars in a completely original way, suggesting neither spire nor turret, column nor minaret.

The Tower is 984 feet high; five to eight inches higher in the warm sunshine months. (*Ascents daily* 10.45–6, *in winter not higher than the second platform.*) The view from the top platform is usually clearest an hour before sunset. Here, Gustave Eiffel built himself a flat to which, at the age of sixty-two, he retired like a new Simeon Stylites, in order to conduct experiments in aerodynamics.

The second platform allows the visitor to piece together the various parts of Paris which have been visited separately. It also allows him to rebuild in imagination to-morrow's Paris. For already plans are being made to change the outskirts almost as radically as Haussmann changed the medieval city. The first complex of tall buildings and shopping centre has already been completed at the end of the Rue de Rennes, near the Gare Montparnasse. Others are planned. It is hoped to pull down slums in eastern Paris and rebuild in such a way as to increase the area of grass and tree (Paris has only four square metres of greenery per inhabitant; London and Rome nine; Washington fifty). But the Paris préfecture, with more power than any other city junta in the world, is determined that the centre shall remain a city built to human scale. However many skyscrapers go up on the fringes, none are likely to be built in central Paris.

At a time when the capitals of the world are becoming more and more alike, responsible Parisians have decided that the centre of their city will retain its character. The respect we English show for the incidentals of history—judges' wigs and

State opening of Parliament—the French reserve above all for the look of their capital.

But how to solve the problem of growth? One interesting plan, entitled **Paris Parallèle**, proposed a new city of one million inhabitants (mainly families engaged in business and administration) some fifteen to twenty-five miles south-west of Paris. This would be a 'vertical' city of tall buildings, leaving 'horizontal' Paris intact. Motor-roads would connect the two, and most of the land in between would be declared a green belt.

This apparently excellent solution to Paris's perennial problem of crowded streets and traffic jams is too revolutionary to stand much chance of being adopted. Instead, French planners seem to favour enlarging provincial towns at about one hundred miles' distance from the capital, so that Paris will eventually be surrounded by a green belt, and outside that, an hour and a half's drive away, by a ring of small cities.

The **Champ de Mars** is, strictly speaking, the parade-ground of the École Militaire, but also an essential part of Exhibition Paris. Here in 1783 the first scientifically conceived balloon was released, landing three-quarters of an hour later near Gonesse where peasants took the billowing, bumping shape for a fabulous monster and attacked it with stones and sticks. The following year the Champ de Mars witnessed Blanchard's epoch-making balloon flight and ten years later Robespierre's fantastic Feast of the Supreme Being, complete with oxen-drawn carts and altar of the fatherland. Here, too, Napoleon's Italian trophies were displayed in 1798 and the Second Empire laid out a racecourse, before the days of Longchamp. To-day the Champ de Mars is a quiet, very unmartial park, with flower-beds and avenues conditioned by the great façade to the south-east.

The **École Militaire** is Madame de Pompadour's gift to Paris. It was she who supported the original plan to build a college for five hundred poor young gentlemen, preferably sons of officers killed or wounded on active service; to her Louis XV wrote, 'All right, go ahead with the plan, my little darling, since you insist'; it was the Pompadour who encouraged Gabriel (later to design the two great mansions flanking Place de la Concorde) and even paid the workmen sometimes from her own purse. Despite her patronage funds ran short and Gabriel was finally obliged to reduce his design by almost two-thirds.

The main façade, its central pavilion an odd mixture of Corinthian columns and squared, flattened domes, gives on to the Champ de Mars; the façade on the courtyard (to be seen from Place de Fontenoy) is richer and its attic windows recall the Invalides, which the École Militaire was intended to outshine. It is now the Staff College and the remarkable gilded woodcarving of its Salle des Maréchaux can be seen on Sundays by special permission of the Commandant d'Armes.

Confronting the École Militaire across two centuries is the **Palais de l'UNESCO**, completed in 1957 (*open daily*, 10–12; 3–7). Its three architects, the American Marcel Breuer, the Italian Pier Nervi and the Frenchman Bernard Zehrfuss, were faced with the problem of completing the semi-circle behind the École, half of it already occupied by two seven-story buildings housing Ministries. They chose a Y-shape, whose curved branches form three façades, each of eight stories.

This is democratic architecture: no portico, no *cour d'honneur*, but equally, no underprivileged side walls: each of the six hundred offices has a good view. The trapezoidal building standing apart is a conference hall: two of its walls bare, two others covered, like the secretariat building, with Italian travertin. Outside, a figure by Henry Moore ('Silhouette at Rest') and two ceramic panels by Joan Miró and Llorens Artigas ('Wall of the Sun'; 'Wall of the Moon'); inside, murals by Picasso and a vast photograph by Brassaï. Everyone will doubtless make up his own mind about this experiment in cosmopolitan design: will it, in a hundred years' time, be considered a curio like the Grand Palais, or as a masterpiece in direct line from the École Militaire and Invalides?

For amateurs of modern architecture, there are two other interesting new buildings which, however, happen to stand rather far from central Paris. One is the **Swiss Hostel**, designed in 1931-2 by Le Corbusier as part of the Cité Universitaire. Here a double row of heavy pieces of a complex moulded section carries a dormitory block that is boldly cantilevered out from them both front and back, the smooth, severe rectilinear structure being balanced by curved walls of rubble masonry. The second is the **Palais du Centre National des Industries et des Techniques**, on the western outskirts, at the Rond Point de la Défense. It is even newer than the UNESCO building and was also partly designed by Zehrfuss. Constructed of concrete, steel and glass, it dispenses altogether with walls, and its roof, the largest in the world, is supported at only three points. The Palais des Industries has three sides and yet another new building, NATO headquarters, has the ground plan of a big A. In Paris, this seems to be the age of the triangle.

From Place de Fontenoy, Rue d'Estrées leads to Boulevard des Invalides. Following this already familiar street, we turn right at Rue de Varenne. No. 77 is the **Hôtel Biron**, to my mind one of the pleasantest places in the world and therefore a fitting finale to any stay in Paris. (Used as the **Musée Rodin**. *Open daily except Tuesday*, 10–12.30; 2–5.) The house itself is not only beautiful—an early work by Gabriel—but of unusual historic interest. Built for a Languedoc wig-maker who had made a fortune in Law's Company of the Indies, it was soon bought by the Duc de Biron, marshal, peer of France and amateur gardener, whose tulip-beds were as famous as his sumptuous parties. After the Revolution, by a curious twist it passed into the hands of a saint—Madame Sophie Barat—who here installed a convent of the Sacred Heart. For almost a century girls of the noble Faubourg received their education at the Sacré Coeur, reading sound authors like Fénelon and Bossuet and learning to put on their white gloves as soon as a nun arrived in the room. When religious congregations were dissolved in 1904, the house became the property of the State, which allowed Rodin to use it as a studio on condition that he would bequeath to France the works he still possessed and organise the Rodin Museum at his own expense.

To-day the house and gardens are dominated by the presence, in his sculpture, of Auguste Rodin. He was born in Paris in 1840 and Paris-bred: a big, heavy man with massive head, small bright eyes, bony aquiline nose and—in later life—a bushy beard. After being rejected three times as a pupil at the Beaux Arts, he studied privately in Paris and Brussels, saving enough money to go to Italy, where he was influenced by Donatello and Michelangelo. 'I went to Rome to find what is found everywhere—the latent heroism of all natural movement.'

His earliest important work on display is **The Age of Brass** (1876). So perfect are the dimensions that when it was submitted to the Salon, Rodin was accused of having made a cast from a living body. The charge was unfounded. Like the Impressionists Rodin continued to suffer much from officialdom. 'The Academicians hold the keys of the Heaven of Arts,' he would often exclaim, 'and close the door to all original talent! But,' he would add, 'they themselves can never enter the Heaven of which they hold the keys.'

St John the Baptist (1878) was exhibited the following year at the Ghent Exhibition, where it won the gold medal. In this work Rodin, I think, was the first sculptor to express sanctity through the whole body: hard, lean torso, striding legs, excited, speaking arms. Rodin made himself as familiar with the nude as the Greeks had been; day after day nude models, men and women, were engaged to move about his studio at Meudon, to be sketched à l'improviste.

The Gate of Hell (1880–1917) was commissioned by the State for a projected Museum of the Decorative Arts. Its 186 figures include The Three Shadows (1880), their pointing gesture explained by the fact that in front of them should run a scroll with Dante's inscription: 'Abandon hope all you who enter here', and The Thinker (1879–1900), originally entitled 'The Poet'—that is, Dante.

The Bust of Jules Dalou (1883) depicts a friend and fellow-sculptor, though a rather conventional one, whose biggest work dominates the Place de la Nation. The suggestion of energy in the neck muscles, of nervous movement in the hair swept back above the ears, show Rodin attacking what he believed to be the radical problem of all good sculpture: discovering how an object moulded from the outside could be made to look as if it had grown from an inner necessity.

In Danaïde (1885) Rodin attempts what may be called his central theme: life issuing from matter, the interfusion of mineral, animal and human. 'When I have a beautiful woman's body as a model, the drawings I make of it also give me pictures of insects, birds and fishes . . . There is no need to create. To create, to improvise are words that mean nothing. Genius only comes to those who know how to use their eyes and their intelligence. A woman, a mountain or a horse are formed according to the same principles.'

Camille Claudel, Rodin's pupil, sat for the marble Thought (1886). Explaining why he had left the lower part of the marble rough, the sculptor said, 'I wanted the marble below to look as if the blood from the head were circulating through it.' And so it seems to do. But equally, I fancy, the rough stone pulls at the girl's thought, making it meander into reverie and daydream.

The **Burghers of Calais** (1884–6) takes as its subject an incident in the Hundred Years War, when six men of Calais marched off (as they feared) to death by hanging in order to save their town from destruction. The figures were first executed in the nude, and the municipality found fault with the burghers' 'insufficiently heroic' attitude. However, the group was finally set up, and a replica stands in London near the Houses of Parliament.

Polyphemus (1888) is shown in the act of breaking the rock he intends to hurl at Acis and Galatea. This handling of a familiar myth shows Rodin's originality in relation to his contemporaries. While they sought to tell a story or express an abstract idea, Rodin cuts through literary and allegoric associations (most of his works he left untitled, allowing friends to name them) and finds a much more fundamental subject matter: energy and movement.

The bronze **Prodigal Son** (before 1889) and **Despair** (1890) come from the right-hand part of the stupendous Gate at which he worked for almost forty years. 'After "The Burghers of Calais" my aim was to find ways of exaggerating logically —that is, by reasonable amplification of the modelling. That, also, consists in the constant reduction of the face to a geometrical figure, and the resolve to sacrifice every part of the face to the synthesis of its aspect . . . In sculpture the projection of the sheaths of muscles must be accentuated, the shortenings heightened, the holes made deeper. Sculpture is the art of the hole and the lump, not the straightness of smooth faces.'

At his figure of **Balzac** (1897) Rodin slaved for seven years. Working from thick-set, medium-sized models with heavy limbs and short arms, he completed no less than seven portraits in different positions. After these studies he created a Balzac much like the one in Nadar's daguerreotype. But he felt this was not final, and returned to the pen-portrait by Lamartine, to the lines: 'He had the face of an element,' and 'he possessed so much soul that his heavy body seemed not to exist.' This is the Balzac he has left us, flashing with creative force. And it was refused by the Société des Gens de Lettres, which had placed the commission!

The marble **Bust of Bernard Shaw** (1906) is so faithful a resemblance that Charlotte Shaw confessed to Rodin that it sometimes frightened her. Rilke, Rodin's secretary at the time, tells how Rodin began work by taking the measurement from the top of the head to the tip of the beard with big iron callipers, then from nose to back of head and ear to ear, from behind. 'After he has made a quick incision for the eyebrows so that something resembling a nose is formed, and has determined the position of the mouth by a slit such as children make in a snowman, he begins, with the model standing quite close, to shape four profiles, then eight, then sixteen, making the model turn after every three minutes . . . You feel somehow that his lightning, hawk-like swoops only fashion one of all the faces that pour into him.'[1]

Finally, a work in stone, **The Cathedral** (1908): a gesture of prayer which also suggests the high-pointed Gothic arch. Rodin was passionately fond of the French cathedrals and his own art too is founded on deep religious awareness. His sister was a nun and Rodin for a short time, at the age of twenty-three, joined the Eudists before discovering that he did not have a vocation. With Rodin, the virtue of humility becomes reverence for Nature, reverence for the body in all its parts, reverence for every detail that expresses spirit. Hence the importance in his work of hands: outstretched, loving hands and hands that sleep, hands turned to claws by pain and gentle hands, St John's prophetic, pointing finger and the leaden clenched fists of the burghers of Calais.

One thinks of Rodin, of the hands that made these hands, of the hundred lives those hands lived in order to create this walled city, this garden peopled with people so living that it is the passer-by, the spectator, the mother seated knitting on a bench who look unreal. One imagines Rodin sitting or standing here, or in his garden at Meudon, a craggy figure sucking the barley-sugar, specially sent from Dijon, which he always carried about with him: drinking an infusion of lime or camomile, borage or cherry-stalks—these herbal remedies were part of his reverence for Nature—pencil or clay in his fingers, ceaselessly observing the human body; in Rilke's words, 'slowly learning to live, to be patient, to work and never to overlook the slightest thing that can give rise to joy.'

All who knew him speak of Rodin's *joie de vivre*, his underlying gaiety. We feel this gaiety ourselves in his statues. Can Rodin's gaiety have anything to do with the gaiety implied by the phrase 'gay Paris'? We may incline to dismiss the idea as far-fetched, and the phrase as cant, but I think that would be

[1] *Selected Letters of Rainer Maria Rilke*, translated by R. F. C. Hull.

a mistake. 'As long as Paris exists,' Nostradamus predicted four centuries ago, 'there will be gaiety in the world,' and we have come to know at first hand that Paris is indeed a gay city, yet the nature of that gaiety has so far proved elusive. The time has come to try to define it.

Parisians work hard and put a great deal into their work. Whether selling a bottle of perfume or dressing a shop-window, designing or modelling a hat, sticking up a poster or preparing *faisan trufflé*, the Parisian does it 'with style', that is, in a way which seeks both objective perfection and the expression of his own individuality. He treats work as a way of winning new ground, a continual extension of frontiers. But this was precisely Rodin's philosophy. Work and again work —incessant work. Few have worked so hard as he. And from work came joy: the joy of new discovery, the joy of self-expression.

The gaiety of Paris, is, I believe, largely the gaiety of people who find themselves in their work. Agreed that many Parisians have routine jobs, roles which allow little personal nuance, there are, all the same, sufficient craftsmen and artists (in the broad sense) to set a tone. It is they who put the sparkle into the champagne. It is they who make it good to be in Paris, they who have designed the long tree-lined vistas, filled the shops with finery and laid out houses and gardens such as the Musée Rodin. But being artists, they have also been passion-ate, impulsive and insubordinate. It is because of their passionately held political beliefs that Paris has killed its king, racked its noblemen, shot its archbishop, murdered Pro-testants and even now, at any moment, may rise again in sudden anger to tear down the Government. This is one of the patterns I see in Paris: a wonderful, deep, centuries-long surge of creative power, and beneath, a dark, destructive undertow. But destructive only for a moment, if we are to believe the city's motto: *Fluctuat nec Mergitur*.

'*On ferme, on ferme.*' The keepers make their last tour. It is time to leave Rodin's world and step out once again into the streets of Paris, to wander back, perhaps through Faubourg St Germain to see the sun set along the river, or up to St Germain des Prés and coffee at the *Deux Magots*, or, farther still, to Notre Dame and the island where Paris began. It is time to take a last look before the journey home. The gilded dome of the Invalides, the unequal towers of St Sulpice, the five arches of the Pont Royal: certain landmarks have become familiar; and certain moments—the curtain-line of the latest Anouilh, the smell of croissants and horse-chestnut leaves and warm air from the grilles of the Métro, the notes of an accordion, the candle-flame in a La Tour painting—these have become good memories, ineffaceable memories. One returns home, yes, but one never quite leaves Paris.

Appendices

Places of Interest not mentioned in the text

ARÈNES DE LUTÈCE, 14 Rue des Arènes (Métro: Monge).
Roman remains of the second and third centuries. 36 tiers
of seats overlook what was probably an arena for games
and gladiatorial combats. Open from early morning to dusk,
or until 11 in June, July and August.

ARSENAL LIBRARY, 1–3 Rue de Sully (Métro: Sully Morland).
The second largest library in France, housed in the former
residence of the Grand Master of the Arsenal. Illuminated
MSS and theatrical collection. The eighteenth-century
apartments retain their furniture. Open 10–5 daily except
Sundays and holidays. Closed 1–15 September. The apartments are open on Thursdays only, 2–4.

CHURCH OF ST MERRI, 76 Rue de la Verrerie (Métro: Châtelet).
Flamboyant Gothic church, built 1520–1612 on the site of
St Merri's seventh-century oratory. Interesting carved key-
stones, vaulting, rose-windows and woodwork.

CHURCH OF ST PAUL ST LOUIS, 99 Rue St Antoine (Métro:
St Paul). Built for the Jesuits by Louis XIII in 1627–41;
earliest example of the Jesuit style in France. Contains an
early Delacroix, 'Christ in the Garden of Olives,' and three
paintings attributed to Simon Vouet.

CHURCH OF ST ROCH, 296 Rue St Honoré (Métro: Tuileries).
Built 1653–1754, the church is of little interest architec-
turally but contains a statue of Cardinal Dubois by Coustou,
a group of the Nativity by the Anguier brothers, 'Healing
of the "Mal des Ardents"' by Doyen and a bust of Le
Nôtre by Coysevox. The walls of the church are marked
with part of Napoleon's 'whiff of grapeshot', with which on
5th October 1795 he crushed a Royalist rising.

FONTAINE DES QUATRE SAISONS, 57–59 Rue de Grenelle (Métro:
Bac). When the noble Faubourg complained that it lacked
water, the elder Turgot provided this stately public fountain. Bouchardon's sculptures (1739–45) show Paris
between the Seine and Marne. The wings are decorated
with the Seasons and *génies*.

HÔTEL DE BRUANT, 1 Rue de la Perle (Métro: St Sébastien
Froissart). Built for himself in 1685 by Libéral Bruant. The
façade is one of the most beautiful in the Marais.

HÔTEL DE CHALONS-LUXEMBOURG, 26 Rue Geoffroy l'Asnier (Métro: St Paul). Louis XIII house notable chiefly for its gateway, built in 1659, framed with Ionic pilasters, its tympanum decorated with a lion's head and coat of arms.

HÔTEL DE DELISLE-MANSART, 22 Rue St Gilles (Métro: Chemin Vert). A small house in the Marais built for himself by the architect Delisle-Mansart.

HÔTEL DE JUIGNÉ, 5 Rue de Thorigny (Métro: St Sébastien Froissart). Built in 1656 by Jean Boullier for one of Louis XIV's tax-collectors, hence its other name: Hôtel Salé. The interior, notable for its wrought-iron staircase, can be visited on Thursday afternoons from November to the end of June.

HÔTEL LAMOIGNON, 24 Rue Pavée (Métro: St Paul). Built in 1580 for Diane de France, whose taste for hunting appears in the allegories on the pediment. The architect is believed to have been Jacques Androuet du Cerceau. A literary meeting-place in the seventeenth and again in the nineteenth century.

MOSQUE, Place du Puits de l'Ermite (Métro: Censier Daubenton). Built 1922-5. The patio was inspired by that of the Alhambra in Granada. Next to the Muslim Institute. Open 2-5 daily except Friday.

MUSÉE BOURDELLE, 16 Rue Antoine Bourdelle (Métro: Montparnasse Bienvenue). Antoine Bourdelle (1860–1929) is best known for his high-reliefs on the Théâtre des Champs Elysées. His towering, monumental figures sometimes achieve grandeur, sometimes are emptily grandiose. 500 of his sculptures have been arranged in his former studio (a typical Montparnasse studio of the period), to which new rooms have been added: it is the only Paris museum built purposely for what it contains. As well as the permanent collection, first-rate exhibitions of contemporary sculpture are shown twice yearly. Open 10–12; 2-5 (6 in summer) except Tuesdays.

MUSÉE MARMOTTAN, 2 Rue Louis Boilly (Métro: Muette). 65 paintings by Claude Monet, mostly done during the last years of his life. The subjects include willows, irises, wistaria, large water lilies, Japanese bridges, portraits and landscapes. The collection was bequeathed to the Museum in 1966 and has been on display since 1971. Open 10–6 except Monday.

PARC DES BUTTES CHAUMONT (Métro: Buttes Chaumont). A picturesque park laid out by Napoleon III and Haussmann on the site of disused gypsum quarries. A lake, waterfall, rocks, grottoes and Roman-style temple. Open 5 to dusk.

PARC MONCEAU (Métro: Villiers, Monceau). Laid out by Philippe Egalité in 1778. Of the original 'fantasies' a pyramid and naumachia remain. Particularly pleasant on Sundays when children from the 8th arrondissement play here. Open 8 to dusk.

PÈRE LACHAISE CEMETERY (Métro: Père Lachaise, Philippe Auguste). The property, which formerly belonged to the Jesuits, owes its name to Louis XIV's confessor. Transformed into a cemetery in 1803. Among the monuments and tombs are those of Abélard and Héloïse, Molière, La Fontaine, Cherubini, Balzac (bust by David d'Angers) and Oscar Wilde (by Epstein). Open daily 7.30–6 (8–5 in winter).

RUE MOUFFETARD (Métro: Monge). A Roman road to Italy via Fontainebleau and Lyons, with curious shop-signs (No. 6, No. 69 and No. 122), old houses and an excellent street market.

STATUE OF JOAN OF ARC, Place de Rivoli (Métro: Tuileries). A bronze-gilt statue by Frémiet near the spot where Joan of Arc fell wounded while attacking the now demolished Porte St Honoré, part of the city's western defences. Annual pilgrimage on 30th May.

STATUE OF MARSHAL NEY, corner of Boulevard du Montparnasse and Avenue de l'Observatoire (Métro: Port Royal). Rude's monument to one of Napoleon's marshals was erected near his place of execution. The statue's energy and suggestion of movement appealed to Rodin, who considered it the most beautiful in Paris.

TOUR DE JEAN SANS PEUR, 20 Rue Etienne Marcel (Métro: Etienne Marcel). Early fourteenth-century tower belonging to the former Hôtel de Bourgogne, where plays of Corneille and Racine were staged. Notable for its decorated spiral staircase.

100 Hotels

The hotels are listed, within each arrondissement, by price.

1st Arrondissement

Louvre – Tuileries – Palais Royal – Place Vendôme – Les Halles

luxury	RITZ, 15 Place Vendôme
****	VENDÔME, 1 Place Vendôme
****	SAINT JAMES ET D'ALBANY, 211 Rue St Hònoré
***	CASTILLE, 37 Rue Cambon
***	MONT THABOR, 4 Rue du Mont Thabor
**	LOUIS LE GRAND, 3 Rue Rouget de Lisle
**	SAINT ROMAIN, 5 Rue St Roch
*	NANTES, 55 Rue St Roch

2nd Arrondissement

Grands Boulevards – Bourse – Rue de la Paix – Le Sentier

****	WESTMINSTER, 13 Rue de la Paix
****	LOUVOIS, 1 Rue Lulli
***	NOAILLES (de), 9 Rue de la Michodière
**	OPÉRA COMIQUE, 4 Rue d'Amboise
*	GRAMONT, 22 Rue de Gramont

4th Arrondissement

Notre Dame – Île St Louis – Hôtel de Ville – Palais de Justice

*	BRETONNERIE, 22 Rue Ste Croix de la Bretonnerie
*	MALHER, 5 Rue Malher
*	SAINT LOUIS, 75 Rue St Louis en l'Île
*	GRAND TURENNE, 6 Rue de Turenne
*	IDÉAL, 22 bis Rue de la Verrerie

*   SANSONNET, 48 Rue de la Verrerie
*   SPÉRIA, 1 Rue de la Bastille

5th Arrondissement

Quartier Latin – La Sorbonne – Panthéon – Arènes de Lutèce

**   CLAUDE BERNARD, 43 Rue des Ecoles
**   MONT BLANC, 28 Rue de la Huchette
*   HARPE, 6 Rue de la Harpe
*   SELECT, 1 Place de la Sorbonne
*   LABYRINTHE, 5 Rue Linné
*   SPHINX, 21 Rue Galande

6th Arrondissement

St Germain des Prés – Luxembourg – St Sulpice – Les Beaux Arts-Facultés

****   LITTRÉ, 9 Rue Littré
****   LUTÉTIA, 43 Boulevard Raspail
****   RELAIS BISSON, 37 Quai des Grands Augustins
***   VICTORIA PALACE, 6 Rue Blaise Desgoffe
***   ANGLETERRE (*d'*), 44 Rue Jacob
***   MADISON, 143 Boulevard St Germain
***   NICE ET DES BEAUX ARTS (*de*), 4 bis Rue des Beaux Arts
***   PARIS DINARD, 29 Rue Cassette
***   PAS DE CALAIS, 59 Rue des Saints Pères
***   SAINTS PÈRES (*des*), 65 Rue des Saints Pères
***   SÉNAT (*du*), 22 Rue St Sulpice
**   AVENIR (*de l'*), 65 Rue Madame
**   BONAPARTE, 61 Rue Bonaparte
**   TRIANON PALACE, 1 bis et 3 Rue de Vaugirard
**   SAINT GERMAIN DES PRÉS, 36 Rue Bonaparte
**   NICE (*de*), 155 Boulevard du Montparnasse
**   RÉCAMIER, 3 bis Place St Sulpice
**   RÉSIDENCE MONTPARNASSE, 14 Rue Stanislas
**   SAINT GEORGES, 49 Rue Bonaparte
**   STUDIO, 4 Rue du Vieux Colombier
*   DEUX CONTINENTS, 25 Rue Jacob
*   PARNASSE, 126 Rue du Cherche Midi

7th Arrondissement

Tour Eiffel – Invalides – École Militaire – Palais Bourbon

****	PONT ROYAL,	7 Rue Montalembert
****	PALAIS D'ORSAY,	7–9 Quai Anatole France
***	MONTALEMBERT,	3 Rue Montalembert
***	SAINT SIMON,	14 Rue Saint Simon
***	QUAI VOLTAIRE,	19 Quai Voltaire
**	SOLFÉRINO,	91 Rue de Lille
*	ORSAY,	50 Rue du Bac
*	VALENCE (*de*),	10 Rue de Lille

8th Arrondissement

Champs Elysées – Étoile – Concorde – Madeleine – St Lazarre

luxury	CRILLON (*de*),	10 Place de la Concorde
luxury	GEORGE V,	31 Avenue George V
luxury	LANCASTER,	7 Rue de Berri
luxury	ROYAL MONCEAU,	35–39 Avenue Hoche
****	CLARIDGE,	74 Avenue des Champs Elysées
****	QUEEN ELIZABETH,	41 Avenue Pierre Ier de Serbie
****	CASTIGLIONE (*de*),	40 Rue du Faubourg St Honoré
***	ARCADE (*de l'*),	7 Rue de l'Arcade
***	ELYSÉES PALACE,	12 Rue de Marignan
***	RÉSIDENCE SAINT PHILIPPE,	123 Rue du Faubourg St Honoré
**	BERRI,	8 Rue Frédéric Bastiat
**	LAVOISIER,	21 Rue Lavoisier

9th Arrondissement

Opéra – Grands Boulevards – Place Pigalle

****	AMBASSADOR,	16 Boulevard Haussmann
****	SCRIBE,	1 Rue Scribe
***	SAINT PÉTERSBOURG,	33 Rue Caumartin
***	PROUST,	68 Rue des Martyrs
**	CAUMARTIN,	27 Rue Caumartin

** FRANCE ET D'ALBION (*de*), 11 Rue Notre Dame de Lorette

16th Arrondissement

Palais de Chaillot – Bois de Boulogne – Passy

luxury RAPHAËL, 17 Avenue Kléber
**** LA PÉROUSE, 40 Rue La Pérouse
**** IÉNA (*d'*), 28 Avenue d'Iéna
**** BALTIMORE, 88 bis Avenue Kléber
*** RÉGINA DE PASSY, 6 Rue de la Tour
*** UNION ÉTOILE, 44 Rue Hamelin
*** SYLVA, 3 Rue Pergolèse
*** ALEXANDER, 102 Avenue Victor Hugo
*** BELMONT (*Le*), 30 Rue de Bassano
** FARNÈSE, 32 Rue Hamelin
** KEPPLER, 12 Rue Keppler
** MARCEAU (*Villa*), 37 Avenue Marceau

17th Arrondissement

Étoile – Porte Maillot – Parc Monceau

**** SPLENDID, 1 bis Avenue Carnot
*** BALMORAL, 6 Rue de Général Lanrezac
*** CÉCILIA, 11 Avenue MacMahon
*** RÉGENCE ÉTOILE (*La*), 24 Avenue Carnot
** ASTRID, 27 Avenue Carnot
** DEMOURS (*Le*), 14 Rue Pierre Demours
** MICHELLE, 129 Avenue de Villiers
** TRIUMPH, 1 bis Rue Troyon
** VILLIERS CHAMPERRET, 139 Avenue de Villiers

18th Arrondissement

Montmartre – Sacré Coeur

*** TERRASS, 12 Rue Joseph de Maistre
** ALSINA, 39 Avenue Junot
** BOURGES, 100 Boulevard Rochechouart
** BECQUEREL, 4–6 Rue Becquerel
** LUXIA, 8 Rue Seveste

Restaurants

The leading 'gastronomic temples', and some of their best known dishes. All are expensive or very expensive, and it is necessary to book. Many are closed in August.

ALLARD, 41 Rue St André des Arts—326-48-23. Canard aux olives, game in season

CHEZ ALBERT, 122 Avenue du Maine—783-47-62. Homard poché aux herbes, carré d'agneau aux aromates

CHEZ GARIN, 9 Rue Lagrange—033-13-99. Truite soufflée

CHEZ MICHEL, 10 Rue Belzunce—878-44-14. Caneton grillé, shellfish

DROUANT, Place Gaillon—73-53-72. Coquille de homard, sole au champagne

GRAND VÉFOUR, 17 Rue de Beaujolais—742-58-97. Lamproie bordelaise, ortolans, bécasse bordelaise in season.

LA BOURGOGNE, 6 Avenue Bosquet—705-96-78. Traditional Burgundy dishes

LA COQUILLE, 6 Rue Debarcadère—380-25-95. Fish and shell-fish

LA MARÉE, 1 Rue Daru—924-52-42. Belons au champagne, demoiselle de Cherbourg.

LAPÉROUSE, 51 Quai des Grands Augustins—326-68-04. Gratin de langoustines, canard nantais

LASSERRE, 17 Avenue Franklin D. Roosevelt—359-53-43. Feuilleté de langoustines Kermor, pannequet soufflé flambé

LEDOYEN, Carré Champs Elysées—265-47-82. Sole soufflée à l'armoricaine, canard sauvage in season

LUCAS CARTON, 9 Place de la Madeleine—265-22-90. Casso-lette queues d'ecrevisses, bécasse flambée

MAXIM'S, 3 Rue Royale—265-27-94. Canetons aux pêches, crêpes Veuve Joyeuse

RÉGENCE PLAZA, 27 Avenue Montaigne—359-85-23. Soufflé de homard Plaza, soufflé glacé Clermont

RELAIS DES PYRÉNÉES, 1 Rue Jourdain—636-65-81. Basque specialities

RELAIS PARIS-EST, Gare de l'Est—607-72-23. Noisettes d'agneau charmereine

RITZ, 15 Place Vendôme—073-28-30. Gratin de langoustines Espadon, crêpes Roxelane

TAILLEVENT, 15 Rue Lamennais—359-39-94. Terrine de brochét, ris de veau florentine

TOUR D'ARGENT, 15 Quai de la Tournelle—033-23-32. Filets de sole cardinal, caneton Tour d'Argent

VIVAROIS, 192 Avenue Victor Hugo—870-94-31. Coq au pommard, gratin à la mode du Dauphine

Inexpensive Places to Eat

Self-service cafeterias or small bars

Latin Quarter – St Germain des Prés – Montparnasse – Grenelle:
BIARD, 63 Boulevard Saint Michel
BRETONNIÈRE, 7 Rue Sainte Croix
CAPOULADE, 63 Boulevard Saint Michel
GLOBBE CONVENTION, 349 Rue de Vaugirard
LA SOURCE, 35 Boulevard Saint Michel
LATIN, 96 Boulevard Saint Germain
LATIN CLUNY, 98 Boulevard Saint Germain
LIBRE SERVICE, Place Edmond Rostand
LIBRE SERVICE, 77 Rue Père Corentin
MONGE, 83 Rue Monge
MONTPARNASSE, 47 Boulevard Montparnasse
SAINT GERMAIN, 168 Boulevard Saint Germain

Place de la République:
BONNE NOUVELLE, 26 Boulevard Bonne Nouvelle
BORDAIS, 149 Rue Amelot
ENGHIEN, 19 Rue d'Enghien
GARE DU NORD, 25 Rue de Dunkerque
GONCOURT, 77 Rue du Faubourg du Temple
STRASBOURG, 1 Boulevard de Strasbourg

Opéra – Palais Royal – Bourse:
BERLITZ, 24 Passage des Princes
BOURSE, 2 Rue du 4 Septembre
CAUMARTIN, 33 Rue Caumartin

CLICHY, 88 Rue de Clichy
GARE ST LAZARE, 2 Rue d'Amsterdam
GRAND VATEL, 275 Rue Saint Honoré
HAUSSMANN, 12 Boulevard Haussmann
ITALIENS, 9 Boulevard des Italiens
LA BIELLA, 73 Rue de Provence
LE NÈGRE, 17 Boulevard Saint Denis
LE RALLYE, 35 Boulevard des Capucines
LIBRE SERVICE DES GALERIES LAFAYETTE, Boulevard Haussmann
LIBRE SERVICE DES MAGASINS DU LOUVRE, Place du Palais Royal
L'INCROYABLE, 23 Rue Montpensier
OPÉRA, 23 Boulevard des Capucines
PALAIS BERLITZ, 19 Rue de la Michodière
RÉGENCE, 161 Rue Saint Honoré
REX, 2 and 6 Boulevard Poissonière
ROYAL, 12 Boulevard Montmartre
TUILERIES, 208 Rue de Rivoli

Etoile – Champs Elysées – St Lazare – Madeleine – Passy:
AUBERGE EXPRESS, 124 Rue de la Boétie
CAFÉTÉRIA MARBEUF, 5 Rue Marbeuf
CHICKEN SELF, 67 Rue Pierre Charron
CLICHY, 3 Place Clichy
ELYSÉE, Avenue des Champs Elysées
HAVRE, 5 Rue du Havre
LES ESSAIS, 40 Avenue Montaigne
LIBRE SERVICE, 34 Avenue des Champs Elysées
LUCE, 45 Avenue de Leningrad
SELF SERVICE, 8 Rue du Havre
SORESPA, 65 Avenue des Champs Elysées
WASHINGTON, 5 Rue de Washington

Museums

The times listed below are subject to alteration, usually unpredictably and without warning. They should be checked in the current number of *Une Semaine de Paris.*

	MÉTRO STATION	TIMES OF OPENING
General		
THE LOUVRE	Place du Carrousel Palais Royal	*10–5 except Tues.*
MUSÉE DES MONUMENTS FRANÇAIS	Place du Trocadéro Trocadéro	*10–5 except Tues.*

The Art of an Epoch

MUSÉE DE CLUNY (*Middle Ages*)	6 Place Paul Painlevé	St Michel	*10–12.45 and 2–5 except Tues.*
PETIT PALAIS (*Renaissance, French art 19th and 20th centuries*)	Avenue Alexandre III	Champs Elysées Clémenceau	*Visible when an important exhibition is held in the Petit Palais*
MUSÉE NISSIM DE CAMONDO (*18th century*)	63 Rue de Monceau	Villiers	*Weekdays, except Tues. 2–5; Sun. 10–12; 2–5*
MUSÉE JACQUEMART ANDRÉ (*18th century*)	158 Boulevard Haussmann	St Philippe du Roule	*2–6 except Tues.*
MUSÉE COGNACQ-JAY (*18th century*)	25 Boulevard des Capucines	Opéra	*10–12, 2–5 except Tues.*
GALERIE DU JEU DE PAUME (*Impressionism*)	Jardin des Tuileries	Concorde	*10–5 except Tues.*
MUSÉE DE L'ORANGERIE (*Monet's 'Les Nymphéas'*)	Jardin des Tuileries	Concorde	*10–5 except Tues.*
MUSÉE D'ART MODERNE	Avenue de New York	Iéna	*10–5 except Tues.*

The Art of the Far East

MUSÉE GUIMET (*Asiatic art, particularly Indo-Chinese sculpture*)	6 Place d'Iéna	Iéna	*10–5 except Tues.*
MUSÉE CERNUSCHI (*Arts of China and Japan*)	7 Avenue Vélasquez	Monceau, Villiers	*10–12, 2–5*
PETIT PALAIS (*Chinese vases*)	Avenue Alexandre III	Champs Elysées Clémenceau	*Visible when an important exhibition is held in the Petit Palais*

Historical Museums

ARCHIVES NATIONALES (*Museum of the History of France*)	60 Rue des Francs Bourgeois	Rambuteau, Hôtel de Ville	*2–5 except Tues.*
MUSÉE CARNAVALET (*Museum of the History of Paris*)	23 Rue de Sévigné	St Paul	*10–12, 2–6 except Tues.*
MUSÉE DU COSTUME DE LA VILLE DE PARIS	11 Avenue du Président Wilson	Iéna, Alma Marceau	*10–12, 2–5 except Tues.*
MUSÉE NATIONAL DE LA FRANCE D'OUTRE-MER (*French colonial history*)	293 Avenue Daumesnil	Porte Dorée	*2–6 except Tues.*
MUSÉE DU VIEUX MONTMARTRE	12 Rue Cortot	Lamarck	*2–5 except Tues.*

		MÉTRO STATION	TIMES OF OPENING
Historical Museums			
MUSÉE DE LA PRÉFECTURE DE POLICE (*The police, past and present*)	36 Quai des Orfèvres	Cité	*Thurs.: 2–5*
MUSÉE DE L'ASSISTANCE PUBLIQUE (*Poor Law administration history*)	47 Quai de la Tournelle	Maubert Mutualité, Cité	*10–12, 2–5 except Tues.*

Scientific Museums

MUSÉE DE L'HOMME (*Anthropology and Ethnology*)	Palais de Chaillot	Trocadéro	*10–5 except Tues.*

		MÉTRO STATION	TIMES OF OPENING
PALAIS DE LA DÉCOUVERTE (*Contemporary science, planetarium*)	Avenue Franklin D. Roosevelt	Champs Elysées Clémenceau, Franklin Roosevelt	*10–12, 2–6 except Fri.*
MUSÉE NATIONAL D'HISTOIRE NATURELLE	57 Rue Cuvier	Jussieu, Gare d' Orléans Austerlitz	*1.30–5 except Tues. The zoo is open 9–5 (7 in summer)*
CONSERVATOIRE NATIONAL DES ARTS ET MÉTIERS (*Scientific instruments, machines, models*)	292 Rue St Martin	Arts et Métiers	*1.30–5.30 except Mon.; 10–5 Sun.*
MUSÉE DES PHARES ET BALISES (*Lighthouses and beacons*)	43 Avenue du Président Wilson	Trocadéro	*Opening times vary. Tel.* KLE 83–04

The Arts of War

MUSÉE DE L'ARMÉE (*Weapons, armour, trophies*)	Hôtel des Invalides	Invalides	*10–12.15, 1.30–5 except Tues.; 1.30–5 Sun.*
MUSÉE DE LA MARINE (*Warships, pleasure boats*)	Palais de Chaillot	Trocadéro	*10–5 except Tues.*
MUSÉE DE LA LÉGION D'HONNEUR (*History of the Orders of Chivalry*)	2 Rue de Belle- chasse	Solférino	*Thurs. and Sat. 2–5*

Arts and Education

MUSÉE PÉDAGOGIQUE (*Children's work, documents*)	29 Rue d'Ulm	Odéon	*9–12, 2–6 except Sat. afternoon*
MUSÉE DE LA PAROLE (*Recordings by famous men*)	19 Rue des Bernardins	Maubert	*Thurs. 2.30–5.30*
MUSÉE INSTRUMENTAL DU CONSERVATOIRE (*Musical instruments*)	14 Rue de Madrid	Europe	*Thurs. and Sat.: 2–4*
MUSÉE DE L'OPÉRA (*Operatic history, including Carpeaux's bust of Garnier and Renoir's portrait of Wagner*)	Place Charles Garnier	Opéra	*10–5 except Sun.*
MUSÉE DE L'ÉCOLE DES BEAUX-ARTS (*Prize-winning paint- ings, mouldings*)	17 Quai Malaquais	St Germain des Prés	*By appointment with the director*
MUSÉE DES ARTS ET TRADITIONS POPULAIRES (*French folklore*)	Palais de Chaillot	Trocadéro	*Temporary exhibi- tions announced in the Press*

The Story of an Object

CABINET DES MÉD- AILLES ET DES ANTIQUES (*Medals, cameos, jewellery*)	Bibliothèque Na- tionale, 58 Rue de Richelieu	Bourse	*10–4 except Sun.*
MUSÉE DE LA MON- NAIE (*Medals, coins*)	11 Quai de Conti	Odéon, Pont Neuf	*11–5, except Sat. and Sun.*
MUSÉE POSTAL (*Complete collection of French stamps*)	4 Rue St Romain	Vaneau	*2–6, except Tues.*

		MÉTRO STATION	TIMES OF OPENING
MUSÉE DES ARTS DECORATIFS (*The story of French and foreign furniture*)	Palais du Louvre, Pavillon de Marsan, 107 Rue de Rivoli	Palais Royal, Tuileries	*10–12, 2–5 except Tues.*
MUSÉE DE LA MANUFACTURE DES GOBELINS (*Tapestry*)	42 Avenue des Gobelins	Gobelins	*2–4 on Wed., Thurs. and Fri.*

Houses of Artists, etc.

MUSÉE RODIN	77 Rue de Varenne	Invalides	*10–12.30; 2–5 except Tues.*
MUSÉE BOURDELLE	16 Rue Antoine Bourdelle	Montparnasse Bienvenue	*10–12, 2–5 except Tues.*
MUSÉE BALZAC	47 Rue Raynouard	Passy	*1.30–5 except Tues.*
MUSÉE CLEMENCEAU	8 Rue Franklin	Trocadéro Passy	*Sun., Thurs. and Sat.: 2–5*
MUSÉE DELACROIX	6 Place Furstenberg	St Germain des Prés	*May–November:*
MUSÉE VICTOR HUGO	6 Place des Vosges	Bastille, St Paul, Chemin Vert	*10–12, 2–5 (6 in summer) except Tues. and public holidays*

Theatres, Music-Halls, Chansonniers

	ADDRESS	TELEPHONE	MÉTRO STATION
Opera Houses			
OPÉRA	Place de l'Opéra	073–95–26	Opéra
OPÉRA COMIQUE	5 Rue Favart	742–72–00	Richelieu Drouot
State-subsidised Theatres			
COMÉDIE FRANÇAISE	Place du Théâtre Français	742–22–70	Palais Royal
THÉÂTRE NATIONAL POPULAIRE	Palais de Chaillot	553–27–79	Trocadéro
THÉÂTRE NATIONAL DE L'ODÉON	1 Place Paul Claudel	326–58–13	Odéon
THÉÂTRE DE LA VILLE	2 Place du Châtelet	326–35–39	Châtelet
THÉÂTRE DE L'EST PARISIEN	17 Rue Malte Brun	636–79–09	Gambetta
Theatres			
AMBASSADEURS	1 Avenue Gabriel	265–97–60	Concorde
ANTOINE	14 Boulevard de Strasbourg	208–77–71	Strasbourg
ATELIER	Place Charles Dullin	606–49–24	Pigalle
ATHÉNÉE	4 Square de l'Opéra	073–82–23	Madeleine, Opéra
BOUFFES-PARISIENS	4 Rue Monsigny	073–87–94	4 Septembre
CHARLES DE ROCHEFORT	64 Rue du Rocher	522–08–40	Villiers
CHÂTELET	Place du Châtelet	488–44–80	Châtelet
COMÉDIE DES CHAMPS ELYSÉES	15 Avenue Montaigne	359–37–03	Alma Marceau
ÉDOUARD VII	8 Place Édouard VII	073–67–90	Opéra
ÉLYSÉE MONTMARTRE	72 Boulevard Rochechouart	606–38–79	Pigalle

EUROPÉEN VAUDEVILLE	5 Rue Biot	522–53–32	Clichy
FONTAINE	10 Rue Fontaine	784–74–40	Blanche
GRAMONT	30 Rue Gramont	742–62–61	Richelieu Drouot
GYMNASE	38 Boulevard Bonne Nouvelle	770–16–15	Bonne Nouvelle
HÉBERTOT	78 bis Boulevard des Batignolles	387–23–23	Rome
HUCHETTE	23 Rue de la Huchette	326–38–99	St Michel
KALEIDOSCOPE	5 Rue Frederic Sauton	633–26–96	Maubert Mutualité
MADELEINE	19 Rue de Surène	265–07–09	Madeleine
MARIGNY	Avenue de Marigny	256–04–41	Champs Elysées
MATHURINS	36 Rue des Mathurins	265–90–00	Havre Caumartin
MICHEL	38 Rue des Mathurins	265–35–02	Havre Caumartin
MICHODIÈRE	4 bis Rue de la Micho- dière	742–95–22	Opéra
MODERNE	15 Rue Blanche	874–94–28	Trinité
MOGADOR	25 Rue de Mogador	285–28–80	Trinité
MONTPARNASSE	31 Rue de la Gaîté	633–41–77	Gaîté, Montparnasse
NOUVEAUTÉS	24 Boulevard Poisson- nière	770–52–76	Montmartre
OEUVRE	55 Rue de Clichy	874–42–52	Trinité
PALAIS ROYAL	38 Rue Montpensier	742–84–29	4 Septembre
PIGALL'S	77 Rue Pigalle	526–04–43	Pigalle
PLAISANCE	111 Rue de Château	273–12–65	Gaîté
POCHE MONTPARNASSE	75 Boulevard Mont- parnasse	548–92–97	Montparnasse
PORTE SAINT MARTIN	16 Boulevard St Martin	607–37–53	Strasbourg St Denis
POTINIÈRE	7 Rue Louis le Grand	073–54–74	Opéra
SAINT GEORGES	51 Rue Saint Georges	878–63–47	St Georges
TERTRE	81 Rue Lepic	606–11–82	Blanche
THÉÂTRE DE PARIS	15 Rue Blanche	874–20–44	Trinité
THÉÂTRE RIVE GAUCHE	101 Boulevard Raspail	548–87–93	Rennes
THÉÂTRE 347	20 bis Rue Chaptal	874–28–34	Pigalle
VARIÉTÉS	7 Boulevard Mont- martre	488–09–92	Montmartre

Music Halls

ALCAZAR	62 Rue Mazarine	326–53–35	Odéon
BOBINO	20 Rue de la Gaîté	033–30–49	Edgar Quintet
CASINO DE PARIS	16 Rue de Clichy	874–94–42	Trinité
FOLIES BERGÈRE	32 Rue Richer	770–41–21	Cadet, Montmartre
LA GRANDE EUGÈNE	12 Rue de Marignan	359–58–64	Marbeuf
MAYOL	10 Rue de l'Echiquier	770–95–08	Bonne Nouvelle
OLYMPIA	28 Boulevard des Capucines	742–25–49	Opéra

Chansonniers

AUX DEUX ANES	100 Boulevard de Clichy	606–10–26	Clichy
A DIX HEURES	36 Boulevard de Clichy	606–07–48	Pigalle
CAVEAU DE LA RÉPUBLIQUE	1 Boulevard Saint Martin	272–44–45	République

Shops

The following are among the well-known shops of Paris.

Departmental Stores
GALERIES LAFAYETTE 40 Boulevard Haussmann
LE BAZAR DE L'HÔTEL DE VILLE 52–64 Rue de Rivoli
LE PRINTEMPS 64 Boulevard Haussmann
LES TROIS QUARTIERS 17 Boulevard de la Madeleine

Antiques
On the Right Bank: Rue du Faubourg St Honoré, Rue de Berri, Rue Royale; on the Left Bank: Rue du Bac, Rue de Grenelle, Rue des Saints Pères.

Children's Clothes
HÉLÈNE VANNER 402 Rue St Honoré

Costume Jewellery
CHEZ AMARYLLIS 36 Rue du Faubourg St Honoré

Food and Wine
CORCELLET 18 Avenue de l'Opéra
FAUCHON 26 Place de la Madeleine

Glassware and Porcelain
BACCARAT 30 bis Rue de Paradis
DAUM 32 Rue de Paradis
Other shops in Rue de Paradis, Rue Drouot, Rue d'Hauteville

Gloves
FABRICE 215 Rue St Honoré
HERMÈS 24 Rue du Faubourg St Honoré
NICOLET 18 Rue Duphot
ROGER FARÉ 58 Rue du Faubourg St Honoré

Hairdressers
ALEX TONIO 12 Rue de la Paix
ANTOINE 5 Rue Cambon

CARITA 11 Rue du Faubourg St Honoré
GUILLAUME 5 Avenue Matignon
JEAN CLÉMENT 24 Rue Clément Marot
PIERRE JACY 45 Avenue Franklin Roosevelt
YVONNE GRAND 3 Avenue Matignon

Handbags
LE GOUT DU JOUR 12 Rue Cambon
VIOLETTE CORNILLE 32 Rue La Boétie

Hats
ALBOUY 49 Rue du Colisée
JANETTE COLOMBIER 4 Avenue Matignon
PAULETTE 63 Avenue Franklin Roosevelt
ROSE VALOIS 18 Rue Royale

And in the streets off Rond Point des Champs Elysées

Instituts de Beauté
ELIZABETH ARDEN 7 Place Vendôme
HARRIET HUBBARD AYER 120 Rue du Faubourg St Honoré
HELENA RUBINSTEIN 52 Rue du Faubourg St Honoré
PEGGY SAGE 7 Place Vendôme

Jewellery
BOUCHERON 26 Place Vendôme
CARTIER 13 Rue de la Paix
STERLÉ 43 Avenue de l'Opéra
VAN CLEEF ET ARPELS 22 Place Vendôme

Lingerie
CHRISTIANE THIESSE 270 Rue St Honoré
MILLE ET UNE NUITS 6 Rue de Castiglione
SCANDALE 73 Rue du Faubourg St Honoré

Materials
Rue Charles Nodier, Rue Pierre Picard, Rue de Steinkerque
and Marché St Pierre (at foot of steps leading to the Sacré
Coeur).

Men's Haberdashers
BERKELEY 44 Rue François Ier
BOIVIN JEUNE 10 Rue de Castiglione

CHARVET 8 Place Vendôme
DORIAN GUY 36 Avenue George V
POIRIER 12 Rue Boissy d'Anglas
RENÉ ET REGARD 9 Avenue Matignon
SULKA 2 Rue de Castiglione

Perfumes
CARVEN 6 Rond Point des Champs Elysées
GUERLAIN 68 Avenue des Champs Elysées and 2 Place Ven-
dôme
LANCÔME 29 Rue du Faubourg St Honoré
PATOU 7 Rue St Florentin

Ready-made Dresses
JAMIQUA 6 Rue Marbeuf
MINNY 37 Avenue Victor Hugo
RAFFAELLE 12 Avenue Victor Hugo

And in the Champs Elysées, Lido Arcade, Rue Tronchet,
Boulevard des Capucines, Boulevard Haussmann, Avenue
Victor Hugo.

Reproductions of Works of Art
BRAUN 18 Rue Louis le Grand
GALERIE DE FRANCE 3 Rue du Faubourg St Honoré
MAEGHT 13 Rue de Téhéran

Shoes
GEORGETTE 22 Rue Cambon
LÉANDRE 4 Rue de Miromesnil
PERUGIA 2 Rue de la Paix

Sweaters
JONES 39 Avenue Victor Hugo
RAMUZ 261 Rue St Honoré

Table Linen
NOËL 90 Rue La Boétie
PAULE MARROT 16 Rue de l'Arcade

Toys
FARANDOLE 48 Avenue Victor Hugo
LE NAIN BLEU 408 Rue St Honoré

RÉCRÉATION 99 Rue du Faubourg St Honoré

Umbrellas
VEDRENNE 9 Rue St Roch

Couturiers

BALMAIN	44 Rue François Ier	225–68–04
CARVEN	6 Rond Point des Champs Elysées	225–66–50
CHANEL	31 Rue Cambon	073–60–21
COURRÈGES	40 Rue François Ier	359–72–17
DIOR	30–32 Avenue Montaigne	359–93–64
EMANUEL UNGARO	2 Avenue Montaigne	256–27–70
FÉRAUD	88 Rue du Faubourg Saint Honoré	265–27–29
GRÈS	1 Rue de la Paix	073–01–15
JEAN PATOU	7 Rue Saint Florentin	073–08–71
LANVIN	22 Rue du Faubourg Saint Honoré	265–27–21
NINA RICCI	20 Rue des Capucines	073–67–31
PIERRE CARDIN	118 Rue du Faubourg Saint Honoré	225–06–23
TED LAPIDUS	37 Avenue Pierre Ier de Serbie	225–52–44
TORRENTE	28 Avenue Matignon	225–81–27
YVES SAINT LAURENT	30 bis Rue Spontini	727–43–79

Art Galleries

Some of the more Interesting among Paris's 360 galleries:

SIMONE BADINIER	1 Rue Laffitte
CLAUDE BERNARD	5 Rue des Beaux Arts
BRETEAU	70 Rue Bonaparte
JEANNE BUCHER	9 ter Boulevard du Montparnasse
IRIS CLERT	28 Rue du Faubourg St Honoré

CORDIER	8 Rue Miromesnil
CREUZE	4 Avenue de Messine
DU DRAGON	19 Rue du Dragon
JACQUES DUBOURG	126 Boulevard Haussmann
PAUL FACCHETTI	17 Rue de Lille
KARL FLINKER	34 Rue du Bac
DE FRANCE	3 Rue du Faubourg St Honoré
GALERIE J	8 Rue de Montfaucon
KLÉBER	24 Avenue Kléber
MAEGHT	13 Rue de Téhéran
DENISE RENÉ	124 Rue La Boétie
ST PLACIDE	41 Rue St Placide
STADLER	51 Rue de Seine
STIEBEL	30 Rue de Seine

Principal Salons

LE SALON (*Artistes Français et Société Nationale des Beaux-Arts*)	Grand Palais	*June*
SALON D'AUTOMNE	Grand Palais	*October*
SALON DES INDÉPENDANTS	Grand Palais	*March or April*
SALON DE MAI	Palais de New York	*May*
SALON D'HIVER	Palais de New York	*December*
SALON DE L'ÉCOLE FRANÇAISE	Palais de New York	
SALON DES TUILERIES	Palais de New York	
SALON DES ARTISTES DÉCORATEURS	Grand Palais	*June-July*
SALON DES HUMORISTES	11 Rue Royale	*April*
SALON DE LA FRANCE D'OUTRE-MER	Grand Palais	

Markets, Fairs and Shows

BIRD MARKET	Place Louis Lépine	*Sundays*
DOG AND DONKEY MARKET	106 Rue Brancion	*Sundays 1–4*
FLEA MARKET (*Antiques, silver, rugs—almost anything you can name*)	Portes de Clignancourt and St Ouen (Marché Biron and Marché Paul Bert form the best introduction to this market of a thousand stalls)	*Sat., Sun. and Mon. (Monday least crowded)*
FLOWER MARKETS	Place Louis Lépine	*Weekdays*
	Place de la Madeleine	*Tues., Wed., Fri., Sat.*
STAMP MARKET	Avenue Gabriel and Avenue Marigny	*Thurs., Sun. and holidays*
WINE MARKET	Place Jussieu (Visit by special permission: Préfecture de la Seine, 2 Rue Lobeau)	*Weekdays* 6.30–12 2–8
GINGERBREAD FAIR (FOIRE AU PAIN D'ÉPICE)	Avenue du Trône, Place de la Nation, Cours de Vincennes	*One month from Easter*
HAM FAIR (FOIRE AUX JAMBONS, *first held:* 1222)	Boulevard Richard Lenoir	*Eve Palm Sunday to Easter Sunday*
INTERNATIONAL FAIR (FOIRE DE PARIS)	Parc des Expositions	*May*
JUNK FAIR (FOIRE À LA FERRAILLE)	Boulevard Richard Lenoir	*Palm Sunday to Easter; and in first half Oct.*
POETS' FAIR	Place des Vosges	*End of May*
CONCOURS LÉPINE (*New Inventions*)	Parc des Expositions	*March*
DOG SHOW	Salle Wagram	*December*
DOMESTIC ARTS SHOW	Grand Palais	*March*
MOTOR CAR SHOW	Grand Palais	*October*
MUSHROOM SHOW	Jardin des Plantes	*October*
ROSE SHOW	Bagatelle	*June*

Useful Addresses

AIR FRANCE	119 Avenue des Champs Elysées	BAL 70–50
	2 Rue Scribe	OPE 41–00
AMERICAN CATHEDRAL	23 Avenue George V	ELY 17–90
AMERICAN CHURCH IN PARIS (*non-denominational*)	65 Quai d'Orsay	INV 38–90
AMERICAN CONSULATE	2 Rue de Presbourg	BAL 52–03
AMERICAN EMBASSY	2 Avenue Gabriel	ANJ 74–60
AMERICAN EXPRESS CO.	11 Rue Scribe	OPE 42–90
AUSTRALIAN CONSULATE	13 Rue Las Cases	INV 19–95
B.E.A.	129 Avenue des Champs Elysées	RIC 46–30
	38 Avenue de l'Opéra	RIC 46–30
BATEAUX MOUCHES	Port de la Conférence	BAL 96–10
BRITISH CONSULATE	37 Rue du Faubourg St Honoré	ANJ 27–10
BRITISH EMBASSY	35 Rue du Faubourg St Honoré	ANJ 27–10
BRITISH EMBASSY CHURCH	5 Rue d'Aguesseau	
BRITISH METHODIST CHURCH	4 Rue Roquépine	ANJ 71–62
BRITISH RAILWAYS	12 Boulevard de la Madeleine	OPE 56–70
CANADIAN CONSULATE	38 Avenue de l'Opéra	OPE 15–83
CAR HIRE (S.A.L.A.M.)	13 Rue de Magdebourg	POI 38–58
CHURCH OF SCOTLAND	17 Rue Bayard	PAS 60–28
COOK (THOMAS) & SON	2 Place de la Madeleine	OPE 40–40
GREAT SYNAGOGUE	44 Rue de la Victoire	TRU 86–05
INFORMATION OFFICE OF THE FRENCH TOURIST ORGANISATION	8 Avenue de l'Opéra	OPE 99–34
IRISH CONSULATE	12 Avenue Foch	PAS 73–58
LOST AND FOUND OFFICE (BUREAU DES OBJETS TROUVÉS)	36 Rue des Morillons	LEC 60–67

NEW ZEALAND CON- SULATE	9 Rue Léonard de Vinci	KLE 66–50
OFFICE DU TOURISME UNIVERSITAIRE	137 Boulevard St Michel	DAN 60–97
PAN AMERICAN AIR- WAYS	138 Avenue des Champs Elysées	BAL 88–00
	1 Rue Scribe	BAL 88–00
PAWN SHOP (CRÉDIT MUNICIPAL)	62 Rue Pierre Charron	ELY 79–17
POST OFFICE (CENTRAL OFFICE)	52 Rue du Louvre	GUT 84–60
PRÉFECTURE DE POLICE	7 Boulevard du Palais	DAN 44–20
ROTARY CLUB DE PARIS	Hôtel Régina, 2 Place des Pyramides	RIC 18–68
ST GEORGE'S ANGLICAN CHURCH	7 Rue Auguste Vacquerie	PAS 22–51
SOUTH AFRICAN CONSULATE	51 Avenue Hoche	WAG 66–97
THIRD CHURCH OF CHRIST SCIENTIST	45 Rue La Boétie	BAL 29–14
T.W.A.	101 Avenue des Champs Elysées	BAL 15–11
	5 Rue Scribe	OPE 49–79

Some Books about Paris

General

VICTOR HUGO *Notre Dame de Paris* (1831).

HILAIRE BELLOC *Paris* (1900). Good about the Roman and medieval city.

HENRY JAMES *The Ambassadors* (1903).

E. V. LUCAS *A Wanderer in Paris* (1909). Charming conversational guide-book with a strong Edwardian flavour.

CARL VAN VECHTEN *Peter Whiffle* (1922). Witty novel by an American dilettante.

LOUIS ARAGON *Le Paysan de Paris* (1926). The city seen by a surrealist.

GEORGE ORWELL *Down and Out in Paris and London* (1933). Life as a *plongeur*.

JEAN COCTEAU *Portraits-Souvenir 1900-14* (1935).

HENRY BIDOU *Paris* (1937). Historical panorama.

LÉON-PAUL FARGUE *Le Piéton de Paris* (1939). Contains this
definition: 'Le Parisien est un monsieur qui va au Maxim's,
sait dire deux ou trois phrases bien senties à sa marchande
de tabac, et se montre généralement très gentil avec les
femmes. Il aime les livres, goûte la peinture, connaît les
restaurants dignes de porter ce nom, ne fait pas trop de
dettes, sinon pas du tout, et laisse des histoires de femmes à
arranger à ses fils.'

FRANCIS CARCO *Bohème d'Artiste* (1940).

RICHARD LE GALLIENNE *From a Paris Garret* (1943).

JACQUES HILLAIRET *Evocation du Vieux Paris* (3 vols. 1952–4).
Scholarly, detailed history of the city, street by street.

JOHN RUSSELL *Paris* (1960). Highly civilised, witty and tren-
chant. For the connoisseur of Paris.

SYLVIA BEACH *Shakespeare and Company* (1960). Literary life
between the wars.

Works of Art

SOMMERVILLE STORY *Rodin* (Phaidon, 1939).

ANTHONY BLUNT *Art and Architecture in France 1500–1700*
(Pelican History of Art, 1953).

GERMAIN BAZIN *Impressionist Paintings in the Louvre* (Thames
& Hudson, 1958).

Les Merveilles du Louvre (Hachette, Collection Réalités, 2
vols. 1958).

PIERRE VERLET and FRANCIS SALET *La Dame à la Licorne* (Braun
et Cie,1960). Faithful colour reproductions and a scholarly
but lively text: a model of its kind.

Index